The International Criminal Court and Türkiye

The establishment of the International Criminal Court (ICC) is a landmark development in the field of international criminal law, marking a significant step forward in the pursuit of global justice. Having gained the recognition of 125 states, the ICC stands as the world's first and only permanent international tribunal capable of trying individuals for the gravest crimes of international concern. This book provides a comprehensive analysis of the challenges and opportunities associated with becoming a member of the ICC, using Türkiye as a case study to explore broader issues relevant to other states that have not yet joined the Court. It argues that the concerns behind Türkiye's reluctance to sign the founding treaty of the ICC are not substantial enough to justify avoiding the Court's jurisdiction and that non-accession does not guarantee immunity from ICC oversight. While primarily focused on Türkiye, the book offers insights that could inform the decisions of other non-signatory states, particularly those with similar reservations about the Court. It demonstrates that the advantages Türkiye stands to gain by joining the ICC are largely applicable to other non-signatory states as well. Through this analysis, the book underscores the ICC's critical role as a global institution and its invaluable contribution to advancing international criminal justice. Presenting a valuable overview of the world's first and only permanent international criminal court, the work will be a valuable resource for academics, researchers and policymakers working in the fields of International Law and International Relations.

Şehmus Kurtuluş is Visiting Professor at the Peter A. Allard School of Law, University of British Columbia, Canada.

The International Criminal Court and Türkiye

Overcoming Accession Concerns and Exploring Shared Benefits

Şehmus Kurtuluş

Routledge
Taylor & Francis Group
LONDON AND NEW YORK

First published 2026
by Routledge
4 Park Square, Milton Park, Abingdon, Oxon OX14 4RN

and by Routledge
605 Third Avenue, New York, NY 10158

Routledge is an imprint of the Taylor & Francis Group, an informa business

British Library Cataloguing-in-Publication Data
A catalogue record for this book is available from the British Library

Library of Congress Cataloging-in-Publication Data
Names: Kurtuluş Şehmus, author.
Title: The International Criminal Court and Türkiye : overcoming accession concerns and exploring shared benefits / Kurtuluş Şehmus.
Description: Abingdon, Oxon [UK] ; New York, NY : Routledge, 2025. | Includes bibliographical references and index.
Identifiers: LCCN 2025022018 (hardback) | ISBN 9781041076704 (paperback) | ISBN 9781003641643 (ebook)
Subjects: LCSH: International Criminal Court. | International criminal courts—Turkey. | International and municipal law—Turkey. | Turkey—Foreign relations—History. | Rome Statute of the International Criminal Court (1998 July 17) | Terrorism (International law) | Aggression (International law)
Classification: LCC KZ7312 .K89 2025 | DDC 345.561/01—dc23/eng/20250508
LC record available at https://lccn.loc.gov/2025022018

ISBN: 978-1-041-07666-7 (hbk)
ISBN: 978-1-041-07670-4 (pbk)
ISBN: 978-1-003-64164-3 (ebk)

DOI: 10.4324/9781003641643

Typeset in Galliard
by Apex CoVantage, LLC

This book is dedicated to Mustafa Kemal Atatürk, the founding father of modern Türkiye, whose visionary reforms established a secular republic and whose unwavering fight against imperialism continues to inspire me. His vision not only shaped the nation but also opened doors for future generations, including myself, through initiatives like the YLSY scholarship program, which enabled me to pursue my master's and doctoral studies.

This book is also dedicated to the memory of Sabahaddin Kurtuluş and Hikmet Kurtuluş, both of whom were ruthlessly executed by a firing squad of the PKK; the former for daring to be a primary school teacher in a small village in eastern Türkiye in the 1990s, and the latter simply for being his wife. Although Sabahaddin and many other teachers who fell victim to terrorism were unable to witness the graduation of their students and children, they became an inspiration to so many who pursue education as a noble profession.

Finally, this book is dedicated to my wife, Derya, and my son, Ege, whose presence filled this journey with love and purpose.

Contents

About the Author

Dr. Şehmus Kurtuluş is Visiting Professor at the University of British Columbia. His primary research interests sit at the intersection of international law, international relations and human rights. Dr. Kurtuluş also researches in the areas of comparative constitutional law and comparative politics. His work has appeared in the Leiden Journal of International Law, International Relations Journal and Istanbul Law Review, among others.

Şehmus Kurtuluş
The University of British Columbia, Peter A. Allard School of Law, Canada

Acknowledgements

This book is largely based on my doctoral dissertation, which I successfully defended in 2015 at *Case Western Reserve University School of Law*. The conversion of my dissertation into a monograph was carried out during my time as Visiting Professor at the *University of British Columbia School of Law*.

I could not have accomplished this book without the constructive support of Professor *Michael P. Scharf*. As my dissertation advisor, he was extremely kind and caring. I feel highly honored and privileged to have worked under his watch.

Similarly, I would like to extend my sincere appreciation to Professor *Lewis R. Katz* for supporting me all the way through. I am grateful for his unwavering support and guidance, which helped me to stay focused and determined.

Likewise, I owe a big thank you to Professor *Avidan Y. Cover*, who agreed to be my co-advisor and provided valuable feedback on my dissertation. I appreciate his continual support and encouragement.

A special thanks go to *Adria Sankovic*, the "LL.M. Mom" of Case Western Reserve University School of Law, who was the first person to encourage me to be a part of the Case Western Reserve University family. I owe her a debt of gratitude for believing in me. May she rest in peace.

I wish to extend my warmest thanks to *Elizabeth H. Woyczynski* for always being there for me. Her care and help made my life in Cleveland easier and more enjoyable. I would not have seen the light without the support from her and other persons mentioned earlier.

My aspiration to earn a doctoral degree from such a distinguished university would not have been realized without the invaluable YLSY scholarship awarded by the *Ministry of National Education of Türkiye*. Likewise, I am grateful to the administration of *Case Western Reserve University School of Law* for awarding me a generous tuition exemption in the second year of my doctoral program.

I would also like to express my gratitude to the *University of British Columbia School of Law* for providing an environment conducive to the development of my dissertation into a monograph and to Professor *Julen Etxabe* for extending the invitation to serve as Visiting Professor at this esteemed institution.

Finally, I extend my heartfelt gratitude to Alison Kirk and the three anonymous reviewers, whose valuable insights and constructive criticisms have greatly enriched the quality and depth of this book. Their insightful feedback and attention to detail have been invaluable in shaping the final manuscript.

Credits

Several chapters of this book were previously published in earlier versions and have been revised and/or adapted for inclusion here. I would like to thank the editorial teams and publishers for granting permission to use the following materials:

Chapter II. [Omission of the Crime of Terrorism from the Rome Statute]: An earlier version of this chapter was published in Şehmus Kurtuluş, Reassessment of Turkey's Objections to the Exclusion of Terrorism from the Rome Statute, Uluslararası İlişkiler/International Relations, 16(64), pp. 145–161 (2019). https://doi.org/10.33458/uidergisi.653027.

Chapter III. [Inclusion of the Non-international Armed Conflicts within the Jurisdiction of the ICC]: The original version of the first sub-section (Characterization of the Violence between Türkiye and the PKK) of this chapter was published in Şehmus Kurtuluş, Characterization of the Violence between Türkiye and the PKK, Leiden Journal of International Law, 37(1), 274–293 (2024). DOI: https://doi.org/10.1017/S0922156523000456.

Chapter IV. [The Prosecutor's Powers and The Possibility of Politicized Prosecutions]: The original version of this chapter was published in Şehmus Kurtuluş, A Critique of the Concerns on the *Proprio Motu* Powers of the ICC Prosecutor, İstanbul Hukuk Mecmuası/İstanbul Law Review, 81(2), 437–456 (2023). https://doi.org/10.26650/mecmua.2023.81.2.0005.

Chapter VI [Implications for the Cyprus Question]: The original version of this chapter was presented at the 3rd International Conference on Management, Business, Economics, Social Sciences and Humanities Research in 2015 and subsequently published in Şehmus Kurtuluş, Cyprus Question: An Obstacle to Turkey's Long – Awaited Accession to the Rome Statute of the International Criminal Court?, International Journal of Social Sciences and Humanities Research, 3(5), 42–49 (2015).

Abbreviations

AMICC	American Non-governmental Organizations Coalition for the International Criminal Court
ASP	Assembly of State Parties
BIAs	Bilateral Immunity Agreements
CIA	Central Intelligence Agency (United States)
ECHR	European Convention for the Protection of Human Rights and Fundamental Freedoms
ECtHR	European Court of Human Rights
EU	European Union
EUROPOL	European Police Office
ICC	International Criminal Court
ICCPR	International Covenant on Civil and Political Rights
ICRC	International Committee of the Red Cross
ICTY	International Criminal Tribunal for the Former Yugoslavia
IDF	Israeli Defence Forces
IDPs	Internally Displaced Persons
IPC	Immovable Property Commission
ISIS	Islamic State of Iraq and the Levant
JIHIDEM	Gendarmerie Human Rights Violations Investigation and Examination Centre
KDP	Kurdistan Democratic Party (Iraq)
LGBT	Lesbian, Gay, Bisexual, and Transgender
LRA	Lord's Resistance Army
NATO	North Atlantic Treaty Organization
OTP	Office of the Prosecutor of the International Criminal Court
PKK	Partiya Karkeren Kurdistan – Kurdistan Workers' Party
PRIO	Peace Research Institute Oslo
PUK	Patriotic Union of Kurdistan (Iraq)
PYD	Partiya Yekîtiya Demokrat – Democratic Union Party (Syria)
TİHK	Turkish Human Rights Institution

UN	United Nations
UPDF	Uganda People's Defence Forces
U.S./U.S.A.	United States (of America)
YPG	Yekîneyên Parastina Gel – People's Defense Units (Syria)

1 Introduction

The Rome Statute of the International Criminal Court (Rome Statute or "the Statute"), adopted on 17 July 1998 and entered into force on 1 July 2002,[1] established the world's first and the only permanent international criminal tribunal capable of trying individuals, from senior commanders to the heads of states, for the most serious crimes that are of international concern.[2] Establishment of the International Criminal Court (ICC or "the Court") is perhaps the greatest development in the field of international criminal law and one of the most significant steps in the advancement of international law. By now, 125 states, almost two-thirds of the world's nations, have already accepted the jurisdiction of the ICC to investigate and prosecute crimes of the greatest concern to the international community, namely, war crimes, crimes against humanity, genocide and aggression.[3]

Of 148 states present at the Rome Diplomatic Conference of Plenipotentiaries (Rome Conference), where the Rome Statute was drafted, 120 states voted in favor of the Statute, with only 7 casting votes against.[4] Türkiye was among 21 states that abstained from adopting the Rome Statute. Although Türkiye participated vigorously in the Rome Conference and took some significant steps towards the activation of the ICC jurisdiction, such as the constitutional amendment that paved the way for the extradition of the Turkish nationals to the ICC, it did not sign the final text of the Rome Statute because several matters in the Statute had not been resolved in a completely

1 United Nations Treaty Collection, Rome Statute of the International Criminal Court, U.N. Doc. A/CONF.183/9, 17 July 1998 [hereinafter Rome Statute].

2 Marlies Glasius, *The International Criminal Court: A Global Civil Society Achievement* i (Routledge Chapman & Hall 2006).

3 Rome Statute, *supra* note 1, art. 5(1).

4 John T. Parry, *Evil, Law and the State: Perspectives on State Power and Violence* (Editions Rodopi B.V. 2006) 152. The states that voted against are China, the United States, Libya, Iraq, Israel, Qatar and Yemen. *See* Anthony Lewis, *At Home Abroad; A Turn in the Road*, www.nytimes.com/1998/07/20/opinion/at-home-abroad-a-turn-in-the-road.html (accessed 20 July 1998).

DOI: 10.4324/9781003641643-1

satisfactory manner for Türkiye.[5] The statements made by the representatives of Türkiye at the Rome Conference and at the 2010 Kampala Review Conference reveal some of Türkiye's reservations on the final text of the Rome Statute of the International Criminal Court underlying Türkiye's reluctance to sign the Rome Statute. Before addressing these reservations and the actual concerns that lie at the bottom of formal reservations, it would be useful to discover Türkiye's long-standing policy to remain engaged with the international human rights mechanisms and to explore the historical and political motivations behind this policy.

It should first be noted that, as one of the founding members of the United Nations and one of the states that voted in favor of the Universal Declaration of Human Rights when it was first introduced in 1948, Türkiye is a party to most of the core UN treaties designed to protect fundamental rights and freedoms, from "Convention against Torture and Other Cruel, Inhuman or Degrading Treatment or Punishment" (and its optional protocol) to "International Covenant on Civil and Political Rights" (and its two additional optional protocols). Türkiye has also accepted the compulsory jurisdiction of the European Court of Human Rights (ECtHR), which hears applications against signatory states for the breach of a broad range of rights and freedoms and issues binding judgments upon them. As will be detailed in the following chapters, the founding treaty of the ECtHR, in fact, imposes much more extensive burdens on States Parties than the Rome Statute of the International Criminal Court and sets much lower thresholds for the admissibility of claims.

Türkiye's policy to remain engaged with the international (mostly western) institutions is a direct result of its long-standing westernization project which dates back to the time of the Ottoman Empire (1299–1922), the predecessor of the Republic of Türkiye. While the westernization and modernization endeavors in the Ottoman Empire traces its origins to the 18th century,[6] these endeavors materialized into a concrete political move in 1839 through a proclamation called the Imperial Edict of Reorganization which launched a period of reform. The Imperial Edict of Reorganization (also known as the Rescript of Gülhane or Imperial Edict of Tanzimat) promised reforms in areas including justice, taxation, governance and conscription and included clauses on such human rights as the right to a fair and public hearing, prohibition of discrimination on grounds of religion and legal principles like *nullum crimen sine lege* (no crime without law).[7] Though the Imperial Edict launched a period

5 Cesran International, *International Criminal Court (ICC)*, http://cesran.org/international-criminal-court-icc (accessed 1 April 2015).

6 Murat Bardakçı, Biz, yediğimiz soğanı bile reformlardan daha fazla önemsemiştik [We Valued Even the Onions We Ate More Than the Reforms], *HaberTurk*, 4 November 2009, www.haberturk.com/yazarlar/murat-bardakci/222810-biz-yedigimiz-sogani-bile-reformlardan-daha-fazla-onemsemistik (accessed 1 January 2024).

7 Yavuz Özdemir, Erol Çiydem and Elif Aktaş, Tanzimat Fermanı'nın Arka Planı [Background of Tanzimat Edict], (1) *Kastamonu Education Journal* 328–329 (2014).

of reforms, the primary motivation behind this and the following edict (the Reform Edict of 1856) was not to westernize and democratize the empire but rather to secure its territorial integrity against nationalist movements and to gain the support of the European states on certain issues.

Westernization has become a key component of the Turkish foreign policy only after the proclamation of the Republic in 1923. It was the reforms of the Mustafa Kemal Atatürk, the Commander-in-Chief of the Turkish War of Independence and the founder of the Republic, that truly secularized and westernized the fledgling Republic of Türkiye. The reforms of Atatürk were designed to build a secular, democratic and modern state and to raise the newly established republic to the level of a modern civilization under the guidance of reason and science. He believed that Türkiye's modernization could best be achieved by adopting itself to the "western" norms and by taking a respectable place among the civilized (mostly western) nations of the world. Joining the key western (usually European) international institutions has since then been the most prominent dimension of the Turkish foreign policy.

In line with the Westernization/Europeanization project, Türkiye has continuously sought to be an active member of the western political, economic and military alliances. It joined the Council of Europe in 1950 and the North Atlantic Treaty Organization (NATO) in 1952 shortly after they were established in 1949. Türkiye has also acceded to a significant number of international human rights instruments, including the European Convention for the Protection of Human Rights and Fundamental Freedoms (ECHR), for the purpose of securing its ground among European countries. It became the 11th state party to the ECHR by ratifying it in May 1954 before Netherlands, Belgium, Italy and France – four of the six founding members of the European Economic Community, the predecessor of the European Union.[8]

In 1959, Türkiye made its first application to join what was then the European Economic Community. The European Economic Community responded to this application by suggesting an association that would prepare Türkiye for full membership both economically and politically. As a result, an agreement creating an association between Türkiye and the European Economic Community (commonly known as Ankara Agreement)[9] was signed with the ultimate (conditional)[10] goal being Türkiye's full membership. Türkiye has been

8 Arthur Henry Robertson, The European Court of Human Rights, (2) *The International and Comparative Law Quarterly* 396 (1959).

9 The official name of the agreement is "Agreement Establishing An Association Between the European Economic Community and Turkey." Official Journal of the European Communities, Agreement establishing an Association between the European Economic Community and Turkey, No. L 361/29, 12 September 1963 [hereinafter Ankara Agreement].

10 Article 28 of the Ankara Agreement states that "As soon as the operation of this Agreement has advanced far enough to justify envisaging full acceptance by Turkey of the obligations arising out of the Treaty establishing the Community, the Contracting Parties shall examine the possibility of the accession of Turkey to the Community." Ankara Agreement, art. 28.

an associate member of the European Union (and its predecessors European Economic Community and European Community) since the entry into force of the Ankara Agreement in 1964.[11]

The belief that Türkiye's democratization, modernization and economic prosperity could best be achieved by Europeanization has made the goal of full membership of the EU the highest strategic priority of the Turkish foreign policy. Fulfillment of the Copenhagen criteria (the overall criteria which applicant countries to the EU must satisfy to become a member state) is, therefore, of utmost importance for the achievement of the Turkish foreign policy objectives.

When evaluating the extent to which Türkiye meets the Copenhagen Criteria's political dimension,[12] European Commission, the executive branch of the EU, addresses, among others, Türkiye's decisions to accede to or withdraw from the international human rights instruments. The Commission's 2021 report on Türkiye's progress towards accession, for instance, has rightly described Türkiye's withdrawal from "Council of Europe Convention on Preventing and Combating Violence Against Women and Domestic Violence" (Istanbul Convention) as an action that "raised further concerns about its adherence to international human rights standards."[13] Türkiye's ratification of international human rights conventions, on the other hand, is described as reform measures to fulfill political criteria of Copenhagen.[14]

In the reports of the European Commission, Rome Statute of the International Criminal Court is also addressed as one of the "major international human rights instruments" Türkiye invited to join.[15] Accession to the Rome Statute is, in fact, a common policy adopted by all members of the EU under the "Common Foreign and Security Policy," a mechanism developed by the Union for adopting common guidelines on external policy and security issues. Indeed, among all EU members and membership candidates, Türkiye is the only country that has not yet joined the International Criminal

11 Türkiye applied to be a full member in 1987 and was officially recognized as a candidate country in 1999, and accession negotiations were officially opened in 2005. The Customs Union between Türkiye and the Union, on the other hand, has been in force since 1 January 1996.

12 Copenhagen political criteria can be summarized as the achievement of "stability of institutions guaranteeing democracy, the rule of law, human rights and respect for and protection of minorities." Eur-Lex Access to European Union Law, *Accession Criteria (Copenhagen Criteria)*, https://eur-lex.europa.eu/EN/legal-content/glossary/accession-criteria-copenhagen-criteria.html (accessed 1 January 2024).

13 European Commission, *Turkey 2021 Report* (October 2021), p. 21, https://neighbourhood-enlargement.ec.europa.eu/document/download/892a5e42-448a-47b8-bf62-b22d52c4ba26_en?filename=Turkey%202021%20report.PDF.

14 *See* for example Erich Hochleitner, *The Political Criteria of Copenhagen and their application to Turkey*, Working Paper (Austrian Institute for European Security Policy 2005), pp. 8, 16.

15 European Commission, *Turkey Regular Report 2002* (October 2002) 25, https://neighbourhood-enlargement.ec.europa.eu/document/download/9018e458-daec-4fc1-8cbf-85839fdcdddb_en?filename=tu_en.pdf.

Court, accession to which is considered "as an essential component of the Union's democratic model and values."[16] In this regard, Türkiye's accession to the founding treaty of the ICC, of which the European Commission and the European Parliament have been strong supporters, would have a very positive impact on full membership negotiations.

Before moving on to address Türkiye's concerns with regard to the accession to the Rome Statute of the International Criminal Court, it would also be useful to study the Kurdistan Workers' Party (PKK), an armed violent group that is denounced as a terrorist organization by the European Union, NATO and much of the international community (including the United States, Canada, Japan, Australia, New Zealand and so on), as Türkiye's views on the ICC have been mostly influenced by its prolonged fight against this terrorist organization.

The PKK was founded in 1978 with the stated aim of establishing a separate Kurdish state[17] in an area spanning four different countries – southeastern Türkiye, northwestern Iran, northern Syria and northern Iraq, where Kurds form the predominant ethnic group – and launched terrorist attacks within Türkiye on 15 August 1984. Terrorist attacks of the PKK have taken place in many forms, including mass killings in rural areas, suicide attacks in metropolitan centers, ambushes, assassinations, road side bombings, kidnappings, etc., and have targeted civilians, as well as security forces.[18] Teachers, engineers, doctors, who worked in the southeastern provinces of Türkiye, and their families have often been targeted by the PKK simply for being an officer of the Turkish state and for improving the living conditions of the region, thereby making the PKK recruitment more difficult. In only three years (between 1992–1994), 95 teachers[19] were systematically killed by the PKK due to the notion that Kurdish children who have been deprived of education would be more vulnerable to PKK recruitment.

While the PKK's treacherous attacks against the Turkish security forces have targeted village guards, military and police officers of both Turkish and

16 Coalition for the International Criminal Court, *Target Countries–URC-Turkey*, http://www.iccnow.org/?mod=urc1010 (accessed 1 January 2015).

17 In the 1990s, the PKK's stated aim to create an independent Kurdish State shifted towards autonomy for the Kurds within Türkiye.

18 The founding leader of the PKK acknowledged that "Turkish authorities had correctly estimated, or even under-estimated, the number of people killed and wounded in the PKK's armed actions since 1978 – with the deaths amounting to 4,472 civilians, 3,874 servicemen, 247 police officers and 1,225 village guards in 6,036 armed attacks, 3,071 bombings, 388 armed robberies and 1,046 abductions." European Court of Human Rights, *Öcalan v. Turkey*, Appl. No. 5980/07, "Press release issued by the Registrar – Decision," 16 July 2010, https://hudoc.echr.coe.int/eng-press#{%22display%22:[%221%22],%22dmdocnumber%22:[%22871381%22],%22itemid%22:[%22003-3206766-3569334%22]} (accessed 1 January 2024).

19 Ataol Behramoğlu, Öğretmen öldürmek [Killing of Teachers], *Cumhuriyet*, 19 August 2017, https://www.cumhuriyet.com.tr/yazarlar/ataol-behramoglu/ogretmen-oldurmek-806610 (accessed 1 January 2024).

Kurdish ethnicity, its indiscriminate attacks have victimized civilian Turkish citizens of both Kurdish and Turkish ethnicity. The PKK often kidnaps, executes or assassinates Kurdish civilians and attacks Kurdish villages with the objective of securing political ends, such as deterring them from criticizing the PKK. In fact, Türkiye's Kurds who refuse to support the cause and methods of the PKK constitute the biggest civilian group targeted directly and deliberately by the PKK, as they mostly live in the southeastern provinces of Türkiye, where most of the PKK's terrorist acts has taken place.

Even though the PKK's stated (original) aim to create an independent Kurdish state allegedly shifted in the 1990s towards autonomy for the Kurds and recognition of Kurdish cultural rights within Türkiye,[20] it has always been the Kurds who suffered the most from the terrorist activities of the PKK and from the negative economic, political and social consequences of these activities. The PKK will be discussed further in Chapter 2 and 3, which will address, respectively, Türkiye's objections to the exclusion of a separate crime of terrorism from the Rome Statute and to the inclusion of non-international armed conflicts within the jurisdiction of the ICC.

This book will examine the concerns underlying Türkiye's reluctance to sign the Rome Statute and will explore the compelling benefits that Türkiye could gain by being a State Party to the ICC. It will suggest that limited subject matter and temporal jurisdiction of the Court and the high threshold criteria set out in the Rome Statute should allay Türkiye's concerns about the final outcome of the Rome Conference. After concluding that Türkiye's objections and concerns do not constitute an insurmountable obstacle for its accession to the Rome Statute, the book will encourage the Turkish government to join the ever-growing ICC family without further delay.

The book consists of nine chapters. Following this introduction, **Chapter 2** will address Türkiye's objections to the exclusion of the crime of terrorism from the subject matter jurisdiction of the ICC, which was one of the biggest disappointments of the Turkish delegation to the Rome Conference. It will suggest that exclusion of a separate crime of terrorism from the Rome Statute should not hinder Türkiye's consideration of accession for several reasons.

First, most of the PKK's terrorist acts, from which Türkiye's efforts to include terrorism in the Rome Statute stemmed, already fall within at least one of the existing core crimes of the Rome Statute, namely, crimes against humanity and war crimes. The lack of the reference to terrorism in the Rome Statute does not prevent the ICC from investigating and prosecuting the terrorist acts. If an investigation were to be triggered today, the ICC would most likely consider most of the terrorist acts of the PKK as falling within the subject-matter jurisdiction of the ICC.

20 European Court of Human Rights, *supra* note 18; Michael Gunter, The PKK-KDP Conflict Robert, in W. Olson, *The Kurdish Nationalist Movement in the 1990s: Its Impact on Turkey and the Middle East*, ed. Robert Olson (University Press of Kentucky 1996) 53.

Second, irrespective of whether the PKK's terrorist acts would fall within the subject matter jurisdiction of the Rome Statute, such jurisdiction would not be triggered by Türkiye because it could lead the ICC to characterize Türkiye's fight against the PKK as an armed conflict subject to international humanitarian law norms – a characterization that Türkiye has strongly opposed. Türkiye's counter-terrorism operations against the PKK satisfy the legal criteria for the determination of a non-international armed conflict, and thus, there is a strong possibility that the Office of the Prosecutor (OTP) would treat these operations as an armed conflict if a preliminary examination were to be started. Because of the probability of such classification, which Türkiye strongly opposes, Türkiye would not wish to trigger an ICC investigation into the crimes committed by the PKK, even if terrorism was expressly included in the Rome Statute.

Third, Chapter 2 argues that regardless of whether the terrorist acts that victimized Türkiye would fall within the subject matter jurisdiction of the Rome Statute, an ICC investigation into those acts would be found inadmissible before the Court because Türkiye has already been conducting genuine criminal investigations against the perpetrators. An examination of the existing national proceedings and investigations against PKK members show that Türkiye is able and willing to conduct effective prosecutions against terrorist crimes taking place in its territory. Thus, even if the crime of terrorism *per se* had been included in the Rome Statute in a way to cover the PKK's crimes that do not amount to any of the currently existing crimes, those acts would most likely be inadmissible under the complementarity principle of the Court because of Türkiye's ability and willingness to prosecute them.

Chapter 2 finally attempts to explain that Türkiye could, in fact, benefit from joining the ICC in its fight against the PKK by acquiring the right to trigger a preliminary examination. Although it is true that Türkiye would not be eager to trigger a preliminary examination into the activities of the PKK for the reasons that will be detailed in Chapter 2, Türkiye's ability to trigger such examination could still have a deterrent effect on the PKK's senior members, their abettors and the states that solicit, abet or fund the crimes of the PKK, as they would fear facing charges before the Court. Moreover, in the highly unlikely event that a preliminary examination is triggered by Türkiye or by the Prosecutor *proprio motu* (on her own motion), articulation of the PKK's most serious crimes in the Preliminary Examination Reports by the Office of the Prosecutor would remind the European countries of their responsibilities regarding the unlawful PKK activities taking place in their territory, and it would send a clear signal that the international community is watching. Thus, Chapter 2 concludes that the lack of the reference to terrorism in the Rome Statute should not hinder Türkiye's consideration of accession.

Chapter 3 establishes that the ICC's jurisdiction over war crimes committed as part of a non-international armed conflict, which was another objection that Türkiye voiced during the Rome negotiations, would not undermine Türkiye's fight against the terrorist groups, contrary to concerns raised by the opponents of the Statute. The chapter focuses on Türkiye's worst-case scenario, in which the Court considers Türkiye's fight against the PKK as a non-international armed conflict subject to Article 8(2)(c) and (e) – the articles that deal with the crimes committed as part of a non-international armed conflict – and explains that the ICC's jurisdiction over non-international armed conflicts should not hinder Türkiye's consideration of accession to the Rome Statute because possible allegations against the Turkish security forces would not meet the legal criteria to justify initiation of a formal investigation, and thus, joining the Court would not hamper Türkiye in its measures of legitimate repression.

Chapter 3 begins with the effort to characterize the violence between Türkiye and the PKK. It submits that given the organization of the PKK and the intensity of the violence produced, the violence between Türkiye and the PKK constitutes a non-international armed conflict subject to international humanitarian law, and thus, the Rome Statute provisions on non-international armed conflicts would be applicable to the conflict between Türkiye and the PKK if the preconditions of the Rome Statute were to be met.

Second, Chapter 3 explains that most of the allegations against Turkish security forces concern the incidents that occurred prior to the entry into force of the Rome Statute in 2002, and thus, they are outside the temporal jurisdiction of the Court. Furthermore, when Türkiye accedes to the Rome Statute, the ICC will have jurisdiction only with respect to the allegations concerning the incidents that occurred after the Statute enters into force for Türkiye, unless Türkiye accepts the jurisdiction of the Court for the acts that took place prior to its ratification but after 2002.[21]

Third, Chapter 3 submits that even if the temporal jurisdiction requirement was satisfied, allegations against Turkish nationals would be found inadmissible before the ICC due to "complementarity" principle and the "gravity" threshold of the Rome Statue. It draws attention to the fact that the ICC does not intervene when the national authorities are able and willing to prosecute the acts in question and when the acts in question fail to appear to be grave enough to trigger a formal ICC investigation.

Fourth, Chapter 3 submits that Türkiye's counter-terrorism operations would not face accusations of excessive use of force because, "in the context of a non-international armed conflict, the Rome Statute does not contain a provision for the war crime of intentionally launching a disproportionate attack."[22] Fifth, Chapter 3 explains that even if other requirements were satisfied, most of the allegations against the Turkish Armed Forces would not

21 Rome Statute, *supra* note 1, art. 11(2).

22 International Criminal Court – Office of the Prosecutor, *Report on Preliminary Examination Activities 2013* (November 2013), at 12, para. 47, http://www.icc-cpi.int/en_menus/icc/press%20and%20media/press%20releases/Documents/OTP%20Preliminary% 20Examinations/OTP%20-%20Report%20%C20Preliminary%C20Examination%C20Activities% 202013.pdf.

satisfy *actus reus* of the crimes enumerated in the Rome Statute. It emphasizes that Türkiye's efforts to fight against terrorism without committing abuses and without victimizing indigenous civilians has been complementary to its efforts to reduce the ability of the PKK to recruit new members. Türkiye's success in bringing its counter-terrorism laws and practices in line with the international standards has been instrumental in gaining further assistance and closer cooperation from other countries in its fight against the PKK. After drawing attention to the fact that joining the ICC could even be conducive to Türkiye's effective fight against terrorism, Chapter 3 concludes that the ICC's jurisdiction over internal armed conflicts should not hinder Türkiye's consideration of accession to the Rome Statute.

Chapter 4 deals with Türkiye's hesitations about the ICC Prosecutor's *proprio motu* powers to initiate an investigation. Chapter 4 first argues that the Prosecutor's power to initiate investigations *proprio motu* is not only crucial for the effective operation of the Court but also instrumental in encouraging domestic prosecutions. It then attempts to explain that prosecutorial powers are not placed in the hands of the Prosecutor without judicial checks. First, the Rome Statute requires the prosecutor to request authorization from the Pre-Trial Chamber before initiating a formal investigation on her own motion. The Prosecutor cannot proceed with an investigation without an authorization from the Pre-Trial Chamber of the Court.

Second, the safeguards and the high threshold criteria set out in the Rome Statute, which are actually the main restraints placed on the Prosecutor's discretion, avert the possibility of the Prosecutor to bring arbitrary charges. Third, there is also political restraint placed on the office of the Prosecutor by the states whose cooperation is needed in order to access the defendants and the evidence. The effective functioning of the ICC relies heavily on the cooperation with states. After drawing attention to the fact that the Prosecutor of the ICC is elected by secret ballots of State Parties with equally weighted votes, Chapter 4 concludes that the judicial checks and the filtering mechanism of the Rome Statute should allay Türkiye's fears over politicized prosecution.

Chapter 5 handles the objections and hesitations of states, including Türkiye, to the ICC's ability to exercise jurisdiction over the nationals of the states that are not party to the Rome Statute in some circumstances, for example, when a non-party state national commits an ICC crime on the territory of a State Party or when a situation is referred to the Court by the Security Council. The chapter explains why the ICC's jurisdiction over the non-party state nationals is not a legal or political obstacle to Türkiye's accession to the Rome Statute. First, once the Rome Statute comes into force for Türkiye, the Court's jurisdiction over non-party states will no longer be an issue for Türkiye, as it will no longer be a non-party. While it is understandable for those countries that would most likely not join the Court in the foreseeable future, such as the United States, to perceive the ICC's jurisdiction over non-party states as a threat, it should not be a concern for a state, such as Türkiye, which already stated that it "will soon approve the Rome Statute after completing its internal preparations."[23]

Second, Chapter 5 argues, Türkiye preserves very little by remaining an outsider and that Türkiye's non-accession does not guarantee that the ICC will not exercise jurisdiction over Turkish nationals. The ICC would have jurisdiction over the acts committed by Turkish nationals on the territory of a state that is either party to the Court or otherwise accepts the jurisdiction of the Court on an *ad hoc* basis, regardless of whether Türkiye is a party or consents to the jurisdiction of the Court. In such case, an investigation could be triggered by the Prosecutor *proprio motu* or by a State Party referral. The ICC would also have jurisdiction over the acts committed by Turkish nationals in a situation referred to it by the Security Council, regardless of where the crimes were committed, as no precondition is required when a situation, in which an ICC crime appears to be committed, is referred to the Court by the Security Council.

Chapter 5 also compares the Turkish and American positions with respect to their concerns regarding the ICC's jurisdiction over the nationals of non-party states in an attempt to explain why Türkiye should not follow in the footsteps of the U.S. – its only western ally that has not yet ratified the Rome Statute – on the issue of ICC accession. It states that, as opposed to Türkiye, the United States enjoy the privileges of being a permanent member of the Security Council, such as the right to veto any resolution that provides the ICC with the jurisdiction over U.S. nationals. Furthermore, the United States concluded Bilateral Immunity Agreements ("BIAs") with over a hundred states to ensure that they would not hand over the U.S. nationals to the ICC without its permission.[24] Türkiye, on the other hand, does not enjoy such protections as BIAs and the privileges of being a permanent member of the Security Council and, therefore, should not follow in the footsteps of the U.S. on the issue of ICC accession.

In the context of the comparison between the Turkish and American positions, Chapter 5 also draws attention to the fact that the United States has much more compelling reasons for not joining the ICC than Türkiye, such as its expansive military operations across the globe. The U.S. fears that large number of American troops could be subject to the Court's jurisdiction and that its officials could be deprived of the type of due process rights guaranteed to Americans under the U.S. Constitution, such as the right to a jury trial or the protection against self-incrimination.

Another compelling U.S. concern that is not shared by Türkiye is the concerns over infringement of national sovereignty. Infringement of sovereignty

23 Coalition for the International Criminal Court, *supra* note 16.

24 American Non-Governmental Organizations Coalition for the International Criminal Court (AMICC), *A Campaign for US Immunity from the ICC*, www.amicc.org/usicc/biacampaign (accessed 1 January 2024).

has not been one of the reasons for Türkiye's objections to the ICC's jurisdiction over the nationals of non-parties or to the Prosecutor's powers. Türkiye has already accepted the compulsory jurisdiction of the ECtHR, which hears applications against signatory states for the breach of a broad range of rights and freedoms and issues binding judgments upon them, at the expense of significant privileges of its sovereignty. Thus, joining a court that tries its nationals would not be an unprecedented (so called) "infringement" of Türkiye's sovereignty.

Chapter 5 finally notes that accession to the Rome Statute could benefit Türkiye more vis-a-vis the U.S., especially given Türkiye's foreign policy priorities, such as its European Union (EU) membership bid. For all these reasons detailed in Chapter V, the chapter concludes that Türkiye's attitude towards the ICC (and towards the issues such as the ICC's jurisdiction over the nationals of non-parties) should differ from that of the U.S.

Chapter 6 discusses possible implications of Türkiye's ICC accession for the Cyprus question. It argues that Türkiye's accession to the Rome Statute is not likely to impact the possibility of the Cyprus question being brought before the Court for several reasons. First, the Republic of Cyprus, which is recognized by the U.N. as the de jure government of the whole island, is already party to the Rome Statute, and thus, it can already attempt to refer the situation in Cyprus to the ICC regardless of whether Türkiye is a State Party or not. In other words, even if Türkiye remains a non-party, the Court could still determine that it has territorial jurisdiction over Türkiye's activities in the northern part of Cyprus because the Republic of Cyprus is internationally recognized as the legitimate government of the entire island.

Second, neither the acts of the Turkish Cyprus (and Türkiye) nor those of the Greek Cyprus (and Greece) on the island of Cyprus would be found admissible before the ICC because they clearly fail to satisfy the subject matter and temporal jurisdiction and the gravity requirement of the ICC. Most notably, Türkiye's military intervention, which ensued following a Greek-led coup that sought to unify the island with Greece, took place in 1974, 50 years ago. Therefore, the acts of the parties during and in the aftermath of the intervention fall outside the temporal jurisdiction of the ICC, which cannot prosecute the incidents that occurred prior to the entry into force of the Rome Statute in 2002. Moreover, the fact that nearly all decision-makers and senior officials involved in the 1974 events are no longer alive presents another jurisdictional challenge, rendering a formal ICC investigation highly unlikely and almost infeasible.

Third, Chapter 6 submits that given the political constraints and the risk of obstructing the re-unification talks, the situation in Cyprus would not be a case the Prosecutor would be eager to get involved by a preliminary examination that is clearly not likely to turn into a formal investigation, even if the preconditions to the exercise of the ICC's jurisdiction were clearly satisfied. The statehood questions, involvement of the Guarantor States and the re-unification efforts between the Greeks and Turks make the situation in Cyprus too sensitive to intervene.[25]

Despite the Rome Statute's high threshold criteria that make an ICC investigation into the situation in Cyprus highly unlikely, some still view the Cyprus question as one of the greatest fears of Türkiye about joining the ICC.[26] Chapter 6, therefore, primarily focuses on the allegations against Türkiye, which, as a Guarantor State exercising its legal right under the Treaty of Guarantee, conducted a military intervention in Cyprus in 1974 "to prevent a Greek takeover of the island"[27] and to safeguard the Turkish Cypriots from being driven off the island. After submitting that an ICC investigation into the situation in Cyprus is highly unlikely due to, *inter alia*, the limited subject matter and temporal jurisdiction of the ICC, as well as the politically sensitive nature of the situation, Chapter 6 also notes that most of the allegations against Türkiye have already been addressed by the European Court of Human Rights (ECtHR), drawing attention to the remedies provided to the victims of some of the acts in question.

Chapter 6 submits that what makes an ICC investigation into the situation in Cyprus highly unlikely and almost infeasible is not the difficulty of establishing territorial or personal jurisdiction but rather factors such as the OTP's caution in selecting cases, the limited temporal and subject matter jurisdiction of the Court, the gravity of the allegations falling below the high thresholds of the Rome Statute, as well as statehood issues and political constraints. In any event, even if Türkiye remains a non-party, the Court could still assert territorial jurisdiction over the alleged acts of Turkish nationals on the island due to the Greek Cyprus's accession to the Rome Statute in 2002.

Chapter 6, therefore, concludes that the Cyprus question should not be viewed as an obstacle to Türkiye's consideration of accession to the Rome Statute. It recommends that instead of being an onlooker to such disputable but possible future considerations, Türkiye should consider being an influential insider of the ICC to better explain its legitimate legal arguments on the issues, such as the situation in Cyprus; to impact the international community's perception of the Cyprus question on its behalf; and to make sure that its side of the issues is well understood.

Chapter 7 suggests a Security Council referral is the only way a state could be subject to the ICC's jurisdiction over the crime of aggression absent its consent. Given that a Security Council referral of a situation would provide the ICC with the competence to prosecute even the nationals of non-State Parties, a state's accession to the Rome Statute would not actually impact the

25 *BBC*, Cyprus Reunification Talks to Resume, www.bbc.com/news/world-europe-26093114 (2 February 2014).

26 Tulin Daloglu, *Why Turkey May Not Want to Join the ICC*, www.al-monitor.com/pulse/tr/originals/2014/09/turkey-icc-rome-statue-human-rights.html (accessed 5 September 2014).

27 Patrick W. Nee, *Key Facts on Turkey: Essential Information on Turkey* (The International Publishing Company 2013) 1.

possibility of it being exposed to the jurisdiction of the Court in respect of an act of aggression as long as that state does not opt in to the aggression amendments. Thus, non-party states' fear that their nationals could face accusations of the crime of aggression should not hinder their consideration of accession to the Rome Statute, as they will have, as States Parties, the option not to accept the Kampala Amendments. Chapter 7 will show that, absent a Security Council referral, the ICC may exercise jurisdiction over the crime of aggression only if it is committed on the territory "and" by the nationals of a State Party that has accepted the Kampala Amendments. The chapter will explain that the states' concerns regarding the ICC's jurisdiction over the crime of aggression are less meaningful given that even the States Parties are afforded the right to opt out of the jurisdiction of the Court over this crime.

Chapter 7 will also show that, as evidenced by the practice of the U.N. Office of Legal Affairs, the states that join the ICC after the adoption or the entry into force of the Kampala Amendments will not be regarded as having ratified these amendments and thus will not be bound by them. The chapter will conclude that Türkiye's possible fears that its nationals could face accusations of the crime of aggression should not hinder its consideration of accession to the Rome Statute because such accession would not impact the possibility of Türkiye being exposed to the jurisdiction of the ICC with regard to an act of aggression so long as Türkiye does not opt in to the Kampala amendments.

Chapter 8 explores the benefits that Türkiye could gain by joining the ICC. All the previous chapters have shown that the exercise of the ICC's jurisdiction over Turkish nationals is highly unlikely and that the concerns presented against Türkiye's accession are not so serious as to justify Türkiye's avoidance of the Court's jurisdiction. Chapter 8, on the other hand, explores some of the compelling benefits for Türkiye to join the ICC.

First, by acceding to the Rome Statute, Türkiye would acquire the rights that would allow Türkiye to participate in the further shaping of the of the law and procedures and the staffing of the ICC. It could more effectively suggest amendments to the Rome Statute and cast its vote on the proposals in a way to accomplish changes it considers important for the protection of its interests. By being a State Party to the Court, Türkiye would also acquire the right to participate in electing and removing the judges and the prosecutor of the Court and put forward its nationals as candidates for these positions. Furthermore, as a State Party, Türkiye could more effectively bring issues that bother it to the Court's agenda, create more meaningful communication with the Office of the Prosecutor and sway other members of the Court as an insider. It could become an active participant of the determination process of critical issues simply by joining the Court.

Second, by joining the ICC, Türkiye would enjoy positive political impacts of being a State Party, such as enhancing its reputation internationally. Accession to the Rome Statute, as a demonstration of Türkiye's commitment to further contribute to international peace and the rule of law, could help Türkiye garner greater support from the members of the Assembly of State Parties and the UN General Assembly when contesting prestigious seats, such as a nonpermanent seat at the Security Council. Türkiye's accession to the Rome Statute could also motivate its southern and eastern neighbors to consider ratification and thus could significantly contribute to the advancement of the international rule of law in the Middle East. Given the significant challenges posed by the frequent commission of serious international crimes in its southern neighborhood, advancing justice, accountability and the fight against impunity in this region aligns with Türkiye's best interests.

Third, as a State Party to the Rome Statute, Türkiye would have a stronger hand in its European Union full-membership negotiations. ICC accession is not one of the criteria for joining the EU, but it is a common policy adopted by all members of the Union under the Common Foreign and Security Policy, and it is considered as an essential component of the EU's values. Türkiye's accession to the founding treaty of the ICC, of which the European Commission and the European Parliament have been strong supporters, would have a very positive impact on the Türkiye-EU full membership negotiations. The EU addresses the accession to the Rome Statute as an improvement in the area of human rights. Türkiye's accession to the Court would represent another important step ahead in strengthening the protection of human rights, providing a significant boost to the negotiation process.

Chapter 9 concludes that the ICC is not a threat for Türkiye but an opportunity to enjoy the benefits of being a State Party to the Court. First, Türkiye's objections to the Rome Statute are not so serious as to justify Türkiye's avoidance of the ICC's jurisdiction because, given the procedural protections of the Statute, the exercise of ICC jurisdiction over Turkish nationals is highly unlikely. Second, remaining a non-party is not an effective way of achieving the changes that Türkiye wants to see in the Rome Statute. Third, remaining outside the Court does not guarantee that the Court will not exercise jurisdiction over Turkish nationals.

Fourth, Türkiye's non-party status to the ICC, which was created with the purpose of fighting against impunity and deterring future commission of grave crimes, harms its reputation internationally. Türkiye is already a party to several key international human rights instruments, including the ECHR, which imposes much more extensive obligations than the Rome Statute and lacks its procedural safeguards, such as the gravity threshold and "interests of justice" considerations, to maintain its international image and European relations. Drawing attention to the benefits of being an active member of the Assembly of State Parties, Chapter 9 finally invites the Turkish government to join the ever-growing ICC family without delay.

Bibliography

Agreement establishing an Association between the European Economic Community and Turkey, Official Journal of the European Communities, 12 September 1963, No. L 361/29.

American Non-Governmental Organizations Coalition for the International Criminal Court (AMICC), *A Campaign for US Immunity from the ICC*, www.amicc.org/usicc/biacampaign.
Bardakçı, Murat. *HaberTurk*, www.haberturk.com/yazarlar/murat-bardakci/222810-biz-yedigimiz-sogani-bile-reformlardan-daha-fazla-onemsemistik (accessed 4 November 2009).
BBC, Cyprus Reunification Talks to Resume, www.bbc.com/news/world-europe-26093114 (accessed 2 February 2014).
Behramoğlu, Ataol, *Öğretmen Öldürmek, Cumhuriyet*, https://www.cumhuriyet.com.tr/yazarlar/ataol-behramoglu/ogretmen-oldurmek-806610 (accessed 19 August 2017).
Cesran International, *International Criminal Court (ICC)*, http://cesran.org/international-criminal-court-icc (accessed 1 April 2015).
Coalition for the International Criminal Court, *Target Countries-Turkey*, http://www.iccnow.org/?mod=urc1006.
Daloglu, Tulin, *Why Turkey May Not Want to Join the ICC*, www.al-monitor.com/pulse/tr/originals/2014/09/turkey-icc-rome-statue-human-rights.html (accessed 5 September 2014).
European Commission, *Turkey 2021 Report* (October 2021), p. 21, https://neighbourhood-enlargement.ec.europa.eu/document/download/892a5e42-448a-47b8-bf62-b22d52c4ba26_en?filename=Turkey%202021%20report.PDF.
European Commission, *Turkey Regular Report 2002* (October 2002) 25, https://neighbourhood-enlargement.ec.europa.eu/document/download/9018e458-daec-4fc1-8cbf-85839fdcdddb_en?filename=tu_en.pdf.
European Court of Human Rights, *Ocalan v. Turkey*, Appl. No. 5980/07, Decision, (ECtHR 7 July 2010), https://hudoc.echr.coe.int/eng#{%22itemid%22:[%22001-69022%22]}.
European Union – Eur-Lex Access to European Union Law, *Accession Criteria (Copenhagen Criteria)*, https://eur-lex.europa.eu/EN/legal-content/glossary/accession-criteria-copenhagen-criteria.html.
Glasius, Marlies, *The International Criminal Court: A Global Civil Society Achievement* (Routledge Chapman & Hall 2006).
Hochleitner, Erich, *The Political Criteria of Copenhagen and Their Application to Turkey*, Working Paper (Austrian Institute for European Security Policy 2005), pp. 8, 16.
International Criminal Court – Office of the Prosecutor, *Report on Preliminary Examination Activities 2013* (November 2013), http://www.icc-cpi.int/en_menus/icc/press%20and%20media/press%20releases/Documents/OTP%20Preliminary%20Examinations/OTP%20-%20Report%20%C20Preliminary%C20Examination%C20Activities%202013.pdf.
Nee, Patrick W., *Key Facts on Turkey: Essential Information on Turkey 1* (The International Publishing Company 2013).
Olson, Robert, ed., *The Kurdish Nationalist Movement in the 1990s: Its Impact on Turkey and the Middle East* (University Press of Kentucky 1996).
Özdemir, Yavuz, Erol Çiydem and Elif Aktaş, Tanzimat Fermanı'nın Arka Planı, (1) *Kastamonu Education Journal* 328–329 (2014).
Parry, John T., *Evil, Law and the State: Perspectives on State Power and Violence* (Editions Rodopi B.V. 2006).
Robertson, Arthur Henry, The European Court of Human Rights, (2) *The International and Comparative Law Quarterly* 396 (1959).
United Nations Treaty Collection, *Rome Statute of the International Criminal Court* (17 July 1998).

2 Omission of the Crime of Terrorism from the Rome Statute

When the 1994 Draft Statute for an International Criminal Court was forwarded to the Rome Conference, the inclusion of the crime of terrorism in the Rome Statute was still a matter of dispute. While representatives from Türkiye, Algeria, Kyrgyzstan, Costa Rica, Armenia, India, Tajikistan, Nigeria, Congo, Sri Lanka, Israel, Tunisia, Trinidad and Tobago, New Zealand, Cuba, Egypt, Benin, Comoros, Ethiopia, Jamaica, Thailand and Bolivia made statements in favor of the inclusion of terrorism in the Statute, most of the remaining countries opposed such inclusion. The head of the Turkish delegation to the Rome Conference, Mehmet Güney, voiced his strong support for listing terrorism as one of the crimes within the jurisdiction of the Court throughout the conference.[1] The Turkish delegation's efforts to include terrorism in the Rome Statute were predicated on the belief that such inclusion could strengthen Türkiye's fight against the PKK.

At the conclusion of the Rome Conference, however, terrorism was not expressly listed as one of the crimes within the subject matter jurisdiction of the ICC. Exclusion of a separate crime of terrorism from the Rome Statute was one of the biggest disappointments of the Turkish delegation which "found itself obligated to abstain" from voting to adopt the Rome Statute because "the final outcome was not in keeping with its expectations."[2] Even at the Kampala Review Conference that took place in 2010, 12 years after the adoption of the Rome Statute, the first concern that the head of the Turkish

1 See, e.g., statements made by Mr. Güney at the 7th plenary meeting of the Rome Conference: Official Records of the United Nations Diplomatic Conference of Plenipotentiaries on the Establishment of an International Criminal Court, Official Records Volume II, A/CONF.183/13, 15 June–17 July 1998, at 106, para. 11 [hereinafter Official Records of the Rome Conference].

2 Official Records of the Rome Conference, *supra* note at 124, para. 41. Among the States that made statements in favor of the inclusion of terrorism in the Rome Statute, Costa Rica, Tajikistan, Nigeria, Congo, Tunisia, Trinidad and Tobago, New Zealand, Benin, Comoros, Bolivia and Armenia have joined the Court despite the failure of the attempts to include a separate crime of terrorism in the Statute, while Algeria, Kyrgyzstan, India, Sri Lanka, Israel, Cuba, Egypt, Ethiopia, Jamaica, Thailand and Türkiye are still non-parties to the Statute.

DOI: 10.4324/9781003641643-2

delegation brought up was the exclusion of terrorism from the agenda of the conference.[3]

This chapter begins with a description of the Turkish efforts to include terrorism in the Rome Statute and the motives behind them. It then establishes that although the Turkish delegation to the Rome Conference was disappointed by the exclusion of the crime of terrorism from the Rome Statute, the lack of the reference to terrorism in the Statute was not, in fact, a loss for the delegation.

First, current status of the Rome Statute already covers most of the PKK's terrorist acts, which prompted Türkiye's efforts to include terrorism in the Rome Statute. The lack of the reference to terrorism in the Rome Statute does not prevent the ICC from investigating and prosecuting the terrorist acts. Second, because of the possibility that the ICC could characterize Türkiye's fight against the PKK as an armed conflict subject to international humanitarian law norms despite Türkiye's objections to such characterization, Türkiye would not be eager to trigger an ICC investigation into the crimes committed by the PKK.

Third, irrespective of whether subject matter jurisdiction of the ICC would be satisfied, the situation with respect to the PKK would most likely be found inadmissible before the Court because of the ongoing national proceedings against the PKK perpetrators. For the reasons listed earlier, this chapter will argue, exclusion of a separate crime of terrorism from the Rome Statute should no longer be regarded as one of the obstacles to Türkiye's accession.

This chapter will also draw attention to the fact that staying outside the ICC does not provide any contribution to the efforts to include terrorism *per se* in the Rome Statute. By joining the ICC, however, Türkiye would acquire the right to propose and vote on behalf of amendments to include terrorism per se as a crime within the jurisdiction of the Court and take the opportunity to sway other countries in this direction, if it still wishes so. As will be elaborated in the following chapters, joining the ICC could, in fact, be conducive to Türkiye's struggle against terrorism. Türkiye, by acceding to the Rome Statute, could enjoy positive political impacts of being a State Party, such as enhancing its reputation internationally. Adherence to the Rome Statute, as a demonstration of Türkiye's commitment to further contribute to international peace and the rule of law, could help Türkiye garner greater support from other State Parties in its war against terrorism.

In this regard, Assembly of the State Parties could serve as a platform for Türkiye to impact the international community's perception of the terrorist groups, against which Türkiye is fighting, on its behalf. This is particularly important given the vigorous efforts within the EU to remove the PKK from

3 International Criminal Court, *Statement by Mr. Ismail Aramaz Head of Turkish Delegation*, http://www.icc-cpi.int/iccdocs/asp_docs/RC2010/Statements/ICC-RC-gendeba-Turkey-ENG.pdf (10 June 2010) [hereinafter Statement by Mr. Ismail Aramaz].

the EU list of terrorist groups.[4] Furthermore, Türkiye could benefit from joining the ICC by acquiring the right to trigger a preliminary examination as a State Party. While it is a fact that Türkiye would not be eager to trigger a preliminary examination for the reasons detailed in this chapter, its ability to trigger such examination could still have a deterrent effect on the PKK's senior members, their abettors and the states that solicit, abet, or fund the crimes of the PKK, as they would fear facing charges before the Court.

1. The Turkish Efforts for the Inclusion of Terrorism in the Rome Statute and the Motives Behind Them

After the dismissal of several proposals to include terrorism *per se* under Article 5 of the Rome Statute, Türkiye, together with Sri Lanka, India and Algeria, proposed to list terrorism under the acts amounting to crimes against humanity.[5] The Turkish delegation's efforts to add terrorism to the list of punishable offenses were directly influenced by Türkiye's more than 30-year-old fight against the terrorist PKK. At the 7th plenary meeting of the Diplomatic Conference, Mr. Güney reminded that international law requires states to "refrain from organizing or encouraging terrorist activities in the territory of other States and from tolerating activities in their own territory directed toward that end."[6] Apparently, the delegation believed that inclusion of the crime of terrorism in the Rome Statute would not only make the terrorist attacks by the PKK prosecutable before the ICC but it could also serve as an extra incentive for the European countries to take decisive actions against the PKK activities within their territory or deter foreign countries from using the outlawed PKK to secure political ends.

The PKK "generates most of its revenue in Europe," mainly from criminal activities such as drug trafficking, human trafficking, arms smuggling, illegal immigration, extortion, illegal taxation, etc.[7] EUROPOL's most recent report in 2018 pointed out that the PKK "uses front organisations and charities in the EU" "to systematically and, if need be, forcibly collect funds in the EU to finance its activities."[8] According to this report, "Austria, France, Romania and Switzerland reported activities of the annual *kampanya* to finance PKK and its armed branch *Hêzên Parastina Gel* . . . France [alone] reports an

4 European Police Office, *EU Terrorism Situation and Trend Report 2015* (The Hague: European Police Office 2015) 28.

5 Robert Kolb, The Exercise of Criminal Jurisdiction over International Terrorists, in Andrea Bianchi (ed.), *Enforcing International Law Norms Against Terrorism* (Oxford: Hart Publishing 2004) 279.

6 Official Records of the Rome Conference, *supra* note 1, at p. 106, para. 10.

7 Moyara Ruehsen, Partiya Karkeren Kurdistan (PKK), in Michael Freeman (ed.), *Financing Terrorism: Case Studies* (New York: Routledge 2016) 65.

8 European Police Office, *EU Terrorism Situation and Trend Report 2018* (The Hague: European Police Office 2018) 11.

estimate of EUR 6 million proceeds."[9] The report also stated that "[t]he PKK is believed to use Europe as a base for logistics and procurement of weapons and recruitment . . . France reported the process of recruitment of militants through the organisation *Komalen Ciwan*."[10] Likewise, EUROPOL's report in 2017 pointed out that "Belgium, France, Germany, Italy, Romania and Switzerland reported that the PKK continued its fundraising, propaganda and recruitment activities."[11] The terrorist organization also obtains revenues from special events, sales of publications and commercial establishments in European countries.[12]

Türkiye's Ministry of Foreign Affairs complains in its official website that the PKK "continues its systematic recruitment activities of young persons living in European countries and trains them in various camps."[13] Indeed, EUROPOL's reports confirmed that "the PKK were maybe running a number of ideological training camps for its youth in remote pre-Alpine areas during the second half of 2016."[14] A report of EUROPOL further revealed that some "[o]rganizations within the EU have been identified as providing logistical support to . . . the PKK."[15] An assessment of the EUROPOL's reports suggests that no decisive actions are being taken against the PKK's activities in Europe.

While several European countries are solely accused of turning a blind eye to PKK's activities within their borders, some European countries, such as Greece,[16] have even been accused by the Turkish government of assisting "with fundraising campaigns and diplomatic support" and providing "political and military training to PKK militants."[17] The United States is also accused by Türkiye of "providing material and training support" to an offshoot of a terrorist organization against which Türkiye has been fighting.[18] Indeed, it is not a secret that PYD and its military wing, YPG, "has turned into a key US ally in the struggle against ISIS" in northern Syria.[19] Though the United

9 European Police Office, *supra* note 8, at 46.
10 European Police Office, *supra* note 8, at 46.
11 European Police Office, *EU Terrorism Situation and Trend Report 2017* (The Hague: European Police Office 2017) 39.
12 Ruehsen, *supra* note 7, at p. 65.
13 Republic of Türkiye Ministry of Foreign Affairs, "*PKK*," www.mfa.gov.tr/pkk.en.mfa (accessed 1 January 2024).
14 European Police Office, *supra* note 11, at p. 39.
15 European Police Office, *EU Terrorism Situation and Trend Report 2013* (The Hague: European Police Office 2013) 11.
16 Uğur Bayıllıoğlu, Uluslararası Ceza Mahkemesi ve Türkiye, 56(1) *Ankara Üniversitesi Hukuk Fakültesi Dergisi* 64 (2007).
17 Ruehsen, *supra* note 7, at p. 66.
18 Özlem Kayhan Pusane, How to Profile PYD/YPG as an Actor in the Syrian Civil War: Policy Implications for the Region and Beyond, in Özden Zeynep Oktav, Emel Parlar Dal and Ali Murat Kurşun (eds.), *Violent Non-state Actors and the Syrian Civil War: The ISIS and YPG Cases* (Switzerland: Springer 2018) 84.
19 Pusane, *supra* note 19, at 84.

States' Central Intelligence Agency (CIA) has officially listed PYD as the Syrian wing of the U.S.-designated terrorist group PKK under foreign-based terrorist groups,[20] in the eyes of U.S. government, "the PYD is a different group than the PKK legally, under United States law."[21] Türkiye has long criticized the US, its NATO ally, for arming and training the YPG and the European countries for their reluctance to act against the PKK activities in their territory or to hand over members of this terrorist organization.[22]

Bearing in mind Türkiye's longstanding fight against the PKK and the statements made by the Turkish delegation at the Rome Conference, the delegation may have expected that inclusion of terrorism in the Rome Statute would help Türkiye achieve three international cooperation objectives that it perceived as essential for the defeat of the PKK. The first expectation behind the delegation's efforts to include terrorism in the Rome Statute may have been that foreign states, particularly the States Parties, would refrain from inducing, financing or providing the means for the commission of the PKK's acts in accordance with Articles 25(3)(b) and (c) of the Statute. While Article 25(3)(b) criminalizes the ordering, soliciting or inducing the commission of any of the crimes covered in the Rome Statute, Article 25(3)(c) outlaws aiding and abetting the commission of such a crime "for the purpose of facilitating the commission" of it.[23]

The second motive behind the delegation's efforts to include terrorism in the Rome Statute may have been that the States Parties would have the obligation to arrest the indicted senior PKK members who reside in their territory and extradite them to the ICC in accordance with article 59 of the Statute, in case the Court tries the case and issues warrants of arrest. Lastly, the Turkish delegation may have expected that inclusion of terrorism in the Rome Statute could serve as an incentive for the European countries not to tolerate the PKK activities in their territories in accordance with the preamble of the Statute,

20 See Central Intelligence Agency, "The World Factbook," Where It States, under the Heading "Terrorism," that "Salih MUSLIM Muhammad Leads Kurdistan Workers Party's Syrian Wing, the Syrian Kurdish Democratic Union Party (PYD), https://www.cia.gov/library/publications/the-world-factbook/geos/sy.html (accessed 1 January 2024). While testifying before a Senate panel at the U.S. Congress in 2016, U.S. Secretary of Defense Ashton Carter also confirmed that there are "substantial ties" between the PYD/YPG and the PKK: The Young Europeans, "PKK: US Defense Sec. Ashton Carter corfirms ties with PYD, YPG, PKK TERROR Groups," Online Video Clip, *You Tube*, 13 January 2018, https://www.youtube.com/watch?v=IkDssSVNz4k (accessed 1 January 2024).

21 Ayşe Ömür Atmaca, Turkey-US Relations (2009–2016): A Troubled Partnership in a Troubled World? in Pınar Gözen Ercan (ed.), *Turkish Foreign Policy: International Relations, Legality and Global Reach* (Switzerland: Springer 2017) 73.

22 PKK Terror Group Gets 30 Million Euros a Year from Its Foundations in Europe, *Daily Sabah*, 15 January 2013, https://www.dailysabah.com/war-on-terror/2016/12/11/pkk-terror-group-gets-30-million-euros-a-year-from-its-foundations-in-europe (accessed 1 January 2024).

23 United Nations Treaty Collection, Rome Statute of the International Criminal Court, U.N. Doc. A/CONF.183/9, 17 July 1998, art. 25(3)(b)-(c).

which states that the States Parties are "[d]etermined . . . to contribute to the prevention of" the crimes covered in the Statute.[24] All these potential expectations will be addressed in the following sections of this chapter in the light of the assessment of Türkiye's objections to the exclusion of a separate crime of terrorism from the Rome Statute.

2. The ICC's Already Existing Jurisdiction Over the Terrorist Crimes of the PKK

The first reason why omission of the crime of terrorism from the Rome Statute is not a valid argument against Türkiye's ratification of it is that most of the crimes that the PKK has been committing already fall within the subject matter jurisdiction of the ICC, as they usually comprise the elements of crimes against humanity – one of the four core crimes of the Rome Statute. Official records of the Turkish Ministry of Defense show that the PKK has so far killed more than 14,000 people, a big majority of whom are civilians.[25] Furthermore, this figure does not include the number of the PKK's executions of its own members. The fact that terrorism is not expressly listed as one of the crimes within the subject matter jurisdiction of the ICC would not prevent the Court from exercising its jurisdiction over the PKK's terrorist acts that constitute crimes against humanity as long as they meet high threshold criteria set out in the Rome Statute.

2.1. The PKK's Acts as Crimes Against Humanity

The idea of prosecuting senior PKK officials in an international tribunal is not new. In 1998, following the crisis between Türkiye and Italy over the extradition of the PKK leader to face a trial in Türkiye,[26] Helsinki Watch, a U.S. based non-governmental organization now named Human Rights Watch, called for his trial for crimes against humanity in an international tribunal.[27] However, the idea did not catch on, on the grounds that "such international court to try an individual" did not exist at the time.[28]

24 United Nations Treaty Collection, *supra* note 23, at *preamble*, para. 5.

25 Ali Sarıhan, The Two Periods of the PKK Conflict: 1984–1999 and 2004–2010, in Fevzi Bilgin and Ali Sarıhan (eds.), *Understanding Turkey's Kurdish Question* (MD: Lexington Books 2013) 94–95; PKK 1984'ten Beri 7 Bin Sivili Katletti, *TRT Haber*, 27 August 2015, http://www.trthaber.com/haber/turkiye/pkk-1984ten-beri-7-bin-sivili-katletti-200648.html (accessed 1 January 2024).

26 World: Europe Rome Takes Ocalan Case to Moscow, *BBC*, 30 November 1998, news.bbc.co.uk/2/hi/europe/225063.stm (accessed 1 January 2024).

27 Kemal Kirisci, The Kurdish Question and Turkish Foreign Policy, in Lenore G. Martin and Dimitris Keridis (eds.), *The Future of Turkish Foreign Policy* (Cambridge: The MIT Press 2004) 278.

28 World: Europe Rome Takes Ocalan Case to Moscow, *supra* note 26.

The PKK killed 5,390 civilians from 1984 to 1999 and 1,045 civilians from 2004 to 2010.[29] Even though the number of the civilian deaths decreased after 2004, as part of a tactical plan that aimed to convince Kurdish population to support its attacks, the PKK continued targeting civilians, as well as security forces. Today, the total number of civilians killed in the terrorist acts for most of which PKK claimed responsibility, including suicide bomb attacks in metropolitan centers and mass killings in rural areas, exceeded 7,000.[30]

Widespread killing of thousands of civilians by the PKK could amount to crimes against humanity under the Rome Statute because under paragraph 1 of the Article 7 of the Statute, murder, *inter alia*, is a crime against humanity "when committed as a part of a widespread or systematic attack directed against any civilian population, with knowledge of the attack."[31] In the ongoing ICC investigation into the situation in the Republic of Kenya, 1,133 deaths were enough to indict for a crime against humanity.[32]

An "attack directed against any civilian population," on the other hand, is defined in paragraph 2 of the Article 7 of the Rome Statute as "a course of conduct involving the multiple commission of acts referred to in paragraph 1 against any civilian population, pursuant to or in furtherance of a State or organizational policy to commit such attack."[33] The wording of this paragraph clearly shows that, for a crime to rise to the level of crimes against humanity, a State connection is not required, so long as an organizational policy exists. In other words, Article 7 (2) makes it clear that non-State entities as well as States could commit a crime against humanity so long as they have an organizational policy.

Al-Qaeda, for example, has been described by many commentators as a non-State entity that has an organizational policy.[34] Professor Michael P. Scharf and Michael A. Newton explain why, according to commentators, al-Qaeda's attacks of 11 September 2001 could be deemed a crime against humanity: 1) they targeted civilians, 2) they resulted in the deaths of significant number of people, 3) they were part of a string of attacks, and 4) they constituted a systematic attack.[35]

As will be detailed further in the following sections, the PKK's repetitive acts are also carried out as part of a plan and policy. The PKK has a

29 Sarıhan, *supra* note 25, at pp. 94–95.
30 TRT Haber, *supra* note 25.
31 Rome Statute, *supra* note 23, art. 7(1).
32 International Criminal Court – Pre-Trial Chamber II, *Decision Pursuant to Article 15 of the Rome Statute on the Authorization of an Investigation into the Situation in the Republic of Kenya*, 31 March 2010, p. 54, para. 131.
33 Rome Statute, *supra* note 23, art. 7(2).
34 Michael P. Scharf and Michael A. Newton, Terrorism and Crimes Against Humanity, in Leila Nadya Sadat (ed.), *Forging a Convention for Crimes against Humanity* (New York: Cambridge University Press 2011) 274.
35 Scharf and Newton, *supra* note 34, at 274.

hierarchical structure, significant number of members and effective control over its members. The PKK's "capacity to declare and hold ceasefires" with the instruction of its captured leader shows that the PKK is "under 'responsible command.'"[36] Considering the criteria mentioned by Prof. Scharf and Newton, a large number of the attacks of the PKK could also be considered as crimes against humanity because they 1) targeted civilians, 2) resulted in the deaths of significant number of people, 3) were part of a string of attacks and 4) constituted a systematic attack. For the purpose of the Rome Statute, a crime against humanity means any of the acts enumerated in the Article 7 of the Statute "when committed as part of a widespread or systematic attack directed against any civilian population, with knowledge of the attack."[37] Among those, "murder,"[38] "severe deprivation of physical liberty in violation of fundamental rules of international law,"[39] "[e]nforced disappearance of persons"[40] and "inhumane acts . . . intentionally causing great suffering, or serious injury to body or to mental or physical health"[41] are only some of the typical crimes of the PKK.

While an isolated, one-time attack does not rise to the level of a crime against humanity,[42] the PKK's acts are carried out as part of a sustained campaign of terrorist organizational policy and thus could be deemed "widespread or systematic." A wave of the PKK's terrorist attacks, which result in hundreds of civilian deaths, could, therefore, be classified as the crime against humanity of murder and of attempted murder. Abductions by the PKK are another example that could be considered by the ICC as crimes against humanity, namely, as "severe deprivation of physical liberty" under the Article 7(1)(e) and as "inhumane acts . . . intentionally causing great suffering, or serious injury . . . to mental . . . health" under the Article 7(1)(k).[43]

It is important to note that neither the Rome Statute nor the customary international law require crimes against humanity be committed within the context of an armed conflict. Article 6 of the 1945 Charter of the International Military Tribunal (Nuremberg) did require a nexus between crimes against humanity and "international" armed conflict.[44] Article 5 of the 1993

36 William Abresch, A Human Rights Law of Internal Armed Conflict: The European Court of Human Rights in Chechnya, 16 *European Journal of International Law* 755 (2005).

37 Rome Statute, *supra* note 23, art. 7(1).

38 Rome Statute, *supra* note 23, art. 7(1)(a).

39 Rome Statute, *supra* note 23, art. 7(1)(e).

40 Rome Statute, *supra* note 23, art. 7(1)(i).

41 Rome Statute, *supra* note 23, art. 7(1)(k).

42 Lucy Martinez, Prosecuting Terrorists at the International Criminal Court: Possibilities and Problems, 34(1) *Rutgers Law Journal* 18(2002).

43 Rome Statute, *supra* note 23, art. 7(1)(k).

44 International Criminal Tribunal for the Former Yugoslavia, *Prosecutor v. Dusko Tadić*, Decision on the Defense Motion for Interlocutory Appeal of Jurisdiction, 2 October 1995, Case No. IT-94-1-I, para. 140 [hereinafter *Tadić* Interlocutory Appeal Decision]. The jurisdiction of the Nuremberg Tribunal over crimes against humanity was actually linked to the existence

Statute of the International Criminal Tribunal for the Former Yugoslavia (ICTY), on the other hand, required crimes against humanity be committed in an armed conflict, "whether international or internal in character."[45] As of customary international law, the Appeals Chamber of the ICTY stated, in *Prosecutor v. Tadic*, that "customary international law no longer requires any nexus between crimes against humanity and armed conflict"[46] and that this requirement "has been abandoned in subsequent State practice with respect to crimes against humanity."[47]

Article 3 of the 1994 Statute of the International Criminal Tribunal for Rwanda, which dealt with crimes against humanity, did not retain any reference to armed conflict at all.[48] Likewise, Article 7 of the Rome Statute defined crimes against humanity in a manner that did not require a connection to an armed conflict, meaning that the ICC has jurisdiction over crimes against humanity committed in situations not involving armed conflict. Indeed, when assessing whether the legal criteria established by the Rome Statute for crimes against humanity is met in a situation, the ICC does not take into account whether or not an armed conflict exists.[49] Considering the ICC's jurisdiction over crimes against humanity is not linked to the existence of an armed conflict, most of the terrorist acts of the PKK are highly likely to be considered by the Court as crimes against humanity, whether or not Türkiye's counter-terrorism operations against the PKK would be classified as an armed conflict.

The jurisprudence of the ICC provides plentiful examples of situations and cases where leaders and members of non-State entities have been charged with and found guilty of crimes against humanity. One of the most recent examples of such conviction can be seen in the situation in Uganda (in the case of the *Prosecutor v. Dominic Ongwen*) in which Trial Chamber IX found Dominic Ongwen, one of the top commanders of an anti-state armed group in Uganda, guilty of 30 counts of crimes against humanity.[50] Likewise, the Office of the Prosecutor has determined in its Preliminary Examination Reports that "the information available provides a reasonable basis to believe that crimes

of an international armed conflict by the Berlin Protocol of October 6, 1945. Protocol Rectifying Discrepancy in Text of Charter, 6 October 1945, reprinted in *Trial of the Major War Criminals Before the International Military Tribunal: Nuremberg*, 14 November 1945–1 October 1946, Vol. 1. 17–18.

45 UN Security Council, *Statute of the International Criminal Tribunal for the Former Yugoslavia (as amended on 17 May 2002)*, art. 5, 25 May 1993.

46 *Tadić* Interlocutory Appeal Decision, *supra* note 44, at para. 78.

47 *Tadić* Interlocutory Appeal Decision, *supra* note 44, at para. 140.

48 UN Security Council, *Statute of the International Criminal Tribunal for Rwanda (as last amended on 13 October 2006)*, 8 November 1994.

49 *See*, for example, the OTP's analysis on the situation in Honduras in its 2014 Preliminary Examinations Report. International Criminal Court – Office of the Prosecutor, *Report on Preliminary Examination Activities 2014*, 2 December 2014, p. 8, para. 31.

50 International Criminal Court, Trial Chamber IX, Situation in Uganda in the Case of the *Prosecutor v. Dominic Ongwen*, "*Trial Judgment*," 4 February 2021 para. 3116.

against humanity under article 7 of the Statute have been committed in the situation in Colombia" by non-State entities.[51] With respect to the situation in Afghanistan, the Office has determined that there is a reasonable basis to believe that crimes against humanity had been committed by non-State armed groups, particularly the (then non-State group) Taliban.[52]

2.1.1. *The Example of the Situation in Uganda*

The first matter into which the ICC was asked to open an investigation through a self-referral is the situation in Uganda.[53] The Government of Uganda referred the situation concerning the Lord's Resistance Army (LRA), a terrorist group which aimed at overthrowing the Government of Uganda,[54] to the ICC in December 2003, and the Prosecutor initiated an investigation on 29 July 2004 following his determination that there is a sufficient basis to believe that crimes within the jurisdiction of the Court had been committed.[55] The Prosecutor charged Joseph Kony, the leader of the LRA, "with criminal responsibility for six attacks" that constituted crimes against humanity and war crimes.[56] Pre-Trial Chamber II of the ICC established, in 2005, that "there are reasonable grounds to believe that" Joseph Kony "committed, . . . ordered or induced the commission of crimes within the jurisdiction of the Court, namely, crimes against humanity and war crimes."[57]

In a later (2016) decision, the Chamber drew attention to the fact that "LRA was an organised armed group with a sufficient degree of organisation to enable it to plan and carry out military operations for a prolonged period of

51 *Report on Preliminary Examination Activities 2017*, International Criminal Court – Office of the Prosecutor, 4 December 2017, p. 29, para. 127. Colombia has experienced over 50 years of violent conflict between state forces and paramilitary groups, the FARC-EP and the ELN, as well as between such paramilitary groups, and the situation remained under preliminary examination for 17 years from June 2004 to October 2021. International Criminal Court – Office of the Prosecutor, *Report on the Situation in Colombia*, 30 November 2023, para. 1.

52 *Report on Preliminary Examination Activities 2017*, International Criminal Court – Office of the Prosecutor, 4 December 2017, p. 53, para. 241.

53 International Criminal Court, Press Release, *President of Uganda Refers Situation Concerning the Lord's Resistance Army (LRA) to the ICC* (29 January 2004), ICC-20040129–44, www.icc-cpi.int/en_menus/icc/press%20and%20media/press%20releases/2004/Pages/president%20of%20uganda%20refers%20situation%20concerning%20the%20lord_s%20resistance%20army%20_lra_%20to%20the%20icc.aspx.

54 The LRA, the ranks of which are believed to have dwindled to several hundred fighters, is no longer in the U.S.'s list of "active" terrorist groups.

55 International Criminal Court, *supra* note 53.

56 International Criminal Court, Pre-Trial Chamber II, *Warrant Of Arrest For Joseph Kony Issued On 8 July 2005 As Amended On 27 September 2005*, 27 September 2005, ICC-02/04–01/05, p. 12, para. 13.

57 International Criminal Court, Pre-Trial Chamber II, *Warrant Of Arrest For Joseph Kony Issued on 8 July 2005 As Amended On 27 September 2005*, 27 September 2005, ICC-02/04–01/05, p. 12, para. 42.

time."[58] Thus, crimes allegedly committed by the LRA have been considered within the scope of the provisions that govern non-international armed conflicts.[59] The Court issued arrest warrants charging the most senior officials of the LRA with crimes against humanity and war crimes.

Some of the violent crimes committed repeatedly by the LRA are at a level similar to the activities of the outlawed PKK, such as murder, intentionally directing an attack against a civilian population or child recruitment.[60] From a subject matter jurisdiction standpoint, high-level members of the PKK, another terrorist group, could also be accused on similar grounds, and the States Parties in which some of those senior members reside would be obligated to communicate evidence.[61] Yet because of the possibility that Türkiye's fight against the PKK may also be characterized, by the Office of the Prosecutor, as an armed conflict subject to international humanitarian law norms, Türkiye would not want to trigger an ICC investigation into the crimes committed by the PKK, regardless of whether the PKK's acts would fall within the subject matter jurisdiction of the Rome Statute. Exclusion of a separate crime of terrorism from the Rome Statute, therefore, should not be regarded as one of the obstacles to Türkiye's accession.

The conclusion from this section of the chapter is that, under Article 7 of the Rome Statute, crimes against humanity are punishable whether or not they are committed in time of armed conflict and whether or not they are committed by non-State entities. Accordingly, some of the terrorist acts of the PKK could also be considered by the Court as crimes against humanity, whether or not Türkiye's counter-terrorism operations against the PKK would be classified as an armed conflict. The ICC's existing jurisdiction over the PKK's repeated acts that might be qualified as crimes against humanity would be sufficient to empower the Court to exercise its jurisdiction over the senior PKK members and its abettors, if other thresholds of the Rome Statute, such as the issues of admissibility, were to be satisfied. Of course, not all the PKK's acts would be considered by the Court as satisfying the requirements of the crimes against humanity under the Rome Statute. But in any event, the fact that terrorism is not featured as a separate offence in the Rome Statute should

58 International Criminal Court – Pre-Trial Chamber II, *Decision on the Confirmation of Charges against Dominic Ongwen*, 23 March 2016, ICC-02/04–01/15, p. 72.

59 The Chamber stated that "[f]rom at least 1 July 2002 to 31 December 2005 a protracted armed conflict not of an international character between the LRA and armed forces of the government of Uganda together with associated local armed units existed in northern Uganda. The armed hostilities exceeded, in intensity, internal disturbances and tensions such as riots, isolated and sporadic acts of violence." International Criminal Court – Pre-Trial Chamber II, *Decision on the Confirmation of Charges against Dominic Ongwen*, 23 March 2016, ICC-02/04–01/15, p. 71.

60 Alhagi Marong, Unlocking The Mysteriousness of Complementarity: In Search of a Forum Conveniens for Trial of the Leaders of the Lord's Resistance Army, 40 *Georgia Journal of International and Comparative Law* 73 (2011).

61 Rome Statute, *supra* note 23, art. 89(1).

not be a concern for Türkiye because most of the terrorist acts are already covered in the Statute.

Some may argue that the PKK's crimes could fail to satisfy the high threshold criteria of the Rome Statute, such as gravity. However, such criteria would need to be met even if terrorism was expressly covered in the Statute. Therefore, what mattered at this stage was to show that most of the crimes committed by the PKK, from which Türkiye's efforts to include terrorism in the Rome Statute stemmed, could already be considered as falling within one of the already existing core crimes of the Statute. Exclusion of a separate crime of terrorism from the Rome Statute, therefore, should not hinder Türkiye's consideration of accession.

2.2. *The PKK's Acts as War Crimes?*

Acts of terrorism may also rise to the level of war crimes, if committed in the context of an armed conflict, either internal or international. The ICC has jurisdiction over the war crimes enumerated under Article 8 of the Rome Statute, including those committed as part of an armed conflict not of an international character.[62] Though Türkiye does not classify its fight against the PKK as an armed conflict within the meaning of international humanitarian law for the reasons that will be explained in the Chapter 3, there is a strong possibility that the Office of the Prosecutor and/or the chambers of the ICC would treat the violence between Türkiye and the PKK as an armed conflict not of an international character. In such a case, the Court could consider some of the terrorist acts of the PKK as rising to the level of war crimes.

Chapter 3, which focuses on Türkiye's concerns with regard to the inclusion of non-international armed conflicts within the jurisdiction of the ICC, will explain that Türkiye does not characterize its struggle against the PKK as an armed conflict because of such fears as that an armed conflict characterization could offer some advantages to the PKK and its members. Chapter 3 will also explain why most of Türkiye's fears about armed conflict characterization are baseless. However, given the fact that Türkiye's PKK-related concerns may not be easily surmounted, it is clear, at least to this author, that Türkiye would not refer the PKK's terrorist crimes to the ICC, even if the crime of terrorism *per se* had been included in the Rome Statute, because triggering such jurisdiction against the crimes committed by the PKK would automatically lead the Court to make a characterization of the violence between Türkiye and the PKK and could result in an armed conflict characterization despite Türkiye's objections.

Moreover, Türkiye's referral of the terrorist acts of the PKK to the ICC could be construed as one of the indicative factors of the existence of a large-scale violence within its borders, thereby increasing the possibility of the armed conflict characterization of the situation in Türkiye. Such referral could

62 Rome Statute, *supra* note 23, art. 8(2).

also be seen as a sign of Türkiye's inability to put forward an effective fight against the PKK or to perform its judicial duties of prosecuting the terrorist crimes and trying the terrorists. Because of the possibility of such interpretations, Türkiye would not ask for an investigation into the crimes committed by the PKK regardless of whether the PKK's terrorist acts would fall within the subject matter jurisdiction of the ICC. The lack of the reference to terrorism in the Rome Statute, therefore, should no longer be seen as an obstacle Türkiye's consideration of accession to the Rome Statute.

Some may rightly argue that the possibility of armed conflict characterization of the violence between Türkiye and the PKK is likely to constitute greater concern for Türkiye than the exclusion of the crime of terrorism from the Rome Statute. This argument, in fact, supports this chapter's contention that exclusion of the crime of terrorism from the Rome Statute was not a loss for the Turkish delegation to the Rome Conference. As the exclusion of terrorism from the Rome Statute is the focus of this chapter, what matters in this section of the chapter is to show that such exclusion should not be considered as an obstacle to Türkiye's accession, especially given the fact that Türkiye would not be eager to trigger an ICC investigation that could lead to an armed conflict characterization. Türkiye's objections to the inclusion of non-international armed conflicts in the Rome Statute (and the validity of Türkiye's concerns with regard to the possibility of armed conflict characterization of its counter-terrorism efforts) are worthy of their own examination and will be handled in Chapter 3.

Before moving on to examine the admissibility of the PKK's acts before the Court, it should be noted that the PKK's acts are not likely to amount to the crime of genocide – another core crime of the Rome Statute – mainly because of the "intent" of those acts. In order for an attack to constitute genocide, at least one of the acts enumerated under Article 6 of the Rome Statute must be "committed with intent to destroy, in whole or in part, a national, ethnical, racial or religious group."[63] The victims of genocide must be targeted because of their membership in one of the protected groups, and the specific intent must be to destroy, in whole or in part, the group.[64]

While the PKK was founded with the aim of establishing a separate Marxist-Leninist Kurdish state,[65] it did not specifically target members of the one of the groups enumerated under Article 6 of the Rome Statute. The PKK's treacherous attacks against the Turkish security forces targeted village guards,

63 Rome Statute, *supra* note 23, art. 6.

64 Jennifer Trahan, *Genocide, War Crimes, and Crimes against Humanity – A Topical Digest of the Case Law of the International Criminal Tribunal for the Former Yugoslavia* (Human Rights Watch 2006) 167.

65 Tuncay Durna and Süleyman Hançerli, Implementing Democratic Policing in the PKK Terrorism Torn Areas, in Özgür Nikbay and Süleyman Hancerli (eds), *Understanding and Responding to the Terrorism Phenomenon: A Multi-Dimensional Perspective* (IOS Press 2007), 326–338, at 328.

military and police officers of both Turkish and Kurdish ethnicity, and its indiscriminate attacks victimized civilian Turkish citizens of both Kurdish and Turkish ethnicity. The PKK did not hesitate to kidnap, execute or assassinate Kurdish civilians or to attack Kurdish villages with the objective of securing political ends, such as deterring them from criticizing the PKK, an objective that has nothing to do with destroying people with Turkish ethnicity.[66] When targeting the civilians, the PKK does not categorize people as Kurds and Turks but as those who are against and those who are pro-PKK.[67]

3. Admissibility Barriers

Another reason why exclusion of the crime of terrorism from the Rome Statute should not be regarded as one of the obstacles to Türkiye's accession is that, even if the subject matter requirement was satisfied, an ICC investigation against the PKK members would still be inadmissible because of the ongoing competent national proceedings. As will be elaborated later, the commission of a crime within the jurisdiction of the ICC is not sufficient for the initiation of an investigation by the Court. Complementarity and *ne bis in idem* principles are only two of the multifold limitations on the ICC's ability to consider a case.

While the principle of complementarity requires the ICC to defer to the national jurisdictions as long as they are able and willing genuinely to carry out the prosecutions in question, *ne bis in idem* principle of Article 20 of the Statute bars the proceedings against an accused for a crime for which he has already been tried. As such, even if we were to assume that all of the PKK's terrorist acts fall within the scope of the expressly covered crimes, it would then be necessary to consider the admissibility of the situation before the Court.

3.1. The Complementarity Principle

The ICC is complementary to the national courts, and it will only act when the domestic authorities are "unable" or "unwilling" to do so.[68] With regard

66 *See*, e.g., Ihsan Bal, *Why PKK (Kurdistan Worker's Party) Killed School Children in Diyarbakir*, www.turkishweekly.net/columnist/2797/why-pkk-kurdistan-workers-party-killed-school-children-in-diyarbakir.html (accessed 8 January 2014).

67 When Massoud Barzani, former leader of Iraq's Kurdish autonomous region, denounced the PKK actions in March 1992 as "savagery' and "terrorist," Öcalan accused him of cooperating with the Turkish State against the PKK, noting that he (Barzani) signed his own death warrant. Michael Gunter, The PKK-KDP Conflict Robert, in W. Olson, *The Kurdish Nationalist Movement in the 1990s: Its Impact on Turkey and the Middle East*, ed. Robert Olson (University Press of Kentucky 1996) 53.

68 Rome Statute, *supra* note 23, art. 17(1)(a).

to the meaning of the labels "unwilling" and "unable," "Paper on some policy issues before the Office of the Prosecutor"[69] provides that:

> A State is unwilling if the national decision has been made and proceedings are or were being undertaken for the purpose of shielding the person concerned from criminal responsibility; there has been an unjustified delay which is inconsistent with an intent to bring the person concerned to justice; or the proceedings were not or are not being conducted independently or impartially.
>
> To assess whether a State is unable to act, the Policy Paper states that the Prosecutor will need to determine whether "due to a total or substantial collapse or unavailability of its national judicial system, the State is unable to obtain the accused or the necessary evidence and testimony or otherwise unable to carry out its proceedings." This provision was inserted to take account of situations where there was a lack of central government, or a state of chaos due to the conflict or crisis, or public disorder leading to collapse of national systems which prevents the State from discharging its duties to investigate and prosecute crimes within the jurisdiction of the Court.[70]

Complementarity principle requires the ICC to ascertain whether national proceedings are covering the same case as the one before the Court and whether those proceedings are genuine within the meaning of Article 17.[71] Available information indicates that the Turkish authorities have been conducting a large number of proceedings against the members of the PKK for their activities that could be qualified as falling within the subject matter jurisdiction of the Rome Statute. Türkiye's Ministry of Justice revealed that, as of 10 February 2018, 10,079 people are in jail because of their conviction of PKK related crimes, which is an indication for Turkish authorities' ability and willingness to prosecute those who are responsible.[72]

Moreover, on 5 October 2012, an İstanbul Court issued arrest warrants for 58 PKK members, including the acting leader, Murat Karayılan, and other senior members, Cemil Bayık, Remzi Kartal, Mustafa Karasu, Duran Kalkan

69 International Criminal Court-Office of the Prosecutor, *Paper on Some Policy Issues before the Office of the Prosecutor* (2003), https://www.icc-cpi.int/nr/rdonlyres/1fa7c4c6-de5f-42b7-8b25-60aa962ed8b6/143594/030905_policy_paper.pdf.

70 International Criminal Court-Office of the Prosecutor, *supra* note 69, art. 4.

71 Rome Statute, *supra* note 23, art. 17.

72 T.C. Adalet Bakanlığı Basın Ve Halkla İlişkiler Müşavirliği, *Adalet Bakanı Gül: Yargı, Terörle Mücadeleyi Çok Etkin Şekilde Sürdürmektedir* [Minister of Justice Gül: Judiciary continues its fight against terrorism very effectively], 10 February 2018, http://www.basin.adalet.gov.tr/Etkinlik/adalet-bakani-gul-yargi-terorle-mucadeleyi-cok-etkin-sekilde-surdurmektedir (accessed 1 January 2024).

and Zübeyir Aydar.[73] It is also important that the most senior members of the PKK who are not in jail are sought with Interpol Red Notices because, in order for the ICC to find a case inadmissible, existing proceedings must prioritize against those who appear to bear the greatest responsibility for the crimes in question.[74]

In its 2012 Preliminary Examinations Report, the Office of the Prosecutor concluded that it had no reason to doubt the genuineness of convictions rendered *in absentia* by Colombian authorities against the leaders of the rebel armed groups who appear to bear the greatest responsibility for the most serious crimes committed in Colombia.[75] With the same reasoning, the Office of the Prosecutor would most likely defer to the proceedings by the competent Turkish authorities, including the convictions rendered *in absentia*.

3.2. ne bis in idem

Another limitation on the ICC's ability to consider a case is the *ne bis in idem* principle, which bars an ICC trial if the accused has already been tried or is in the process of being tried by another court for the conduct in question, unless the proceedings in the other court were for the purpose of shielding the accused from accountability or lacked impartiality or independence.[76] Abdullah Öcalan, the original leader of the PKK, is now serving life in prison on an island off the coast of Türkiye for "founding an armed gang in order to destroy the integrity of the Turkish state and of instigating various terrorist acts that had resulted in loss of life," which are also basis for most of the crimes committed by the PKK.[77] An ICC investigation against Öcalan with respect to the same conduct would not be permissible under the *ne bis in idem* principle of the Rome Statute.

Öcalan appealed his conviction to the European Court of Human Rights, alleging he did not get a fair trial, which was guaranteed by the Article 6 of the European Convention for the Protection of Human Rights and Fundamental

73 PKK Yönetimine Yakalama Kararı (Arrest Warrants for the PKK Leaders), *Cumhuriyet*, 9 Mayıs 2013, http://www.cumhuriyet.com.tr/haber/diger/420546/PKK_yonetimine_yakalama_karari.html (accessed 1 January 2024).

74 Avrupa Sadece Adi Suçları İade Etmiş (Europe Has Extradited Only for Ordinary Crimes), *Aktif Haber*, 15 January 2015, www.aktifhaber.com/avrupa-sadece-adi-suclulari-iade-etmis-719910h.htm (accessed 1 January 2024).

75 International Criminal Court – Office of the Prosecutor, *Situation in Colombia Benchmarking Consultation*, 15 June 2021, p. 7, para. 16; International Criminal Court – Office of the Prosecutor, *Report on Preliminary Examination Activities 2012*, November 2012, p. 26, para. 109.

76 Rome Statute, *supra* note 23, art. 20.

77 European Court of Human Rights, *Ocalan v. Turkey*, Appl. No. 46221/99, "Judgment," 12 May 2005, para. 18, *available at* http://hudoc.echr.coe.int/sites/eng/pages/search.aspx?i=001-69022#{"itemid":["001–69022"]} (accessed 1 January 2024).

Freedoms, a convention to which Türkiye is a party.[78] The ECtHR found that the national proceedings against Öcalan had not complied with some of the requirements of Article 6 of the ECHR and that a retrial or a reopening of the case would be an appropriate way of addressing that.[79] After examining the execution of the ECtHR's judgment by the Ankara Assize Court, the İstanbul Assize Court found that no additional hearing was necessary because the applicant's sentence would be the same, even without the violations found by the ECtHR.

The Committee of Ministers of the Council of Europe, which has the task of supervising the execution of the judgments of the ECtHR, was asked by the counsel of Öcalan to ensure that Türkiye would reopen his case. The Committee, however, decided to close its examination over the case, concluding that Türkiye had fulfilled its obligation in accordance with Article 46 of the ECHR because the proceedings carried out by İstanbul Assize Court to review the case were similar to the proceedings for the reopening of the case.[80] Given the conclusion came out of the Committee of Minister, the ICC proceedings against Öcalan and other PKK senior members who have been convicted by Turkish authorities under the supervision of the ECtHR system would be inadmissible under the *ne bis in idem* principle.

In addition, it should be noted that the purpose of Article 20 of the Rome Statute, which sets out the *ne bis in idem* principle, is not to protect the human rights of the defendants at national level. The likelihood that national proceedings were not "conducted independently or impartially in accordance with the norms of due process recognized by international law" can only be relevant to the ICC insofar as it is "inconsistent with an intent to bring the person concerned to justice."[81] That is to say, the PKK members would not be able to seek a new trial before the ICC by arguing that Türkiye did not offer them a fair one.

An examination the existing national proceedings and investigations against PKK members show that Türkiye is able and willing to conduct effective prosecutions against terrorist crimes taking place in its territory. Thus, even if the crime of terrorism *per se* had been included in the Rome Statute in a way to cover the PKK's crimes that do not amount to any of the currently existing crimes, those acts would be found inadmissible before the ICC because of Türkiye's ability and willingness to prosecute them. Thus, exclusion of the crime of terrorism from the Rome Statute was not, in fact, a loss for the Turkish delegation to the Rome Conference and should not have disappointed the delegation to the extent that it would abstain from voting to adopt the Statute.

78 European Court of Human Rights, *supra* note 77, at para. 18.

79 European Court of Human Rights, *supra* note 77, at para. 210.

80 European Court of Human Rights, *Ocalan v. Turkey*, Appl. No. 5980/07, "*Decision*," 7 July 2010, http://hudoc.echr.coe.int/sites/eng/*pages*/search.aspx?i=001-69022 (accessed 1 January 2024).

81 Rome Statute, *supra* note 23, art. 20(3)(b).

4. The Impact of the Preliminary Examinations

Preliminary examinations are launched by the OTP with the purpose of determining whether a situation, in which the OTP is interested, meets the legal criteria established by the Rome Statute to warrant investigation by the Court.[82] The OTP releases periodic reports on its preliminary examination activities, where it provides information on its analysis and includes upgrades regarding the phases each particular examination reached. The preliminary examination reports, particularly the ones that confirm the commission of the ICC crimes and move on to the next phase of the analysis in a given situation, have a significant deterrent effect on the perpetrators and their abettors because of the possibility of facing charges before the Court.[83] While it is true that Türkiye would not be eager to trigger such investigation for the reasons detailed in this chapter, a preliminary examination into the PKK's activities could similarly serve as a warning to the states that allegedly solicit, fund or abet the acts of the PKK and deter them from doing so.

Article 53(1) of the Statute requires the Prosecutor to consider three successive factors while conducting a preliminary examination. First, the Prosecutor must consider whether the jurisdiction requirement – temporal, material and either territorial or personal – is satisfied. Second, the Prosecutor must decide whether the situation is admissible in light of the complementarity and gravity requirements. Finally, the Prosecutor must determine whether a formal ICC investigation into the situation "would not serve the interests of justice." At the conclusion of each preliminary examination, the Office decides whether there is a reasonable basis to proceed with an investigation.

Accordingly, before moving to the admissibility phase of its analysis in a given situation, the OTP has to determine whether a crime within the jurisdiction of the Court has been or is being committed. This means that even the situations, which are most likely to be found inadmissible before the Court due to the complementarity and gravity requirements, will be subject to the analysis of the OTP with a view to assessing whether an ICC crime has been committed. This is especially important in the PKK context because, as discussed in the previous sections, while most of the PKK's terrorist acts fall within the scope of the expressly covered Rome Statute crimes, they are inadmissible before the Court due to the genuine national proceedings against the perpetrators. If Türkiye accedes to the Rome Statute and the OTP decides to open a preliminary examination into the situation with respect to the PKK, the commission of the most serious crimes by the terrorist organization would be confirmed in the jurisdictional phase of the analysis before even moving to the admissibility phase of the examination.

82 ICC-OTP, *Report on Preliminary Examination Activities 2012*, *supra* note 75, at para. 1.

83 *See* Human Rights Watch, *ICC: Course Correction*, http://www.hrw.org/news/2011/06/16/icc-course-correction (16 June 2011).

In the small likelihood that a preliminary examination is launched against Türkiye's will, confirmation of the PKK's most serious crimes in the Preliminary Examination Reports could promote the aims that the representatives of Türkiye at the Rome Conference intended to achieve with their efforts to include terrorism in the Statute. First, a Preliminary Examinations Report that classifies some of the activities of the PKK as crimes against humanity could have a significant deterrent effect on the commission of the future PKK crimes. Second, such report could also deter neighboring and European countries from funding or facilitating the PKK's acts by making clear that they could be subject to the ICC's jurisdiction once a formal investigation is opened. Confirmation of the PKK's crimes in the Preliminary Examinations Reports could also spur the states – especially the European countries where the PKK runs public campaigns, extorts money and recruits new members – to pursue their own investigations into the PKK activities in their territory. Lastly, confirmation of the most serious crimes committed by the PKK could provide a greater incentive for European countries to arrest and extradite the indicted PKK members to Türkiye.

During the reporting periods, the Prosecutor reminds the parties to the conflict of their responsibilities under international law and the Rome Statute and pushes them towards the fulfillment of their obligations to investigate. Thus, the initiation of a preliminary examination process itself, even before confirmation of the commission of an ICC crime, would remind the concerned parties of their responsibilities regarding the unlawful PKK activities taking place in their territory and would send a clear signal that the international community is watching. Given that a preliminary examination into the PKK activities could promote the aims that the Turkish delegation intended to achieve with its efforts to include terrorism in the Statute and that remaining a non-party does not provide any contribution to the attempts to add terrorism to the list of punishable offenses, the lack of the reference to this crime should not hinder Türkiye's consideration of accession to the Rome Statute.

5. Conclusion

The conclusion from the earlier discussion is that the lack of the reference to terrorism in the Rome Statute, which was the primarily expressed concern of the Turkish delegations in Rome and Kampala, should not hinder Türkiye's consideration of accession to the Statute. First, Türkiye would not want to trigger an ICC investigation into the crimes committed by the PKK, mainly because such an investigation could lead to an "armed conflict" characterization. As will be detailed in the next chapter, Türkiye's counter-terrorism operations against the PKK satisfy the legal criteria for the determination of an armed conflict, and thus, there is a strong possibility that the ICC could treat these operations as an armed conflict if an investigation were to be started.

Second, some of acts of the PKK appear to fall within at least one of the already existing core crimes of the Rome Statute. The lack of the reference to terrorism in the Rome Statute does not prevent the ICC from investigating and prosecuting terrorist acts. Third, an ICC investigation into the terrorist acts that victimized Türkiye would be found inadmissible because Türkiye has already been conducting genuine criminal investigations against the perpetrators.

As will be detailed in the following chapters, Türkiye, by acceding to the Rome Statute, could enjoy positive political impacts of being a State Party, such as enhancing its reputation internationally. Accession to the Rome Statute, as a demonstration of Türkiye's commitment to further contribute to international peace and the rule of law, could help Türkiye garner greater support from other State Parties in its war against terrorism. In this regard, Assembly of State Parties (ASP) could serve as a platform for Türkiye to impact the international community's perception of the terrorist groups, against which Türkiye is fighting, on its behalf. By acceding to the Rome Statute, Türkiye could also accelerate its full membership negotiations with the European Union, whose members are all party to the ICC, and use its strengthened corporate dialogue with the European members of the Court to develop closer cooperation in combatting the funding networks of the PKK in European countries.

It is usually expected that most of the states that prefer to ratify the Rome Statute are intent to promote peace and the rule of law at the international level and that they have confidence in their national criminal system. Türkiye's accession to the Rome Statute, as a demonstration of its confidence in its own national criminal justice system, could also help Türkiye to speedily utilize international cooperation measures, such as the extradition of PKK members. Securing the extradition of terror suspects from the European countries is of great importance for Türkiye's fight against terrorism given the large number of the PKK members who reside there. European countries have so far granted less than 3% of the extradition requests by Türkiye.[84] Any step that would enhance Türkiye's reputation internationally, such as the ratification of the Rome Statute, could serve as an extra incentive for European countries to arrest and extradite the indicted PKK members to Türkiye.

The following chapters will also explain that Türkiye is already a party to several key international human rights instruments, including the ECHR, which imposes much more extensive obligations than the Rome Statute[85] and lacks its procedural safeguards, such as the gravity threshold and "interests of justice"[86] considerations, to maintain its international image and European relations. Indeed, Türkiye's policy to remain engaged with the international

84 Europe Refuses to Extradite Terror Suspects to Turkey, *T-Vine*, 5 February 2017, www.t-vine.com/europe-refuses-to-extradite-terror-suspects-to-turkey/ (accessed 1 January 2024).

85 While the ICC has a limited subject matter jurisdiction over the most serious crimes of international concern, ECHR imposes much more extensive burdens on States Parties, from freedom of expression to the right to form and join trade unions.

86 "In deciding whether to initiate an investigation, the Prosecutor" of the ICC shall, "taking into account the gravity of the crime and the interests of victims," "consider whether: . . .

human rights mechanisms is instrumental in gaining further assistance from other countries in its fight against the terrorist groups.

Bibliography

Abresch, William, A Human Rights Law of Internal Armed Conflict: The European Court of Human Rights in Chechnya, 16 *The European Journal of International Law* 755 (2005).

Aktif Haber, *Avrupa Sadece Adi Suclari Iade Etmis*, www.aktifhaber.com/avrupa-sadece-adi-suclulari-iade-etmis-719910h.htm (accessed 15 January 2015).

Bal, Ihsan, *Why PKK (Kurdistan Worker's Party) Killed School Children in Diyarbakir*, www.turkishweekly.net/columnist/2797/why-pkk-kurdistan-workers-party-killed-school-children-in-diyarbakir.html (accessed 8 January 2014).

Bayıllıoğlu, Uğur, Uluslararası Ceza Mahkemesi ve Türkiye, 56(1) *Ankara Üniversitesi Hukuk Fakültesi Dergisi* (2007).

BBC, World: Europe Rome Takes Ocalan Case to Moscow, news.bbc.co.uk/2/hi/europe/225063.stm (accessed 30 November 1998).

Bianchi, Andrea and Yasmin Naqvi, eds., *Enforcing International Law Norms against Terrorism* (Oxford: Hart Publishing 2004).

Central Intelligence Agency, *The World Factbook*, https://www.cia.gov/library/publications/the-world-factbook/geos/sy.html

Cumhuriyet, *PKK Yonetimine Yakalama Karari* [Arrest Warrants for the PKK Leaders], http://www.cumhuriyet.com.tr/haber/diger/420546/PKK_yonetimine_yakalama_karari.html (accessed 9 May 2013).

Daily Sabah, *PKK Terror Group Gets 30 Million Euros a Year from Its Foundations in Europe*, https://www.dailysabah.com/war-on-terror/2016/12/11/pkk-terror-group-gets-30-million-euros-a-year-from-its-foundations-in-europe (accessed 15 January 2013).

Ercan, Pınar Gözen, ed., *Turkish Foreign Policy: International Relations, Legality and Global Reach* (Switzerland: Springer 2017).

European Police Office, *EU Terrorism Situation and Trend Report 2013* (2013).

European Police Office, *EU Terrorism Situation and Trend Report 2015* (2015).

European Police Office, *EU Terrorism Situation and Trend Report 2017* (2017).

European Police Office, *EU Terrorism Situation and Trend Report 2018* (2018).

Freeman, Michael, ed., *Financing Terrorism: Case Studies* (New York: Routledge 2016).

Human Rights Watch, *ICC: Course Correction*, http://www.hrw.org/news/2011/06/16/icc-course-correction (accessed 16 June 2011).

International Criminal Court – Office of the Prosecutor, *Paper on Some Policy Issues before the Office of the Prosecutor* (September 2003), https://www.icc-cpi.int/nr/rdonlyres/1fa7c4c6-de5f-42b7-8b25-60aa962ed8b6/143594/030905_policy_paper.pdf.

International Criminal Court – Office of the Prosecutor, *Report on Preliminary Examination Activities 2012* (November 2012), http://www.icc-cpi.int/NR/rdonlyres/C433C462-7C4E-4358-8A72-8D99FD00E8CD/285209/OTP2012ReportonPreliminaryExaminations22Nov2012.pdf.

---

there are nonetheless substantial reasons to believe that an investigation would not serve the interests of justice." Rome Statute, *supra* note 23, art. 53(1).

International Criminal Court – Office of the Prosecutor, *Report on Preliminary Examination Activities 2014* (December 2014), at 62, para. 262, http://www.icc-cpi.int/iccdocs/otp/OTP-Pre-Exam-2014.pdf.

International Criminal Court – Office of the Prosecutor, *Report on Preliminary Examination Activities 2017* (4 December 2017).

International Criminal Court – Office of the Prosecutor, *Report on the Situation in Colombia* (30 November 2023).

International Criminal Court – Office of the Prosecutor, *Situation in Colombia Benchmarking Consultation* (15 June 2021).

International Criminal Court, *Press Release – President of Uganda Refers Situation Concerning the Lord's Resistance Army (LRA) to the ICC (29 January 2004),* ICC-20040129–44,www.icc-cpi.int/en_menus/icc/press%20and%20media/press%20releases/2004/Pages/president%20of%20uganda%20refers%20situation%20concerning%20the%20lord_s%20resistance%20army%20_lra_%20to%20the%20icc.aspx.

International Criminal Court, Pre-Trial Chamber II, Case No. ICC-02/04–01/05, Warrant of Arrest for Joseph Kony Issued on 8 July 2005 as Amended on 27 September 2005 (ICC 27 September 2005).

International Criminal Court – Pre-Trial Chamber II, Decision on the confirmation of charges against Dominic Ongwen, ICC-02/04–01/15 (23 March 2016).

International Criminal Court, *Statement by Mr. Ismail Aramaz Head of Turkish Delegation*, http://www.icc-cpi.int/iccdocs/asp_docs/RC2010/Statements/ICC-RC-gendeba-Turkey-ENG.pdf (accessed 10 June 2010).

International Criminal Court, *Trial Chamber IX, Situation in Uganda in the Case of the Prosecutor v. Dominic Ongwen*, "Trial Judgment" (4 February 2021).

Martin, Lenore G. and Dimitris Keridis, eds., *The Future of Turkish Foreign Policy* (Cambridge: The BCSIA 2004).

Marong, Alhagi, Unlocking the Mysteriousness of Complementarity: In Search of a Forum Conveniens for Trial of the Leaders of the Lord's Resistance Army, 40 *Georgia Journal of International & Comparative Law* 67, 73 (2011).

Martinez, Lucy, Prosecuting Terrorists at the International Criminal Court: Possibilities and Problems, 34 *Rutgers Law Journal* 1 (2002).

Nikbay, Özgür and Süleyman Hancerli, eds., *Understanding and Responding to the Terrorism Phenomenon: A Multi-Dimensional Perspective* (IOS Press 2007).

Official Records of the U.N. Diplomatic Conference of Plenipotentiaries on the Establishment of an Int'l Criminal Court, 7th plen. mtg., U.N. Doc. A/CONE 183/SR.7.

Oktav, Özden Zeynep, Emel Parlar Dal and Ali Murat Kurşun (eds.), *Violent Non-state Actors and the Syrian Civil War: The ISIS and YPG Cases* (Switzerland: Springer 2018).

Olson, Robert, ed., *The Kurdish Nationalist Movement in the 1990s: Its Impact on Turkey and the Middle East* (University Press of Kentucky 1996).

Online Video Clip, *You Tube*, 13 January 2018, https://www.youtube.com/watch?v=IkDssSVNz4k.

Pre-Trial Chamber II, Decision pursuant to Article 15 of the Rome Statute on the Authorization of an Investigation into the Situation in the Republic of Kenya (ICC 31 March 2010), http://www.icc-cpi.int/iccdocs/doc/doc854287.pdf.

Prosecutor v. Tadic, Case No. IT-94–1-I, Decision on the Defense Motion for Interlocutory Appeal of Jurisdiction, para. 70 (International Criminal Tribunal for the Former Yugoslavia 2 October 1995).

Protocol Rectifying Discrepancy in Text of Charter, 6 October 1945, reprinted in Trial of the Major War Criminals Before the International Military Tribunal: Nuremberg, 14 November 1945–1 October 1946, Vol. 1.

Republic of Türkiye Ministry of Foreign Affairs, *PKK*, www.mfa.gov.tr/pkk.en.mfa.

Sadat, Leila N., ed., *Forging a Convention for Crimes against Humanity* (Cambridge University Press 2011).

T.C.Adalet Bakanlığı Basın Ve Halkla İlişkiler Müşavirliği, *Adalet Bakanı Gül: Yargı, Terörle Mücadeleyi Çok Etkin Şekilde Sürdürmektedir* [Minister of Justice Gül: Judiciary continues its fight against terrorism very effectively], http://www.basin.adalet.gov.tr/Etkinlik/adalet-bakani-gul-yargi-terorle-mucadeleyi-cok-etkin-sekilde-surdurmektedir (accessed 10 February 2018).

Trahan, Jennifer, *Genocide, War Crimes, and Crimes against Humanity – A Topical Digest of the Case Law of the International Criminal Tribunal for the Former Yugoslavia* (Human Rights Watch 2006) 167.

TRT Haber, *PKK 1984'ten Beri 7 Bin Sivili Katletti*, http://www.trthaber.com/haber/turkiye/pkk-1984ten-beri-7-bin-sivili-katletti-200648.html (accessed 27 August 2015).

T-Vine, *Europe Refuses to Extradite Terror Suspects to Turkey*, www.t-vine.com/europe-refuses-to-extradite-terror-suspects-to-turkey/ (accessed 5 February 2017).

UN Security Council, Statute of the International Criminal Tribunal for Rwanda (as last amended on 13 October 2006) (8 November 1994).

UN Security Council, Statute of the International Criminal Tribunal for the Former Yugoslavia (as amended on 17 May 2002) (25 May 1993).

United Nations Treaty Collections, Rome Statute of the International Criminal Court, 17 July 1998, U.N. Doc. A/CONF.183/9.

3 Inclusion of the Non-international Armed Conflicts within the Jurisdiction of the ICC

Majority of the states participating in the Rome Conference strongly favored the inclusion of non-international armed conflicts within the jurisdiction of the ICC on the grounds that armed conflicts not of an international character are the most prevalent form of conflicts[1] and that the worst atrocities take place in non-international armed conflicts.[2] Some states argued that if non-international armed conflicts were to be excluded from the Rome Statute, *raison d'être* of the ICC would be seriously undermined.[3] In this regard, inclusion of non-international armed conflicts in the Rome Statute was considered by some states to be a *conditio sine qua non* for their accession to the Rome Statute.[4]

1 Official Records of the United Nations Diplomatic Conference of Plenipotentiaries on the Establishment of an International Criminal Court, Official Records Volume II, A/CONF.183/13, 15 June–17 July 1998, at 272, para. 62 [hereinafter Official Records of the Rome Conference].

2 Official Records of the Rome Conference, *supra* note, at 70, para. 99. The States that made statements in favor of the inclusion of internal armed conflicts within the Rome Statute are South Africa, Sweden, Canada, Slovenia, Czech Republic, United Republic of Tanzania, Armenia, Namibia, Zambia, Estonia, Argentina, Bangladesh, Georgia, Russia, Philippines, Germany, Spain, Italy, Australia, United Kingdom, Republic of Korea, Chile, Togo, Lesotho, Slovakia, Hungary, Gabon, Ethiopia, Malta, Guinea-Bissau, Trinidad and Tobago, Lithuania, Costa Rica, Brunei Darussalam, Hungary, Bulgaria, USA, Ireland, Finland, New Zealand, Cape Verde, Denmark, Jordan, Ecuador, Uganda, Sierra Leone, Belgium, Japan, Austria, Norway, Croatia, Senegal, Liechtenstein, Switzerland, Brazil, Mali, Uruguay, Colombia, Nicaragua, Israel, Bosnia and Herzegovina, Congo, Sri Lanka, Venezuela, Portugal, Solomon Islands, Brazil, Mozambique, Botswana, Greece, Poland, Indonesia, Burkina Faso, Romania, France, Guatemala and Andorra. Observers for the following international organizations also expressed support for such inclusion: European Community, Latin American Institute of Alternative Legal Services, Agence de cooperation culturelle et technique, International Committee of the Red Cross, United Nations High Commissioner for Human Rights, Office of the United Nations High Commissioner for Refugees, Women's Caucus for Gender Justice, International Commission of Jurists, International Humanitarian Fact-Finding Commission and Women's International League for Peace and Freedom.

3 Official Records of the Rome Conference, *supra* note, at 277, para. 54.

4 Official Records of the Rome Conference, *supra* note, at 283, para. 8.

DOI: 10.4324/9781003641643-3

Only a small minority of states, namely, China, Sudan, Iraq, Iran, Bahrain, Egypt, Algeria, Burundi, Pakistan, Saudi Arabia, Oman, India, Qatar, Syrian Arab Republic, Libyan Arab Jamahiriya, United Arab Emirates, Nepal and Thailand, along with Türkiye, opposed and expressed concerns at the inclusion of non-international conflicts within the Statute. While some of these opposing States argued that such inclusion might lead to interferences in the internal affairs of States;[5] imperil the territorial integrity and political independence of States;[6] and undermine measures to establish peace in internal conflicts,[7] some expressed concern that provisions on war crimes committed during non-international armed conflicts did not reflect customary international law,[8] and thus, the Court's jurisdiction should not be extended to non-international armed conflicts.

Some states changed their position on whether to support or oppose such inclusion during the course of the Rome Conference. Representative of Indonesia, for example, after opining, at the 27th meeting on 8 July 1998, that war crimes committed during non-international armed conflicts "need not be included" in the Rome Statute, as those crimes "could be punished using the provisions of crimes against humanity,"[9] stated, at the 35th meeting on 13 July 1998, that his delegation "was now prepared to accept the inclusion."[10]

Despite serious objections of the opposing states, the war crimes committed during the course of a non-international armed conflict were included in the Rome Statute. Besides including several war crimes applicable to non-international armed conflicts from the Additional Protocol II, the Rome Statute lowered the threshold for situations amounting to a non-international armed conflict and added new crimes to the list of war crimes.[11] Such inclusion was the main reason some states, such as China, voted against the final text of the Rome Conference.[12] In fact, four of the opposing states were among the only seven States that chose to vote against the final version of the Rome Statute at the end of the Conference.[13] Moreover, none of the opposing states have so far joined the Court.

Although the Turkish delegation to the Rome Conference agreed that inclusion of war crimes in the Rome Statute was essential,[14] it drew attention

5 Official Records of the Rome Conference, *supra* note, at 126, para. 75.
6 Official Records of the Rome Conference, *supra* note, at 168, para. 101.
7 Official Records of the Rome Conference, *supra* note, at para. 101.
8 Official Records of the Rome Conference, *supra* note, at 335, para. 4.
9 Official Records of the Rome Conference, *supra* note, at 287, para. 60.
10 Official Records of the Rome Conference, *supra* note, at 338, para. 35. Indonesia has not, nevertheless, joined the Court.
11 Jing Guan, The ICC's Jurisdiction over War Crimes in Internal Armed Conflicts: An Insurmountable Obstacle for China's Accession? 28(4) *Penn State International Law Review* 721 (2010).
12 Guan, *supra* note 11, at 714.
13 Other states that voted against are the United States, Israel and Yemen.
14 Official Records of the Rome Conference, *supra* note 1, at 276, para. 35.

to the necessity of a very high threshold for the prosecution of those crimes.[15] The delegation opposed the inclusion of Article 8(2)(c) and (e),[16] which deal with the crimes committed within the context of a non-international armed conflict, stating that "[t]he future Court should have nothing to do with internal troubles, including measures designed to maintain national security or root out terrorism."[17] Predictably, the Turkish delegation was concerned that inclusion of internal war crimes in the Rome Statute could, in the future, lead to ICC's interference in Türkiye's internal fight against the PKK and that such interference could undermine its fight against terrorism. Inclusion of non-international armed conflicts within the Rome Statute is, therefore, one of the main reasons why Türkiye abstained from adopting the final text of the Rome Statute.

The previous chapter pointed out that Türkiye would not attempt to trigger an ICC investigation into the terrorist activities of the PKK, even if the crime of terrorism *per se* had been included in the Rome Statute and the thresholds of the Rome Statute had been satisfied, mainly because of the fact that such attempt could lead the Court to characterize as an armed conflict subject to international humanitarian law, a characterization that Türkiye has strongly opposed. This chapter will explain the reasons why Türkiye does not classify the violence between Türkiye and the PKK as an armed conflict within the meaning of international humanitarian law and why the ICC is highly likely to consider it as an armed conflict. This chapter will also point out that possible war-related accusations against the Turkish security forces make the PKK issue the most fatal potential conflict between Türkiye and the ICC.

This chapter will then focus on Türkiye's worst-case scenario in which the Court considers Türkiye's fight against the PKK as an armed conflict subject to Article 8(2)(c) and (e) – the articles that deal with the crimes committed as part of an armed conflict not of an international character. It will explain that the ICC's jurisdiction over non-international armed conflicts should not hinder Türkiye's consideration of accession to the Rome Statute because possible allegations against the Turkish security forces would not meet the legal criteria to justify the initiation of a formal investigation, and thus, joining the Court would not hamper Türkiye in its measures of legitimate repression.

First, most of the allegations against Turkish security forces concern the incidents that occurred prior to the entry into force of the Rome Statute, and thus, they are outside the temporal jurisdiction of the ICC. The Court will have jurisdiction only with respect to the allegations concerning the incidents occurred after the entry into force of the Rome Statute for Türkiye. Second, even if the temporal jurisdiction requirement was satisfied, allegations against Turkish nationals would be found inadmissible before the ICC because of the

15 Official Records of the Rome Conference, *supra* note 1, at 330, para. 48.
16 Official Records of the Rome Conference, *supra* note 1, at 169, para. 107.
17 Official Records of the Rome Conference, *supra* note 1, at 124. para. 43.

efficiency and operability of the Turkish criminal justice and due to the gravity threshold of the Rome Statute.

Third, the allegations against the Turkish Armed Forces would not satisfy *actus reus* of the crimes enumerated in the Rome Statute. Therefore, the ICC's jurisdiction over non-international armed conflicts should not hinder Türkiye's consideration of accession. Türkiye could, as a State Party to the Court, continue its lawful fight against terrorism in compliance with the international humanitarian law principles reiterated in the Rome Statute. Türkiye's compliance with the established international law standards has, in fact, been conducive to the effectiveness of the counter-terrorism measures.

1. Characterization of the Violence between Türkiye and the PKK

Armed conflicts, whether international or non-international, are governed by international humanitarian law ("IHL"). The Geneva Conventions and their Additional Protocols (four treaties and three Additional Protocols), which regulate the conduct of armed conflicts and seek to ameliorate the effects of armed conflicts on civilians and soldiers, form the core of IHL. Türkiye, though a party to the four Geneva Conventions of 1949, has not ratified or acceded to any of the three Additional Protocols.[18] Thus, Additional Protocol II[19] ("AP II"), which aims at protecting the victims of non-international armed conflicts ("NIAC"), would not apply to a NIAC in Türkiye except for its provisions that overlap with customary international law. Article 3 common to each of the four Geneva Conventions of 1949 (common Article 3 or "CA3") would be the only Geneva Conventions–based law applicable to a NIAC in Türkiye.

Common Article 3 introduced the phrase "armed conflict not of an international character" into the legal lexicon without proffering a definition of it.[20] The elucidation of requirements for the applicability of the provisions governing NIACs is thus "among the most difficult and controversial issues in international humanitarian law."[21] While the International Committee of the Red Cross (ICRC) seeks broader recognition for the lower thresholds of the

18 Türkiye signed "Protocol additional to the Geneva Conventions of 12 August 1949, and relating to the Adoption of an Additional Distinctive Emblem" (Protocol III) but has not ratified it. International Committee of the Red Cross, "Treaties, States Parties and Commentaries," https://ihl-databases.icrc.org/applic/ihl/ihl.nsf/INTRO/615?OpenDocument (accessed 1 January 2024).

19 Protocol Additional to the Geneva Conventions of 12 August 1949 and relating to the Protection of Victims of Non-International Armed Conflicts, 8 June 1977, 1125 U.N.T.S. 609 [hereinafter Additional Protocol II].

20 Sandesh Sivakumaran, *The Law of Non-International Armed Conflict* (Oxford: Oxford University Press 2012) 161.

21 Theodor Meron, *The Humanization of International Law* (The Netherlands: Martinus Nijhoff Publishers 2006), 29.

armed conflict characterization, states usually tend to refuse the applicability of IHL to the conflicts to which they are a party.

Due to the lack of a definition of a NIAC in CA3, the descriptions provided by the two conventional instruments (Additional Protocol II and the Rome Statute of the International Criminal Court) and by the subsidiary means for the determination of rules of international law (judicial decisions and teachings of publicists)[22] have gained prominence. These sources, however, have set different thresholds for the applicability of the provisions governing NIACs, all of which will be addressed in this section.

The ICTY's famous *Tadić* decision on Interlocutory Appeal of Jurisdiction (1995) established that a NIAC can be identified by hostilities above a certain level of intensity, which take place either between state forces and organized non-State armed groups or solely between organized non-State armed groups.[23] Accordingly, two elements need to be assessed when ascertaining the NIAC nature of a situation: a certain level of intensity of the violence produced and a certain level of the organization of the armed group(s) concerned. Subsequent ICTY jurisprudence has provided the indicative factors that demonstrate the existence of the requisite levels of intensity and organization.

The threshold set for the application of AP II, on the other hand, is considerably higher than that of CA3, as additional requirements, such as territorial control by the armed group(s) concerned, need to be met for the Protocol to apply. The scope of application of AP II, therefore, is much more limited than that of CA3. One can see the conflicts, in which AP II is applicable, as a different type (Additional Protocol II-type) of NIAC.

Ascertaining whether or not Türkiye's counter-terrorism efforts against the PKK trigger the applicability of the international humanitarian law continues to be the subject of dispute. This section will address the question of whether the violence between Türkiye and the PKK constitutes an armed conflict within the meaning of international humanitarian law. The section will first explain the different non-international armed conflict descriptions provided by i) the ICTY's famous *Tadić* decision, ii) Additional Protocol II and iii) the Rome Statute of the ICC and discuss the different applicability thresholds set by these sources. After noting that the terrorist nature of the acts of violence in a situation will not prevent them from being characterized as an armed conflict and that the application of the international humanitarian law norms would not, in fact, affect the legal status of the PKK, this section will examine whether Türkiye's struggle against the PKK could be classified as an armed conflict subject to international humanitarian law norms.

22 Statute of the International Court of Justice, U.N. Charter, Annex I, at 21–30 (1945), art. 38(1).

23 International Criminal Tribunal for the Former Yugoslavia, *Prosecutor v. Dusko Tadić*, Decision on the Defense Motion for Interlocutory Appeal of Jurisdiction, 2 October 1995, Case No. IT-94-1-I, para. 70 [hereinafter *Tadić* Interlocutory Appeal Decision].

While some scholars opined that "it is at least arguable that the situation in south-eastern Türkiye does not amount to a non-international armed conflict within the meaning of the law of armed conflict,"[24] the predominant view is that the situation in Türkiye does constitute a non-international armed conflict subject to IHL. The views against or on behalf of an armed conflict characterization, however, usually fail to engage in a careful and objective analysis of the elements of a NIAC. Most of the views on behalf of an armed conflict characterization, for example, fail to recognize the fact that the PKK has never been able to control a part of Türkiye's territory, a *sine qua non* requirement for the applicability of AP II.

There exists an international court judgment that mentioned IHL as one of the relevant laws to be argued to apply to the situation in Türkiye: in the case of *Benzer and Others v. Turkey* in 2014, the ECtHR cited the common Article 3 of the 1949 Geneva Conventions as one of the international materials "relevant" for the acts committed as part of the violence between the Turkish security forces and the PKK.[25] This reference, however, was made without any analysis as to whether the violence in question could be characterized as an armed conflict subject to IHL; CA3 was simply referred to as one of the potential grounds, which could potentially be presented by the parties in the case as a law regulating Türkiye's counter-terrorism efforts against the PKK. Moreover, the reference to CA3 (as one of the relevant laws to be argued to apply to the situation) has not been repeated in ECtHR's other judgments on Türkiye's counter-terrorism measures.

The following sub-section will explore the constituent elements of a NIAC by setting out the conditions for the applicability of CA3 in light of the *Tadić* decision. The second sub-section will set out the requirements for the applicability of AP II by highlighting the additional requirements for its applicability. The third sub-section will explain the conditions for the applicability of the Rome Statute's provisions governing NIACs. After stressing that the Rome Statute contains two separate lists of war crimes committed as part of NIACs, the third sub-section will discuss and contribute to the two contending views relating to the question of whether the Statute brings only one common (shared) applicability threshold, which is equivalent to that of CA3.

The fourth sub-section will provide an overview of Türkiye's struggle against the PKK and a description of its concerns regarding the armed conflict characterization of the situation thereof. The fifth sub-section will examine whether Türkiye's struggle against the PKK could be classified as an armed conflict under CA3, AP II and the Rome Statute by applying the relevant

24 David Turns, At the "Vanishing Point" of International Humanitarian Law: Methods and Means of Warfare in Non-international Armed Conflicts, (45) *German Yearbook of International Law* 133 (2002).

25 European Court of Human Rights, *Benzer and Others v. Turkey*, "Judgment Final," 24 March 2014, Appl. No. 23502/06, para. 89.

criteria to the factual situation in Türkiye. The final sub-section will draw a number of conclusions.

1.1. The ICTY's Tadić Decision and the Lower (Common Article 3) Threshold for an Armed Conflict Characterization

The ICTY's Appeals Chamber famously held, in *Prosecutor v. Tadić* in 1995, that the requirement for the existence of a NIAC is met when there is a "protracted armed violence between governmental authorities and organized armed groups or between such groups within a State."[26] The Chamber noted that "international humanitarian law applies from the initiations of such armed conflicts and extends beyond the cessation of hostilities until . . . a peaceful settlement is achieved."[27] It was subsequently clarified by the ICTY that the term "protracted" should be interpreted to mean "intense" rather than its ordinary meaning "prolonged."[28] The Trial Chamber of the ICTY elaborated:

> The test applied by the Appeals Chamber to the existence of an armed conflict for the purposes of the rules contained in Common Article 3 focuses on two aspects of a conflict; *the intensity of the conflict and the organization of the parties to the conflict.* In an armed conflict of an internal or mixed character, these closely related criteria are used solely for the purpose, as a minimum, of distinguishing an armed conflict from banditry, unorganized and short-lived insurrections, or terrorist activities, which are not subject to international humanitarian law.
>
> (emphasis added)[29]

According to this test, the intensity of the hostilities and the organization of the parties are the only requirements for the determination of the existence of an armed conflict. Clearly, the threshold set by the Appeals Chamber of the ICTY is considerably lower than that of AP II, as the "territorial control" or "involvement of government forces"[30] are not required. This threshold is usually referred to as "the lower threshold of common Article 3" as opposed to

26 *Tadić* Interlocutory Appeal Decision, *supra* note 23, at para. 70.

27 *Tadić* Interlocutory Appeal Decision, *supra* note 23, at para. 70.

28 Stuart Casey-Maslen and Steven Haines, *Hague Law Interpreted: The Conduct of Hostilities under the Law of Armed Conflict* (Oxford: Hart Publishing 2018) 57. "The criterion of protracted armed violence has therefore been interpreted in practice, including by the *Tadić* Trial Chamber itself, as referring more to the intensity of the armed violence than to its duration.": International Criminal Tribunal for the Former Yugoslavia, *Haradinaj Case*, IT-04–84-T, Judgment, 3 April 2008, para. 49.

29 International Criminal Tribunal for the Former Yugoslavia, Trial Chamber II, *The Prosecutor v. Dusko Tadić*, Opinion and Judgment, 7 May 1997, Case No. IT-94–1-T, para. 562.

30 As suggested by the phrase "or between such groups," involvement of government forces is not required.

the "higher threshold of Additional Protocol II." Accordingly, factors other than the "intensity of the conflict" and "organization of the parties" can only be indicative criteria rather than prerequisites.

As for the requisite degree of intensity of the hostilities, AP II's restriction that the Protocol will only apply in situations distinguishable from "internal disturbances and tensions, such as riots, isolated and sporadic acts of violence and other acts of a similar nature"[31] is also valid for CA3.[32] In this regard, the terrorist nature of the acts of violence in question will not prevent them from being characterized as an armed conflict, as long as they are not "single acts of terrorism"[33] and intensity and organization elements are met. As affirmed by an ICTY Trial Chamber, "it is immaterial whether the acts of violence perpetrated may or may not be characterized as terrorist in nature."[34] In other words, a NIAC characterization does not require the armed group concerned to actually respect the laws of war nor to actually implement the rules governing armed conflicts.

The low threshold for armed conflict characterization set by the *Tadić* decision was reaffirmed by subsequent decisions of the ICTY[35] and subsequently found its way to the Rome Statute (through a proposal from Sierra Leone).[36] The Rome Statute used the same language as the ICTY's *Tadić* decision for addressing NIACs, except that the term "protracted armed violence" was replaced by "protracted armed conflict": "armed conflicts that take place in the territory of a State when there is protracted armed conflict between governmental authorities and organized armed groups or between such groups."[37] Whether this discrepancy (replacement of the word "violence" with "conflict") aimed at bringing an additional threshold or the new sentence merely represents reformulation of the existing threshold has been debated extensively.[38] In order to understand and contribute to these debates, the third sub-section will analyze the articulation of Article 8 of the Rome Statute, which deals with war crimes.

31 Additional Protocol II, *supra* note 19, art. 1(1).

32 Sylvain Vite, Typology Of Armed Conflicts in International Humanitarian Law: Legal Concepts and Actual Situations, 91(873) *International Review of the Red Cross* 23 (2009); International Committee of the Red Cross, How Is the Term "Armed Conflict" Defined in International Humanitarian Law? *Opinion Paper* 3 (2008).

33 International Criminal Tribunal for the Former Yugoslavia, *The Prosecutor v. Ljube Boškoski and Johan Tarčulovski*, Judgement, 10 July 2008, Case No. IT-04–82-T, para. 185–190.

34 International Criminal Tribunal for the Former Yugoslavia, *supra* note, at para. 185.

35 Casey-Maslen and Haines, *supra* note 28, at 57.

36 Official Records of the Rome Conference, *supra* note 1, at 335, para. 8.

37 United Nations Treaty Collection, Rome Statute of the International Criminal Court, U.N. Doc. A/CONF.183/9, 17 July 1998, art. 8(2)(f).

38 *See,* for example, Anthony Cullen, The Definition of Non-International Armed Conflict in the Rome Statute of the International Criminal Court: An Analysis of the Threshold of Application Contained in Article 8(2)(f), 12(3) *Journal of Conflict and Security Law* (2008).

1.2. *Additional Protocol II Threshold for an Armed Conflict Characterization*

As discussed earlier, identification of a NIAC requires the violence concerned to cross a certain level of intensity and the armed group(s) concerned to be sufficiently organized. 1977 Additional Protocol II, however, has introduced additional requirements for its applicability. Article 1(1) of AP II sets out that the protocol applies to non-international armed conflicts:

> which take place in the territory of a High Contracting Party between its armed forces and dissident armed forces or other organized armed groups which, under responsible command, exercise such control over a part of its territory as to enable them to carry out sustained and concerted military operations and to implement this Protocol.[39]

Accordingly, in addition to the intensity of the hostilities and organization of the armed group concerned, AP II requires 1) that the conflict takes place in the territory of a State Party, 2) that the conflict is between state forces and non-State armed group(s) (that state forces be involved in the conflict), 3) that the non-State armed group concerned is under responsible command and 4) that the non-State armed group concerned exercises such control over a part of the territory of the State Party concerned as to enable the group "to carry out sustained and concerted military operations and to implement" the Protocol.[40]

Here, it should be noted that the "sustained and concerted" nature of the conflict and actual implementation of AP II (respect for IHL) by the armed group concerned are not required for the Protocol to be applicable.[41] Having the territorial control sufficient to allow the armed group "to carry out sustained and concerted military operations and to implement" the Protocol is what is required by the language of Article 1(1).[42]

That the violence concerned must reach a degree of intensity that rises above sporadic acts of violence, on the other hand, is still a requirement, as it is one of the constituent elements of a NIAC. That is to say, the ability of the armed group to engage in protracted armed violence is not enough; there should actually be a conflict with a certain degree of intensity. In this regard, Article 1(2) of AP II expressly warns that the "Protocol shall not apply to situations of internal disturbances and tensions, such as riots, isolated and

39 Additional Protocol II, *supra* note 19, art. 1(1).

40 Additional Protocol II, *supra* note 19, art. 1(1). The requirement that the non-State armed group concerned must be under responsible command is not separately listed here, as it is already required by the "organization" element.

41 Sivakumaran, *supra* note 20, at 189.

42 Additional Protocol II, *supra* note 19, art. 1(1).

sporadic acts of violence and other acts of a similar nature, as not being armed conflicts."[43]

1.3. *The Rome Statute Threshold for an Armed Conflict Characterization*

Article 8 of the Rome Statute contains two separate provisions that enumerate a list of offences committed during armed conflicts not of an international character, and each is followed by another section that sets out the scope of application.[44] While Article 8(2)(c) provides a list of serious violations of CA3 (and is followed by Article 8(2)(d), which sets out the scope of application), Article 8(2)(e) enumerates a list of "other serious violations of the laws and customs applicable in armed conflicts not of an international character" (and is followed by Article 8(2)(f), which sets out the scope of application).

Both Article 8(2)(c) (serious violations of CA3) and Article 8(2)(e) (other serious violations of the laws and customs applicable in NIACs) are explicitly stated not to apply "to situations of internal disturbances and tensions, such as riots, isolated and sporadic acts of violence or other acts of a similar nature."[45] This negative formulation is taken directly from Article 1(2) of AP II.[46] However, AP II's other restrictive elements, such as territorial control or involvement of state forces, have not been imported.

It is important to note that Article 8(2)(f), which defines the scope of application of Article 8(2)(e), contains an additional sentence that states that Article 8(2)(e) will apply to "armed conflicts that take place in the territory of a State when there is protracted armed conflict between governmental authorities and organized armed groups or between such groups."[47] This sentence is taken directly from the ICTY's *Tadić* decision, except that the term "protracted armed violence" was replaced by "protracted armed conflict."[48]

The said additional sentence gives rise to the same question asked at the end of the second section: Does this additional sentence and the replacement of the word "violence" with "conflict" represent an additional requirement that would raise the threshold of applicability of Article 8(2)(e) to a level above that of CA3 but below that of AP II, thereby creating a new (intermediate) category of NIAC? Or does it merely rephrase (and clarify) Article 8(2)(d)?

The facts that 1) the Rome Statute included two separate lists of war crimes relating to the situations of armed conflicts not of an international character,[49]

43 Additional Protocol II, *supra* note 19, art. 1(2).

44 Rome Statute, *supra* note 37, art. 8.

45 Rome Statute, *supra* note 37, art. 8(2)(f)

46 The only difference in the sentence is that the Rome Statute uses "or" instead of "and": "violence or other acts.": Rome Statute, *supra* note 37, at 8(2)(f).

47 Rome Statute, *supra* note 37, art. 8(2)(f).

48 *Tadić* Interlocutory Appeal Decision, *supra* note 23, at para. 70.

49 In the early drafts of the Rome Statute "serious violations of common Article 3" and "[o]ther serious violations of the laws and customs applicable in armed conflicts not of an international character" were included in a single provision.

2) the phrase "protracted armed conflict" was preferred instead of "protracted armed violence," and 3) the "protracted armed conflict" requirement referred only to the second list (article 8(2)(e)) exacerbate the doubts about the uniformity of applicability in 8(2)(d) and 8(2)(f) of the Rome Statute. While some scholars, including Marco Sassoli, Antoine Bouvier and Rene Provost, suggested that Article 8(2)(f) of the Rome Statute represents a new (additional) threshold, some scholars, including Theodor Meron, Michael Bothe and Claus Kress, opposed such understanding.[50] The opponents claim that Article 8 of the Rome Statute brings only one common (shared) threshold, which is equivalent to that of CA3 and applies to both Article 8(2)(c) and (e).

The ICC's jurisprudence too implicitly admitted the lack of clarity on the matter without drawing a clear conclusion:

> The Chamber is also mindful that the wording of Article 8(2)(f) of the Statute differs from that of Article 8(2)(d) of the Statute, which requires the existence of a "protracted armed conflict" and thus may be seen to require a higher or additional threshold to be met-a necessity which is not set out in Article 8(2)(d) of the Statute. The argument can be raised as to whether this requirement may nevertheless be applied also in the context of Article 8(2)(d) of the Statute. However, irrespective of such a possible interpretative approach, the Chamber does not deem it necessary to address this argument, as the period in question covers approximately five months and is therefore to be regarded as "protracted" in any event.[51]

Apart from the possibility of establishment of such extension by the jurisprudence of the ICC in the future, this author is of the view that the difference in the wording of Article 8(2)(d) and (f) suggests that the violence that is sufficiently intense but not protracted would fail to satisfy Article 8(2)(f) but could still cross the threshold of the 8(2)(d), and thus, CA3 protections of Article 8(2)(c) would still apply. The reason why the chambers of the ICC have not so far categorized NIACs as those that meet the lower threshold of CA3 and those that cross the so-called intermediate[52] threshold of Article 8(2)(f) may be that all conflicts that have been so far found sufficiently intense by the Court were also protracted in nature anyway. While it is true that the protracted nature of a conflict is one of the indicative factors that may assist

50 Cullen, *supra* note 38, at 435.

51 International Criminal Court, Pre-Trial Chamber II, *Prosecutor v. Jean-Pierre Bemba* Gombo, Decision on the Charges, Case No. ICC-01/05-01/08, 15 June 2009, para. 235.

52 Marco Sassoli, Antoine Bouvier and Anne Quintin, for example, submitted that "[t]he Statute of the International Criminal Court provides an intermediary threshold of application." Marco Sassoli, Antoine A. Bouvier, and Anne Quintin, *How Does Law Protect in War? Cases, Documents and Teaching Materials on Contemporary Practice in International Humanitarian Law* (vol. 1, 3rd ed.) (Geneva: International Committee of the Red Cross 2011) 23.

in the determination of the intensity of the conflict,[53] such nature is, at the same time, a *sine qua non* requirement for the applicability of the Article 8(2)(e) provisions.

The preparatory work of the Rome Statute and the circumstances of its conclusion, which are "supplementary means of interpretation" as specified by the Vienna Convention on the Law of Treaties,[54] also suggest that referral to "protracted armed conflict" was made in order to satisfy the states that favored a higher threshold for the applicability of Article 8(2)(e) and thus to secure their support in the adoption of the Rome Statute. In the early drafts of the Rome Statute, "serious violations of Article 3 common to the four Geneva Conventions of 12 August 1949" and "[o]ther serious violations of the laws and customs applicable in armed conflicts not of an international character" was included in a single provision. Some states present at the Rome Conference (Egypt, Sudan and Bahrain),[55] however, insisted that as opposed to the lower threshold of applicability for the serious violations of common Article 3, the higher AP II threshold of applicability should be set for the "other serious violations."[56]

This suggestion, which was in turn introduced as a proposal by the Conference Bureau,[57] would, if adopted, exclude conflicts fought between non-State armed groups (without the involvement of government forces) and the conflicts in which the anti-government armed group did not exercise territorial control from the jurisdiction of the Court. Thus, a number of states were strongly opposed to the proposal.

In an attempt to balance the expectations of the states favoring broader applicability (without any distinction between the serious violations of CA3 and the other serious violations) with the concerns of the states that preferred the higher AP II threshold for the latter, Sierra Leone introduced a proposal which has subsequently become the final version of Article 8(2)(f).[58] Accordingly, Rome Statute provisions on serious violations other than that of common Article 3, namely, Article 8(2)(e), apply to "armed conflicts that take place in the territory of a State when there is protracted armed conflict

53 Dapo Akande, Classification of Armed Conflicts: Relevant Legal Concepts, in Elizabeth Wilmshurst (ed.), *International Law and the Classification of Conflicts* (Oxford: Oxford University Press 2012) 56.

54 Vienna Convention on the Law of Treaties, U.N. Doc. A/CONF.39/27, 1155 U.N.T.S. 331, 8 I.L.M. 679, opened for signature 23 May 1969, entered into force on 27 January 1980, art. 32.

55 Guan, *supra* note 11, at 722.

56 Theodor Meron, Crimes under the Jurisdiction of the International Criminal Court, in Herman A.M. von Hebel, Johan G. Lammers, and Jolien Schukking (eds.), *Reflections on the International Criminal Court Essays in Honour of Adriaan Bos* (The Hague: TMC Asser Press 1999) 54.

57 Sivakumaran, *supra* note 20, at 192.

58 Official Records of the Rome Conference, *supra* note 1.

between governmental authorities and organized armed groups or between such groups."[59]

In this regard, it should first be noted that the ICC's jurisprudence on the identification and characterization of armed conflicts has not diverged from the ICTY. Chambers of the ICC and the Office of the Prosecutor have consistently cited and relied on the jurisprudence from the ICTY.[60] According to a comprehensive definition adopted and affirmed by the chambers of the ICC, an armed conflict not of an international character is characterized as follows:

> by the outbreak of armed hostilities of a certain level of intensity, exceeding that of internal disturbances and tensions, such as riots, isolated and sporadic acts of violence or other acts of a similar nature, and which takes place within the confines of a State territory. The hostilities may break out (i) between government authorities and organized dissident armed groups or (ii) between such groups.[61]

In line with the jurisprudence of the ICTY and the definition set out earlier, the jurisprudence of the ICC has made it clear that the Court focuses on two aspects of the hostilities in order to distinguish a NIAC from less serious forms of violence: intensity of the confrontations and the organization of the non-State armed group(s) party to the hostilities.[62] Other factors, such as territorial control or involvement of government forces, are not determinative but are usually relevant and important factors.

59 Rome Statute, *supra* note 37, art. 8(2)(f).

60 *See*, for example, the following decisions of the ICC: International Criminal Court, Trial Chamber I, Situation in the Democratic Republic of the Congo, *Prosecutor v. Thomas Lubanga Dyilo*, Judgment pursuant to Article 74 of the Statute, 14 March 2012, para. 506, 535; International Criminal Court, Pre-Trial Chamber II, Situation in the Central African Republic, *The Prosecutor v. Jean-Pierre Bemba Gombo*, Decision Pursuant to Article 61(7)(a) and (b) of the Rome Statute on the Charges of the Prosecutor Against Jean-Pierre Bemba Gombo, 15 June 2009, ICC-01/05–01/08, para. 229; International Criminal Court, The Office of the Prosecutor, Situation in Mali Article 53(1) Report, 16 January 2013, para. 55.

61 International Criminal Court, Pre-Trial Chamber III, The Situation in the Republic of Côte d'Ivoire, Decision Pursuant to Article 15 of the Rome Statute on the Authorization of an Investigation into the Situation in the Republic of Côte d'Ivoire, 15 November 2011, ICC-02–11-Corr, para. 119; International Criminal Court, The Office of the Prosecutor, Situation in Colombia, Interim Report, November 2012, para. 125; Article 53(1) Report (Situation in Mali), International Criminal Court, Pre-Trial Chamber III, para. 56; Judgment pursuant to Article 74 of the Statute (Situation in the Democratic Republic of Congo), International Criminal Court, Pre-Trial Chamber III, para. 533; Decision Pursuant to Article 61(7)(a) and (b) of the Rome Statute on the Charges of the Prosecutor Against Jean-Pierre Bemba Gombo (Situation in the Central African Republic), International Criminal Court, Pre-Trial Chamber III, para. 231.

62 Article 53(1) Report (Situation in Mali), *supra* note 60, at para. 57; Judgment pursuant to Article 74 of the Statute (Situation in the Democratic Republic of Congo), *supra* note 60, at para. 506; Interim Report (Situation in Colombia), *supra* note 60, para. 125.

While the determination of the existence of an armed conflict does not require the violence in question to be protracted in nature, such nature is still a requirement for the applicability of the provisions contained in Article 8(2)(e) (as it is expressly envisaged by Article 8(2)(f)). The Pre-Trial Chamber's observation in the *Prosecutor v. Jean-Pierre Bemba Gombo* that "the period in question covers approximately five months and is, therefore, to be regarded as 'protracted' in any event"[63] indicates that the duration needed to fulfill the "protracted armed conflict" requirement for the purposes of the applicability of the Article 8(2)(e) provisions can be as short as five months or even less depending on other factors.

1.4. Türkiye's Struggle against the PKK and Concerns about the Armed Conflict Characterization

As mentioned in Chapter 1, the PKK is an armed group that is designated as a terrorist organization by much of the international community, including the European Union,[64] NATO,[65] Türkiye,[66] the United States,[67] Canada,[68] Japan,[69] Australia,[70] New Zealand[71] and so on. Its request seeking removal from the EU terrorist list has recently been rejected by the European Court of Justice.[72]

63 Decision Pursuant to Article 61(7)(a) and (b) of the Rome Statute on the Charges of the Prosecutor Against Jean-Pierre Bemba Gombo (Situation in the Central African Republic), *supra* note 60, at para. 235.

64 List of Persons, Groups and Entities, Official Journal of the European Union, Vol. 65, 4 February 2022, p. 4.

65 The organization does not have a list of terrorist entities but refers to the PKK as a terrorist group. *See*, for example, North Atlantic Treaty Organization, "Press conference by NATO Secretary General Jens Stoltenberg following the first session of NATO Ministers of Foreign Affairs, Bucharest, Romania," 29 November 2022, www.nato.int/cps/en/natohq/opinions_209381.htm?selectedLocale=en (accessed 1 January 2024).

66 Republic of Türkiye Ministry of Foreign Affairs, *PKK*, www.mfa.gov.tr/pkk.en.mfa (accessed 1 January 2024).

67 The United States Department of State, *Foreign Terrorist Organizations*, www.state.gov/foreign-terrorist-organizations/ (accessed 1 January 2024).

68 Public Safety Canada, *Currently Listed Entities*, www.publicsafety.gc.ca/cnt/ntnl-scrt/cntr-trrrsm/lstd-ntts/crrnt-lstd-ntts-en.aspx (accessed 1 January 2024).

69 公安調査庁 [Public Security and Intelligence Agency], 地域別テロ情勢等中東・北アフリカ [Terrorism Situation by Region, Middle East/North Africa], 地域別テロ情勢 [Terrorism Situation by Region], トルコ [Türkiye], クルド労働者党 [PKK], https://www.moj.go.jp/psia/ITH/area/ME_N-africa/index.html (accessed 1 January 2024).

70 Australian National Security, *Listed Terrorist Organisations*, https://www.nationalsecurity.gov.au/what-australia-is-doing/terrorist-organisations/listed-terrorist-organisations (accessed 1 January 2024).

71 Police, *Lists Associated with Resolutions 1267/1989/2253 and 1988*, www.police.govt.nz/advice/personal-community/counterterrorism/designated-entities/lists-associated-with-resolutions-1267-1989-2253-1988 (accessed 1 January 2024).

72 Top EU Court Rejects PKK's Request Seeking Removal from Terror List, *Anadolu Agency*, 14 December 2022, www.aa.com.tr/en/europe/top-eu-court-rejects-pkk-s-request-seeking-removal-from-terror-list/2764022 (accessed 1 January 2024).

Abdullah Öcalan, the founding leader of the PKK, who is now serving life in prison in Türkiye, acknowledged:

> Turkish authorities had correctly estimated, or even under-estimated, the number of people killed and wounded in the PKK's armed actions since 1978 – with the deaths amounting to 4,472 civilians, 3,874 servicemen, 247 police officers and 1,225 village guards in 6,036 armed attacks, 3,071 bombings, 388 armed robberies and 1,046 abductions.[73]

Today, the number of civilians killed by the PKK exceeds 7,000.[74]

Türkiye does not characterize its operations against the PKK as an armed conflict subject to the IHL norms but as "domestic counter-terrorism" subject only to international human rights law, on such grounds as that the PKK does not exercise territorial control needed to carry out sustained and concerted military operations, and it is a terrorist organization that does not respect the rules of war.[75] In this regard, Türkiye is concerned that its acknowledgement of the applicability of IHL to its operations against the PKK would entail admitting that Türkiye is unable to stop large-scale violence within its borders and that the PKK wields control over a part of Türkiye's territory.[76]

Türkiye is also concerned that characterization of the violence between Türkiye and the PKK as an armed conflict within the meaning of IHL could offer some advantages to the PKK and impose additional burdens on Turkish security forces. Such characterization could, Türkiye fears, bestow the PKK with moral legitimacy and facilitate the PKK's claims that it has the requisite legal "personality to carry on diplomacy and participate in peace conferences"[77] or it could confer combatant status on the PKK members.

Contrary to the concerns of Türkiye, however, the application of IHL would not, at least legally speaking, affect the legal status of the PKK (and its terrorist activities), as emphasized by the last sentence of CA3.[78] Unlike

73 European Court of Human Rights, *Öcalan v. Turkey*, Appl. No. 5980/07, "Press release issued by the Registrar – Decision," 16 July 2010, available at https://hudoc.echr.coe.int/eng-press#{%22display%22:[%221%22],%22dmdocnumber%22:[%22871381%22],%22itemid%22:[%22003-3206766-3569334%22]} (accessed 1 January 2024).

74 PKK 1984'ten Beri 7 Bin Sivili Katletti (PKK Murdered 7,000 Civilians Since 1984), *TRT Haber*, 27 August 2015, http://www.trthaber.com/haber/turkiye/pkk-1984ten-beri-7-bin-sivili-katletti-200648.html

75 Turns, *supra* note 24, at 133.

76 Turns, *supra* note 24, at 133.

77 William Abresch, A Human Rights Law of Internal Armed Conflict: The European Court of Human Rights in Chechnya, 16 *European Journal of International Law* 756 (2005).

78 Common Article 3 clearly states that its application "shall not affect the legal status of the Parties to the conflict." *Convention [No. I] for the Amelioration of the Condition of the Wounded and Sick in Armed Forces in the Field*, 12 August 1949, art. 3, 75 U.N.T.S. 31, 32 [hereinafter Convention I]; *Convention [No. II] for the Amelioration of the Condition of the Wounded, Sick and Shipwrecked Members of Armed Forces at Sea*, 12 August 1949, art. 3, 75 U.N.T.S. 85, 86–88 [hereinafter Convention II]; *Convention [No. III] relative to the Treatment of Prisoners of War*, 12 August 1949, art. 3, 75 U.N.T.S. 135, 136–138 [hereinafter Convention

IHL of IACs, which confers on a combatant the right to target an enemy combatant and be immune from prosecution for such action, under IHL of NIACs, a person who engages in hostilities against the state forces would not be accorded the status of combatant.[79] Consequently, he would not, if captured, enjoy the rights of the prisoner of war status and would not be immune from criminal prosecution for attacking state forces or properties. Therefore, acknowledging the applicability of IHL of NIACs would not, in fact, require Türkiye to treat the captured PKK militants as prisoners of law nor to accord them immunity from domestic legislation for attacking security forces. Concordantly, Additional Protocol II warns that the Protocol will not affect the responsibility of a government "to defend the national unity and territorial integrity of the State."[80]

Some states, such as Colombia, refused, for years, to join the states that ratified AP II "for fear that to do so would be to recognize the armed groups as belligerents and grant them status."[81] Here, it might be useful to briefly explain the concept of belligerency. Traditionally, recognition of a situation as belligerency was tantamount to recognition of civil war and brought responsibilities for the recognizing states. If a situation meeting certain factual preconditions – such as the existence of hostilities beyond the scope of mere local unrest or occupation of a substantial part of the territory of the state by the insurgents – was recognized as belligerency by the parent state, it was regulated by the full body of the laws of war, and the belligerents were treated as combatants, not as traitors.[82] Third-party states recognizing belligerency, on the other hand, were bound by the law of neutrality and prohibited from offering assistance to belligerents or the state.[83] Although recognition of belligerency has fallen into disuse,[84] "it still exists in international law,"[85] and "a situation may still be recognized as belligerency."[86]

Recognition of the applicability of AP II, however, "is in no way tantamount to recognition of belligerency."[87] The Diplomatic Conference that negotiated and adopted the four 1949 Geneva Conventions passed a resolution, which provided that conditions of recognition of an armed group as belligerent "are

III]; *Convention [No. IV] relative to the Protection of Civilian Persons in Time of War*, 12 August 1949, art. 3, 75 U.N.T.S. 287, 288–290 [hereinafter Convention IV].

79 Marco Sassoli, Use and Abuse of the Laws of War in the War on Terrorism, (22) *Law & Inequality: A Journal of Theory and Practice* 197 (2004).

80 Additional Protocol II, *supra* note 19, art. 3(1).

81 Sivakumaran, *supra* note 20, at 190.

82 Captured belligerents were, therefore, afforded prisoner of war status. Yair M. Lootsteen, The Concept of Belligerency in International Law, 166 *Military Law Review* 109, 110 (2000); Sivakumaran, *supra* note 20, at 15.

83 Sivakumaran, *supra* note 20, at 15.

84 Sivakumaran, *supra* note 20, at 195; Lootsteen, *supra* note 82, at 133.

85 Lootsteen, *supra* note 82, at 133.

86 Sivakumaran, *supra* note 20, at 196.

87 Sivakumaran, *supra* note 20, at 191.

governed by the general rules of international law on the subject and are in no way modified by the Geneva Conventions," demonstrating that rules governing NIACs are "not intended to apply only in situations in which belligerency could be recognized."[88]

It should be noted that the application of CA3 would not, in fact, impose additional burdens on Türkiye, as it is also party to both the European Convention for the Protection of Human Rights and Fundamental Freedoms (ECHR) and the International Covenant on Civil and Political Rights (ICCPR). As stated by the Inter-American Commission on Human Rights, "the provisions of common Article 3 are essentially pure human rights law."[89] In this regard, human rights instruments binding on Türkiye are even more extensive than CA3.[90]

Finally, Türkiye is deeply concerned that the classification of its internal hostilities as an armed conflict and recognition of the applicability of IHL could lead to allegations of war crimes against the Turkish security forces. In this regard, Türkiye is especially concerned that individual abuses by the security personnel will be "turned into gross generalizations of violations of human rights by the PKK propaganda machine" and that Türkiye's counter-terrorism operations, which are already under the scrutiny of the ECtHR, could be undermined by the politically motivated allegations of war crimes.[91] This concern also constitutes one of the biggest obstacles to Türkiye's accession to ICC, as noted in the previous chapter.

The PKK's decades-long experience of spreading disinformation and fake news to gain as much popular support as possible is fueling the Turkish concerns that unfounded allegations may reach the investigation stage before the ICC. In this regard, it is worth noting that the PKK's disinformation and propaganda campaign in Europe began in the 1990s. As correctly pointed out in a much-cited article written in 1995 by Nur Bilge Criss:

> Every murder in the [Türkiye's southeastern] region that might have been caused by blood feuds, honor, or plain personal vendetta was immediately attributed to the state. Struggle for regional leadership within the PKK ranks sometimes ended up in murder, which was again blamed on the state . . . This is not to deny that there have been violations of human rights [by Turkish authorities], but to point out that cases of individual abuse were turned into gross generalizations of violations of human rights by the PKK propaganda machine.[92]

88 Sivakumaran, *supra* note 20, at 161.
89 Meron, *supra* note 21, at 47.
90 Abresch, *supra* note 77, at 747.
91 Nur Bilge Criss, The Nature of PKK Terrorism in Turkey, (18) *Studies in Conflict and Terrorism* 21–23 (1995).
92 Criss, *supra* note 91, at 21. (emphasis added).

Türkiye's refusal to characterize its operations against the PKK as an armed conflict, nevertheless, is not determinative. The following section will deal with the issue of characterization of the violence between Türkiye and the PKK.

1.5. Characterization of the Situation in Türkiye

The previous sub-sections explained that two requirements need to be satisfied for the determination of the existence of an armed conflict: the sufficient degree of organization of the non-State armed group concerned and the sufficient degree of intensity of the violence. The following headings will address, in light of the indicative factors of the constituent elements of a NIAC, the question of whether the violence between Türkiye and the PKK satisfies the two constituent elements and, if so, whether the AP II would be applicable if Türkiye ratifies it.

1.5.1. Organization Requirement

The ICC, whose jurisprudence on the identification of armed conflicts has not diverged from the ICTY, provides an up-to-date list of factors that may be taken into account when assessing the two constituent elements of a NIAC.[93] Accordingly, whether an armed group is organized may be assessed by taking into account, *inter alia,* the following indicators:

> i) the existence of a command structure, the existence of headquarters, the issuing of political statements and the use of official spokespersons; (ii) the military (operational) capacity of the armed group, which may be shown by, for example, the ability to define a unified military strategy, the use of military tactics, the ability to carry out (large-scale or coordinated) operations, the control of territory and having a territorial division into zones of responsibility; (iii) the logistical capacity of the armed group, indicated, among others, by the existence of a supply chain for military equipment, as well as by the group's ability to move troops around and to recruit and train personnel; (iv) the existence of an internal disciplinary system and the ability to implement IHL; and (v) the group's ability to speak with one voice, indicated, for example, by the capacity of the leadership to act on behalf of its members in political negotiations and to conclude agreements, such as ceasefire or peace agreements.[94]

93 See, for instance, International Criminal Court, Trial Chamber VI, Situation in the Democratic Republic of the Congo, *Prosecutor v. Bosco Ntaganda*, Judgment, July 8, 2019, ICC-01/04–02/06, para. 704, 716.

94 International Criminal Court, *supra* note 93, para. 704. The test of whether intensity and organization elements are satisfied "should be applied flexibly" as none of the relevant "factors are individually determinative." Judgment pursuant to Article 74 of the Statute, *Prosecutor v. Thomas Lubanga Dyilo*, *supra* note 60, at para. 537.

The PKK has a significant number of members. The number of active PKK militants between 1991 and 1993, when the PKK was at the summit of its power, is estimated to range from 10,000 to 20,000.[95] The current number of the PKK's armed members, according to the U.S. Department of State's most recent "Country Reports on Terrorism," is estimated to be 4,000 to 5,000.[96] The PKK's "capacity to declare and hold ceasefires" with the instruction of its captured leader suggests that it is "under responsible command."[97] It has effective control over its members and an effective hierarchical structure with identifiable ranks and positions. The PKK also has the capacity to acquire weapons, recruit and train new members. Its attacks are usually carried out as part of an organizational plan and policy.

Though these qualifications together seem to suggest that the PKK is an organized armed group and thus meets one of the two constituent elements of a non-international armed conflict, its failure to meet some of the crucial indicative factors of the organization criterion makes it difficult to determine whether the PKK could be considered "sufficiently" organized to be a party to an armed conflict against Türkiye. Indeed, the PKK's inability to control territory,[98] to implement IHL[99] or to carry out sustained large-scale operations to oust the state's authority[100] as well as that the organization routinely carries out terrorist attacks that target civilians[101] increase the doubts about the sufficiency of its organization.

Nevertheless, this author agrees with the generally accepted view that the PKK is sufficiently organized and under responsible command, as suggested by its significant number of members, effective hierarchical structure, capacity

95 Ümit Özdağ, *Türkiye'de Düşük Yoğunluklu Çatışma ve PKK* [Low Intensity Conflict in Türkiye and the PKK] 81 (Üç Ok Yayıncılık 2005).
96 U.S. Department of State, *Country Reports on Terrorism 2020*, December 2021, 288.
97 Abresch, *supra* note 77, at 755.
98 *See* later section 6.3.
99 *See* later p. 38.
100 *See* later section 6.3.
101 The PKK claimed responsibility for hundreds of terrorist attacks that directly targeted civilians. *See, e.g.*, European Court of Human Rights, *supra* note 73. The members of the group have been convicted for terrorist crimes in hundreds of different cases not only in Türkiye but also in several other countries, including Italy, France, Denmark and Germany. *See, e.g.*, Thomas Van Poecke, Frank Verbruggen and Ward Yperman, "Terrorist offences and international humanitarian law: The armed conflict exclusion clause," International Review of the Red Cross, 103 (916–917) (2021): 318; "*The PKK from its inception has employed classic insurgency tactics, blending violence and terror with political organization. The terror has systematically and primarily been directed first at potential rivals within the Kurdish camp, including other leftist organizations, and then at 'collaborators' – in other words, other Kurds suspected of benefiting from interactions or cooperation with the state. . . . The PKK's effort to lessen Turkish state presence in the southeast by killing Turkish schoolteachers and civil servants, and by burning schools and other public institutions, has particularly enraged the Turkish public.*" Henri J. Barkey and Graham E. Fuller, Turkey's Kurdish Question (Lanham, MD.: Rowman & Littlefield Publishers 1998), 28.

to recruit and train new members and equip them with weapons and uniforms. The group satisfies the majority of the indicative factors emphasized by the jurisprudence of the ICTY and ICC for the determination of the organization of a non-State armed group, such as "the existence of a command structure," "ability . . . to recruit and train personnel" and "ability to speak with one voice, indicated, for example, by the capacity of the leadership to act on behalf of its members in political negotiations."[102] The PKK can, therefore, be considered sufficiently organized to be a party to an armed conflict, thereby satisfying one of the two criteria for the non-international armed conflict characterization.

1.5.2. Intensity Requirement

Whether the degree of intensity required for the non-international armed conflict characterization is crossed in a situation of violence may be determined by taking into account, *inter alia,* the following factors:

> (i) the seriousness and frequency of attacks and armed clashes; (ii) the spread of clashes over territory and the group's ability to control territory over a period of time; (iii) whether any ceasefire orders had been issued or ceasefires agreed to; (iv) the type and number of armed forces deployed, including any involvement of the government; (v) the type of weapons used; (vi) whether the situation had attracted the attention of the UN Security Council or involvement of other international organizations; (vii) whether those fighting considered themselves bound by IHL; and (viii) the effects of the violence on the civilian population, including the extent to which civilians left the relevant area, the extent of destruction and the number of persons killed.[103]

It should be noted that when referring to the relevant factors, the chambers of the ICC and the OTP use such phrases as "non-exhaustive list," "potentially relevant,"[104] "[intensity] *may* be shown by"[105] and "should take into account, *inter alia*."[106] These phrases clearly suggest that the said factors are illustrative and not exclusive. Additionally, that the intensity of the confrontations (as one of the two constituent elements for an armed conflict characterization) is, at the same time, one of the factors to be taken into account to assess whether the armed group concerned is sufficiently organized (the other constituent

102 (*Trial) Judgment, Prosecutor v. Bosco Ntaganda, supra* note 93, at para. 704.
103 (*Trial) Judgment, Prosecutor v. Bosco Ntaganda, supra* note 93, at para. 716.
104 (*Trial) Judgment, Prosecutor v. Bosco Ntaganda, supra* note 93, at para. 537.
105 Interim Report (Situation in Colombia), *supra* note 61, at para. 126. (emphasis added).
106 Judgment pursuant to Article 74 of the Statute, *Prosecutor v. Thomas Lubanga Dyilo, supra* note 60, at para. 538.

element) shows that the two elements and the potentially relevant factors are all usually interactive.

The PKK mostly avoids pitched battles with state forces.[107] It usually employs hit-and-run guerrilla warfare strategy. Its attacks against the security forces take place chaotically, usually as hit-and-run ambushes, suicide or car bomb attacks, sabotage, roadside attacks, abductions and mine traps, each time in different areas.[108] Moreover, the PKK does not usually show considerable resistance to Türkiye's operations in the areas where it hides, except for its ambushes, land mines or booby traps.

Though the types of these attacks may conduce one to consider that there are no serious direct armed clashes that reach the requisite degree of intensity, there have been some periods and several clashes that were intense enough to trigger the applicability of IHL. Especially in the early 1990s and the period between August 2015 and March 2016, the most violent engagements between the PKK members and security forces took place. These periods will be detailed under the following two headings. Before moving to discuss the intensity of the violence in these two periods in detail, it should be noted that once triggered, the international humanitarian law will apply from the initiation of the armed conflict concerned and will extend "beyond the cessation of hostilities until . . . a peaceful settlement is achieved."[109] In other words, once the threshold of intensity is crossed, IHL will continue to apply, even if the violence falls below a certain level of intensity or in the absence of active hostilities until "a lasting cessation of armed confrontations without real risk of resumption."[110]

1.5.2.1. INTENSITY OF THE VIOLENCE PRODUCED IN THE 1990S

The PKK was founded in 1978. Its first attack directly targeting the Turkish security forces was carried out on the night of 15 August 1984.[111] Its biggest and most violent attacks were carried out in the early 1990s. On 15 May 1992, for instance, a group of 600 PKK militants attacked a gendarmerie outpost

107 The group "concentrate not on fighting pitched battles, but on advancing deep behind enemy lines, attacking and then withdrawing swiftly." Joost Jongerden, *The Settlement Issue in Turkey and the Kurds: An Analysis of Spatial Policies, Modernity and War* (Leiden and Boston: Brill 2007) 61.

108 "As a mobile guerrilla force that staged hit-and-run attacks, they did not need to keep enormous stocks of weapons with them at all times. Instead, after an attack, they withdrew to the mountains." Aliza Marcus, *Blood and Belief: The PKK and the Kurdish Fight for Independence* (New York, London: New York University Press 2007), 188.

109 *Tadić* Interlocutory Appeal Decision, *supra* note 23, at para. 70.

110 Christian Schaller, The Temporal Scope of the Laws of Armed Conflict in Multinational Military Operations, in Robin Geiß and Heike Krieger (eds.), *The "Legal Pluriverse" Surrounding Multinational Military Operations* (Oxford: Oxford University Press 2019) 67.

111 Özdağ, *supra* note 95, at 34.

in Taşdelen village of Şırnak province, as a result of which 27 soldiers and 40 PKK militants were killed.[112] Only a few months later, on 29 September 1992, a group of 500 PKK militants attacked a gendarmerie border outpost in the Derecik district of Hakkari province, as a result of which 28 soldiers and 174 PKK militants were killed.[113] This PKK attack is the one with the highest number of soldiers killed since the beginning of the conflict[114] (except for the execution of 33 unarmed soldiers, on 24 May 1993, who were traveling by a civilian bus to surrender to their military units).[115] Super Cobra helicopters and war jets were employed to attack the militants,[116] "many of whom apparently escaped into Iraq after the raid."[117]

Two days later, on 1 October 1992, a group of 100 PKK militants raided the Cevizdalı village of Bitlis province and "killed twenty-nine people, including many women and children."[118] The PKK's adoption of the "murder of civilians as open policy" exacerbated the effects and scope of the conflict.[119] The civilian population of certain southeastern districts was, therefore, profoundly affected by the conflict, especially throughout the 1980s and early 1990s. In 1987 alone, the PKK attacked 14 villages, killing 242 villagers and burning down 137 schools.[120]

The state's forcible evacuation of the more than 2,500 villages and hamlets that were under the threat and/or influence of the PKK during the 1980s and 1990s (especially in the first half of the 1990s) is another indicator of the

112 En kanlı üçüncü saldırı [The Third Bloodiest Attack]. *Habertürk*, 19 October 2011, https://www.haberturk.com/gundem/haber/680803-en-kanli-ucuncu-saldiri (accessed 1 January 2024).

113 Özdağ, *supra* note 95, at 67. The number of PKK militants, according to some sources, was about 300. 82 Are Reported Dead as Kurds Battle Turks, *The New York Times*, 30 September 1992, www.nytimes.com/1992/09/30/world/82-are-reported-dead-as-kurds-battle-turks.html (accessed 1 January 2024).

114 En fazla şehit verilen 4'üncü saldırı [The Fourth Attack with the Highest Number of Martyrs], *CNNTürk*, 19 October 2011, www.cnnturk.com/turkiye/en-fazla-sehit-verilen-4uncu-saldiri (accessed 1 January 2024).

115 Kurdistan Workers' Party (PKK), *The Washington Post*, https://www.washingtonpost.com/wp-srv/inatl/daily/feb99/pkkprofile.htm (accessed 1 January 2024).

116 Ümit Özdağ and Ersel Aydınlı, Winning a Low Intensity Conflict: Drawing Lessons from the Turkish Case, 2(3) *The Review of International Affairs* 96 (2003).

117 *The New York Times*, *supra* note 113.

118 Human Rights Watch, *The Kurds of Turkey: Killings, Disappearances and Torture* (March 1993) 12.

119 Amnesty International, *Turkey: A Policy of Denial* (February 1995) 10. The PKK have often "claimed responsibility for bomb attacks which were clearly directed at civilian targets," "execut[ed] captured village guards . . . their wives and children," "declared a policy of 'executing' teachers and other non-military government officials." Amnesty International, *supra* note 119. In the first ten years of the insurgency between 1984–1994, the PKK killed 124 teachers. Özdağ, *supra* note 95, at 85.

120 Özdağ, *supra* note 95, at 43; Human Rights Watch, *Background*, www.hrw.org/legacy/reports/1997/turkey/Turkey-02.htm (accessed 1 January 2024).

intensity and civilian cost of the violence produced in that period.[121] Likewise, the imposition of emergency rule from 1987 to 2002 in eastern and south-eastern provinces most affected by the conflict is among the indicators of the seriousness of the situation in the 1980s and 1990s.[122]

The PKK carried out 4,198 attacks in 1993,[123] 3,538 attacks in 1994[124] and 2,200 attacks in 1995.[125] 11,546 PKK militants, 3,621 security personnel and 5,014 civilians were already killed by the first half of the 1990s as a result of the PKK attacks.[126] Some of Türkiye's operations, too, have resulted in intense confrontations. Though the PKK has mostly avoided pitched battles in favor of hit-and-run attacks and ambushes,[127] there have been rare cases where the PKK units responded to Türkiye's military operations against the PKK hide-outs with a conventional type of combat "and in turn suffered heavy losses."[128]

On 12 October 1992, only two weeks after the PKK's Derecik attack, for example, 15,000 Turkish ground troops backed by tanks, helicopters and fighter jets[129] entered northern Iraq, "where some PKK holdouts initially refused to put down their weapons."[130] 1,452 PKK militants were killed or wounded, according to Turkish General Staff, as a result of this cross-border operation that lasted 20 days.[131] The PKK acknowledged only 161 casualties.[132] Turkish military destroyed much of the PKK's infrastructure and ammunition depots in northern Iraq[133] and "hoisted the nation's flag in Haftanin,"[134] a PKK holdout nestled in the mountains of northern Iraq, which "had grown into an important gathering and training camp for the PKK."[135] The operation was carried out with the apparent support of the Iraqi Kurdish forces (PUK and KDP) that fought alongside the Turkish military.[136]

121 Özdağ, *supra* note 95, at 43.
122 Özdağ, *supra* note 95, at 43.
123 Özdağ, *supra* note 95, at 76.
124 Özdağ, *supra* note 95, at 85.
125 Özdağ, *supra* note 95, at 93.
126 Özdağ, *supra* note 95, at 93.
127 *See* Jongerden, *supra* note 107, at 61.
128 Özdağ and Aydınlı, *supra* note 116, at 96.
129 Özdağ and Aydınlı, *supra* note 116, at 96; Özdağ, *supra* note 95, at 69.
130 Marcus, *supra* note 108, at 205.
131 İhsan Dörtkardeş, Irak'a yapılan en büyük kara harekatı [The Largest Ground Operation into Iraq], *Doğan Haber Ajansı*, 20 October 2011, https://web.archive.org/web/20160207064531/http://www.dha.com.tr/iraka-yapilan-en-buyuk-kara-harekati_223858.html (accessed 1 January 2024).
132 Marcus, *supra* note 108, at 205.
133 Özdağ and Aydınlı, *supra* note 116, at 96.
134 Marcus, *supra* note 108, at 205.
135 Marcus, *supra* note 108, at 145, 146.
136 Marcus, *supra* note 108, at 33; Gürcan Balik, *Turkey and the US in the Middle East: Diplomacy and Discord during the Iraq Wars* (London and New York: Bloomsbury Publishing 2016) 65.

The PKK, which suffered severe losses in its attempt to fight a conventional type of combat in October 1992, later "returned to areas [in northern Iraq] vacated by Turkish troops"[137] but "never again tried to defend territory and instead relocated fighters as necessary"[138] (except for the clashes in 2015 and 2016, which will be covered in the following heading). The 1990s, nevertheless, saw larger scale cross-border operations targeting the PKK hideouts in northern Iraq. On 20 March 1995, for instance, as many as 35,000 Turkish soldiers entered northern Iraq, launching a new major anti-PKK operation that lasted 43 days[139] in hopes of finally ending the PKK's "ability to use the border strip to launch attacks."[140] It was reported that 568 PKK militants were killed as a result of the operation.[141] Clearly, Türkiye's cross-border operations into the PKK bases in northern Iraq have greatly expanded the geographical scope as well as the human and material costs of the conflict.

1.5.2.2. FIERCE CLASHES BETWEEN AUGUST 2015 AND MARCH 2016

The PKK attempted to prevent policing functions of the Turkish security forces in several neighborhoods of four southeastern provinces in Türkiye by digging trenches and setting up barricades at the doorsteps of the civilian population between August 2015 and March 2016, following the end of a period called "solution process."[142] The solution process, which lasted from March 2013 to July 2015, was a dialogue process that aimed at persuading the PKK, by peaceful means, to lay down its arms. The government's policy of overlooking the PKK mobilization during the solution process encouraged the PKK to spread the conflict to urban areas by erecting barricades on the streets of several Kurdish neighborhoods, planting explosives and booby traps in these barricades and using civilian houses as shelters. The PKK's attempts to keep security forces out of several neighborhoods by building barricades and trenches following the collapse of the solution process were, as will be detailed later, all short-lived and far from successful, but they led to fierce clashes in several neighborhoods.

Curfews were imposed to prevent civilian casualties in the neighborhoods concerned during the operations to remove the trenches and to clear

137 Hugh Pope, Most Turkish Troops Said to Be Out of Iraq: Mideast: Ankara's Army Says It Killed 555 Kurdish Militants and Lost 61 Soldiers, *Los Angeles Times*, 5 May 1995, www.latimes.com/archives/la-xpm-1995-05-05-mn-62674-story.html (accessed 1 January 2024).

138 Marcus, *supra* note 108, at 206.

139 Özdağ, *supra* note 95, at 92.

140 Marcus, *supra* note 108, at 245; Özdağ and Aydınlı, *supra* note 116, at 97.

141 Asa Lundgren, *The Unwelcome Neighbour: Turkey's Kurdish Policy* (London and New York: Bloomsbury Publishing 2007) 79.

142 Adnan Küçükali and Mehmet Balıkçılar, Hendek Terörü Olaylarının Nusaybin'deki Küçük ve Orta Ölçekli İşletmelere Etkisi [Effects of the Trench Terrorism on the Small and Medium-Sized Enterprises in Nusaybin], (22) *Emek ve Toplum* 363 (2019).

these neighborhoods from the PKK militants. While the operations in some neighborhoods lasted for several days, operations in certain neighborhoods lasted for weeks, and the curfews were held even longer to clear leftover explosives. The said operations took place in different neighborhoods of four southeastern provinces (Diyarbakır, Mardin, Şırnak and Hakkari), with the 103-day-long operations in the Sur district of the Diyarbakir province being the longest-lasting.[143] Operations in the Derik, Dargeçit and Nusaybin districts of the Mardin province lasted for 6, 18 and 82 days, respectively.[144] Operations in the İdil, Silopi and Cizre districts of the Şırnak province, on the other hand, lasted for 20, 37 and 78 days, respectively.[145] Finally, operations in the Yüksekova district of the Hakkari province lasted for 37 days.[146]

The PKK's attempts to spread the conflict to urban areas by erecting and defending the barricades on the streets of several Kurdish neighborhoods between August 2015 and March 2016 claimed the lives of 859 security personnel and 335 civilians.[147] 4,571 PKK militants were killed during the operations to remove the barricades and trenches.[148] More than 355,000 civilians left their homes in the conflict area.[149] These figures support this sub-section's argument that there were intense confrontations between August 2015 and March 2016. A great number of buildings had to be demolished after the end of the clashes "because PKK militants had planted bombs in them and dug tunnels beneath them."[150] "During the clean-up of rubble, . . . security forces were detonating around 70 explosives a day planted in the houses. This was one of the main reasons why the whole process took so long in Nusaybin."[151]

143 PKK operasyonlarında 103 günde neler yaşandı? [What Happened in the 103 Days of PKK Operations], *Milliyet*, 10 March 2016, www.milliyet.com.tr/gundem/pkk-operasyonlarinda-103-gunde-neler-yasandi-2207223 (accessed 1 January 2024); Kubilay Aydın, PKK Operasyonlarının Bilançosu [Consequences of the PKK Operations], *Sözcü*, 11March2016,www.sozcu.com.tr/2016/gundem/pkk-operasyonlarinin-bilancosu-1131227/ (accessed 1 January 2024).

144 Sertaç Canalp Korkmaz, Meskûn Mahal Muharebesini Anlamak [Understanding Urban Warfare], *ORSAM* 18 (2018).

145 Korkmaz, *supra* note 144, at 18.

146 Korkmaz, *supra* note 144, at 18.

147 Ministry of Interior of the Republic of Türkiye, Uluslararası Af Örgütü'nün Raporuna İlişkin Basın Açıklaması [Press Release on the Report of the Amnesty International], 23 January 2017, para. 14, www.icisleri.gov.tr/uluslararasi-af-orgutunun-raporuna-iliskin-basin-aciklamasi (accessed 1 January 2024).

148 Küçükali and Balıkçılar, *supra* note 142, at 363.

149 Terör yüzünden 355 bin kişi göç etti [355,000 People Migrated because of Terrorism], *Sözcü*, 27 February 2016, www.sozcu.com.tr/2016/gundem/muezzinoglu-teror-yuzunden-355-bin-kisi-goc-etti-1111739/ (accessed 1 January 2024).

150 Terör yüzünden 355 bin kişi göç etti, *supra* note 149.

151 Managing Turkey's PKK Conflict: The Case of Nusaybin, *International Crisis Group*, 2 May 2017, www.crisisgroup.org/europe-central-asia/western-europemediterranean/turkey/243-managing-turkeys-pkk-conflict-case-nusaybin (accessed 1 January 2024).

The previously described i) human and material costs; ii) temporal and geographical scope of the conflict; iii) effects of the conflict on civilians, including the extent to which civilians left the conflict areas and extent of the destruction; iv) as well as the nature of the state's response and the type of weapons used all suggest that the violence between Türkiye and the PKK is sufficiently intense to constitute an armed conflict within the meaning of IHL. The conclusion for this sub-section is that both the requisite degree of organization criterion and the requisite degree of intensity criterion seem to be fulfilled in the context of Türkiye-PKK confrontations. The violence between Türkiye and PKK, therefore, constitutes a NIAC within the meaning of IHL and is subject to CA3.

As for the applicability of the Rome Statute, sub-section 1.3 explained that the Statute contains two separate lists of war crimes committed as part of NIACs – Article 8(2)(c) and Article 8(2)(e) – and that the protracted nature of a conflict is a *sine qua non* requirement for the applicability of the latter. While the determination of the existence of an armed conflict does not require the violence in question to be protracted in nature, such nature is still a requirement for the applicability of the provisions contained in Article 8(2)(e). Given that the duration needed to fulfill the "protracted armed conflict" requirement for the purposes of the applicability of Article 8(2)(e) can be as short as five months or even less,[152] it is not difficult to conclude that the nearly 40-year-old violence between Türkiye and the PKK is protracted in nature. Both Article 8(2)(c) and Article 8(2)(e) of the Rome Statute would, therefore, be applicable to the situation in Türkiye if the preconditions to the exercise of jurisdiction of the ICC were to be satisfied (e.g., if Türkiye was a State Party).

Additional Protocol II, however, would not be applicable to the situation in Türkiye, even if Türkiye was a party to it, because the PKK has never been able to exercise territorial control needed to implement the Protocol, which will be the subject of the next heading. As there are conflicting views on whether or not the PKK ever exerted territorial control, a separate heading is devoted to the applicability of the AP II to the situation in Türkiye.

1.5.3. Applicability of Additional Protocol II

As detailed in sub-section 1.2, territorial control by the armed group concerned is a *sine qua non* requirement for the applicability of Additional Protocol II. In order for AP II to be applicable to a non-international armed conflict, the armed group concerned must exercise such control over a part of the territory of the state concerned as to enable the group "to carry out sustained and concerted military operations and to implement" the Protocol.[153] Territorial control, on the other hand, can be said to exist only if the armed group in

152 *See* sub-section 1.3 page 74.
153 Additional Protocol II, *supra* note 19, art. 1(1).

question is able "to move freely, access information and resources, and prevent its enemies' movement and access in a particular place and time."[154]

In the late 1980s and early 1990s, the PKK's main goal was to establish a "liberated zone" it had dreamed of since its foundation in an area encompassing three southeastern provinces (Hakkari, Siirt and Van), where it often carried out ambushes and attacked gendarmerie stations.[155] The Turkish security forces, however, usually responded quickly to the sporadic attempts by the PKK to exercise territorial control. The group contested the state for control of several southeastern districts in March 1992, but the state forces managed to maintain control "after a few days of heavy clashes."[156] As will be detailed later, the PKK was never able to take and hold territory[157] or exert complete territorial control over even rural areas, not even in the early 1990s, the period of its greatest success.[158]

Though the PKK carried out large-scale attacks against the gendarmerie border outposts in the early 1990s, the two largest of which mentioned earlier, it was never able to take over the control of outposts or checkpoints of the Turkish security forces, even in the most rural areas.[159] The reason the PKK has relied solely on hit-and-run[160] and terrorist[161] attacks in Türkiye was the fact that it was never able to take and hold territory needed "to carry out sustained and concerted military operations."[162]

One of the PKK's main aims in 1990 was to be able to hold its fourth congress in Türkiye.[163] However, since it could not find a safe haven, even in the rough, mountainous terrains of southeastern Türkiye, the fourth congress was held in northern Iraq.[164] As a matter of fact, the PKK could not hold any of its congresses in Türkiye, despite its great desire.

Some argued that the PKK exerted control over some districts in southeastern Türkiye in the early 1990s. Aliza Marcus, for example, stated in her book that "to break the PKK's control over parts of the southeast, Turkish soldiers conducted frequent house raids, looking for signs of PKK support and weapons."[165] However, the PKK control Marcus mentioned, in which the

154 Michael A. Rubin, Rebel Territorial Control and Civilian Collective Action in Civil War: Evidence from the Communist Insurgency in the Philippines, 64(2–3) *Journal of Conflict Resolution* 463 (2020).
155 Özdağ, *supra* note 95, at 50, 51, and 54.
156 Özdağ and Aydınlı, *supra* note 116, at 96.
157 William Abresch, too, correctly observed that the PKK "was never capable of holding towns." Abresch, *supra* note 77, at 755.
158 Özdağ, *supra* note 95, at 59.
159 Özdağ, *supra* note 95, at 59–60.
160 *See, e.g.*, Marcus, *supra* note 108.
161 *See* footnotes 214 and 232.
162 Additional Protocol II, *supra* note 19, art. 1(1).
163 Özdağ, *supra* note 95, at 54.
164 Özdağ, *supra* note 95, at 55.
165 Marcus, *supra* note 108, at 238.

PKK militants were so invisible that house raids were necessary to find them and their weapons, is not the type of control that would trigger the applicability of AP II.

Those who referred to the PKK's "control" in the early 1990s were, in fact, generally referring to the group's ability to terrorize parts of the southeast and to the Turkish forces' inability to "protect each village."[166] In this regard, the PKK's burning of schools and killing of teachers in rural villages in the late 1980s and early 1990s cannot be considered as territorial control within the meaning of IHL; they can only show the state's failure to take efficient measures to protect those areas from the PKK attacks. Most objective observers do not dispute that the PKK was never able to take and hold territory or gain exclusive territorial control over a part of Türkiye, not even in the early 1990s.

The fact that the PKK is hiding and headquartered in the "uncontrolled,"[167] extremely rugged and remote mountains of northern Iraq since the 1990s is a proof of its inability to build a base or hide within Türkiye, let alone to control a territory therein. Even the most rural areas and the mountainous terrain in east and southeast Türkiye, where the majority of the PKK's attacks took place, are tightly controlled and patrolled by the security forces; and the caves that are used by the PKK members as shelters are destroyed during these routine patrols.[168] Even in the early 1990s, when the PKK lived its "golden years,"[169] the Turkish armed forces routinely patrolled the rural areas of southeastern Türkiye to destroy the caves and dugouts that served as shelters for the PKK militants.

If the PKK had apparent and permanent bases in the area and was patrolling the area in search of Turkish soldiers, then it could be argued that the area was under the PKK's control within the meaning of the applicability of AP II. Clearly, this has never been the case in Türkiye. It has always been Türkiye that patrolled the rural areas of the southeast in search of PKK militants, their hideouts and weapons. The PKK, on the other hand, was the party trying to "infiltrate" the Turkish territory from its bases in the "uncontrolled" mountainous terrain in northern Iraq to conduct hit-and-run attacks against the Turkish state forces.[170]

Some observers refer to the PKK's ability to manage smuggling and drug trafficking activities in the border area as "PKK control in the region,"[171] without discussing whether the group ever gained exclusive territorial control. Türkiye or Iraq's failure to protect these areas from such PKK activities as managing smuggling activities, however, does not indicate the existence of

166 Özdağ and Aydınlı, *supra* note 116, at 92.

167 Yunus Eren, *The Impact of Land Border Security on Terrorism Financing: Turkey's Southeast Land Border and the PKK, Master Thesis*, Naval Postgraduate School (2013) 5.

168 Özdağ, *supra* note 95, at 83–84.

169 Özdağ, *supra* note 95, at 90.

170 Eren, *supra* note 167, at 28.

171 Eren, *supra* note 167, at 63.

territorial control by the PKK within the meaning of applicability of AP II. As explained by Marcus, "it was impossible to fully secure the high mountains and deep ravines that ran along the border."[172] The PKK was far from gaining exclusive and complete territorial control over, even rural areas in northern Iraq.

Türkiye has carried out countless military operations into northern Iraq to eliminate the PKK bases, which are mostly underground and hidden in the Qandil Mountains. The PKK once tried to defend territory in northern Iraq in October 1992, in the face of the aforementioned major cross-border operation into PKK bases there. However, due to the heavy losses, the PKK "never again tried to defend territory and instead relocated fighters as necessary."[173] It should nevertheless be noted that even if the PKK had territorial control in northern Iraq and Türkiye was a party to AP II, that would not be sufficient to trigger the applicability of AP II to the conflict between Türkiye and the PKK because the Protocol requires the non-State armed group concerned to exercise control over a part of the territory of the State Party concerned (in this case Türkiye).[174]

As detailed in the previous heading, the PKK also attempted to control several neighborhoods in Türkiye's four southeastern provinces between August 2015 and March 2016, by digging trenches and building roadblocks and booby traps to keep security forces out. These efforts, however, were all short-lived[175] and were far from successful, as evidenced by the fact that even the entries and exits of the neighborhoods concerned were fully controlled by the security forces, and the PKK militants were only able to move through the tunnels.[176]

It is clear that the PKK's short-lived efforts to protect the barricades and trenches by such methods as using civilian houses as shelters and planting mines or other types of explosives cannot be considered as "territorial control" within the meaning of applicability of AP II. In fact, these efforts were not even based on a realistic evaluation of whether they could actually result in territorial control but were a result of the government's orders to the security forces and local authorities to ignore the PKK mobilization in the region for the purpose of maintaining the solution process.[177]

The PKK deliberately chose the most prominent Kurdish neighborhoods, where it hoped it could easily blend into the civilian population and use civilian houses as cover without any serious objections from the locals. Increasing

172 Marcus, *supra* note 108, at 205.
173 Marcus, *supra* note 108, at 206.
174 *See* sub-section 1.2.
175 *See* sub-section 1.5.2.2.
176 "PKK had dug tunnels in the neighbourhoods [concerned] to move fighters and weapons." International Crisis Group, *supra* note 151.
177 It was the government's unwise policy of loosening the security measures and ignoring the movements of the PKK militants that encouraged the PKK to attempt to control territory.

the likelihood of civilian casualties caused by the counter-terrorism operations, which would serve as a propaganda tool by the PKK, and limiting the military methods that could be deployed by the security forces were the main motivations for the PKK to deliberately risk the lives of civilians of specific Kurdish neighborhoods. The organization used children as human shields and civilian buildings, including houses and schools, as shelters to fire on the security forces, leading to the destruction of hundreds of civilian buildings.[178] Some of the male PKK members, who fired on the security forces from the civilian houses, disguised themselves as civilian women.[179]

The reason barricades were not destroyed within minutes (by, for example, an aerial bombardment) was not the PKK's ability to defend the barricades but the fact that the group was using civilian houses as shelters. An intervention, which would have added to the civilian casualties already caused by the PKK, would have given the PKK what it has always wanted: making the civilians affected by the counter-terrorism operations a potential source of recruitment and support for the PKK. The security forces' efforts not to endanger civilian locals are the main reason why the PKK has not managed to get Türkiye's Kurds (who are estimated to account for 15–18% of Türkiye's population of about 85 million)[180] to support its separatist violence and why Türkiye has not experienced a civil war or a large-scale prolonged armed violence within its borders as neighboring Syria has. Due to the endangered civilian locals' refusal of the PKK's calls to support its efforts to build and stand behind the barricades[181] and the PKK's inability to engage in sustained armed confrontations with the state forces, the PKK's efforts to establish territorial control over certain neighborhoods and to incite a civil war were far from successful.

As for the applicability of Additional Protocol II, the language of the Protocol requires that the level of territorial control achieved by the armed group concerned be sufficient to allow it to implement the Protocol. The PKK's efforts to exercise territorial control were clearly far from enabling it to implement AP II (to house prisoners and convene courts to guarantee their due process and fair trial rights;[182] to take care of the wounded and sick;[183]

178 Aydın, *Sözcü*, *supra* note 143.
179 Hainlere çok yakıştı, 58 terörist etekle yakalandı! [It Looked Well on Traitors: 58 Terrorists Have Been Captured with Skirts on], *Türkiye Gazetesi*, 9 January 2016, www.turkiyegazetesi.com.tr/gundem/337479.aspx
180 Mesut Yeğen (Project Coordinator), Uğraş Ulaş Tol and Mehmet Ali Çalışkan (Researchers), "Kürt Seçmenlerin Oy Verme Dinamikleri: Kuzeydoğu-Ortadoğu ve Güneydoğu Anadolu Alt Bölgelerinde Seçmenin Siyasal Tercihlerinin Sosyolojik Analizi" [Voting Dynamics of Kurdish Voters: Sociological Analysis of the Voters in the Northeastern, Middleastern and Southeastern Sub-regions] (January 2015): 11.
181 "PKK didn't find the answer it was looking for. The people didn't stand behind the trenches and barricades": Cuma Çiçek and Vahap Coşkun, *The Peace Process from Dolmabahçe to Present-Day: Understanding Failure and Finding New Paths* (Barış Vakfi 2016) 21.
182 Additional Protocol II, *supra* note 19, art. 6(2).
183 Additional Protocol II, *supra* note 19, art. 7.

to provide children with proper education, "including religious and moral education";[184] or to remove children "to a safer area within the country and ensure that they are accompanied by persons responsible for their safety and well-being").[185] The recent execution of 13 Turkish citizens, whom the PKK kidnapped as hostages under the guise of prisoners of war and dragged from one cave to another, in a cave in northern Iraq in the face of Türkiye's rescue operation,[186] is an example that demonstrates that the PKK is far from having achieved the territorial control needed to implement the norms of IHL.

In sum, as the discussion earlier clearly suggests, the PKK does not exercise territorial control needed "to carry out sustained and concerted military operations and to implement" AP II.[187] In fact, the PKK has never been able to exercise territorial control over a part of Türkiye's territory, even for a short period of time. The territorial control criterion for the applicability of AP II is not, therefore, met by the PKK, and the Protocol would not apply to the violence between Türkiye and the PKK, even if Türkiye was a party to it.

1.6. Conclusion

This section first explained that, under IHL of NIACs, a person who engages in hostilities against the state forces would not be accorded the status of combatant. Acknowledging the applicability of IHL to the violence between Türkiye and the PKK would not, therefore, require Türkiye to treat the captured PKK militants as prisoners of law or to grant them immunity from domestic legislation for attacking state forces. The section also clarified that the application of IHL would not, contrary to the concerns of Türkiye, affect the legal status of the PKK.

The section has argued that both the requisite degree of organization criterion and the requisite degree of intensity criterion for the armed conflict characterization seem to be fulfilled in the context of Türkiye-PKK confrontations. First, the PKK satisfies the majority of the indicative factors for the determination of the organization of a non-State armed group, such as the existence of a command structure and the ability to recruit and train personnel. Second, human and material costs, the temporal and geographical scope of the conflict, as well as the nature of the state's response and the type of weapons used all suggest that the violence between Türkiye and the PKK is sufficiently intense to constitute an armed conflict within the meaning of IHL. The violence in

184 Additional Protocol II, *supra* note 19, at 4(3)(a).

185 Additional Protocol II, *supra* note 19, art. 4(3)(e).

186 Ragıp Soylu, Turkey: Hundreds Arrested after PKK's Execution of 13 Hostages, *Middle East Eye*, 15 February 2022, www.middleeasteye.net/news/turkey-pkk-execution-hostages-erdogan-lashes-out; "Turkish Army Says 13 Civilians Killed as Anti-PKK Operation Ends," *Al Jazeera*, 14 February 2021, www.aljazeera.com/news/2021/2/14/turkey-completes-northern-iraq-operation-against-pkk-minister

187 Soylu, *supra* note 186, art. 1(1).

question, therefore, constitutes a NIAC within the meaning of IHL and is subject to CA3.

This section has also demonstrated that the Rome Statute provisions on NIACs (Article 8(2)(c) and Article 8(2)(e)) would be applicable to the situation in Türkiye if it were a State Party. It finally submitted that Additional Protocol II would not be applicable to Türkiye's fight against the PKK, even if Türkiye was a State Party, because the PKK has never been able to exercise such control over a part of Türkiye's territory as to enable it to carry out sustained military operations and to implement the Protocol. The section's analysis regarding the fulfillment of AP II-standard is also a challenge to the alternative narrative by other scholars that AP II-standard is also satisfied. In this sense, the Türkiye-PKK conflict provides an excellent practical example of how the two different legal standards for NIACs can indeed produce two different conclusions on the nature of a given situation of violence.

2. Limited Temporal Jurisdiction of the ICC

Most of the allegations against the Turkish Armed Forces concern the incidents that occurred outside the time period over which the ICC can act. For example, village evacuations and resettlements of the displaced population, for which Türkiye has been severely criticized with respect to its fight against the PKK, took place between 1985 and 2001.[188] The jurisdiction of the Court, however, is not retroactive, and thus, the Court won't have jurisdiction over events that took place before the entry into force of the Rome Statute on July 1, 2002.[189] Moreover, when Türkiye accedes to the Rome Statute, the Court will have jurisdiction only with respect to the allegations concerning the incidents occurred after the entry into force of the Statute for Türkiye, unless Türkiye accepts jurisdiction of the Court also for the acts that took place prior to its ratification but after July 1, 2002.[190]

In 2006, Martin Scheinin, the Special Rapporteur on the Promotion and Protection of Human Rights and Fundamental Freedoms While Countering Terrorism, noted with great satisfaction that Türkiye had, at the time of reporting, already pursued a high pace of reform in the area of international humanitarian law and human rights since 2001.[191] The Rapporteur, who visited Türkiye to gather firsthand information about how counter-terrorism measures affect the protection and promotion of human rights, commended

188 Jongerden, *supra* note 107, at 82.

189 Rome Statute, *supra* note 37, art. 11(1).

190 Rome Statute, *supra* note 37, art. 11(2).

191 Martin Scheinin, Preliminary Note by the Special Rapporteur on the Promotion and Protection of Human Rights and Fundamental Freedoms While Countering Terrorism, at 2, para. 5, U.N. Doc. E/CN.4/2006/98/Add.2, (24 March 2006), https://documents-dds-ny.un.org/doc/UNDOC/GEN/G06/119/83/PDF/G0611983.pdf?OpenElement.

Türkiye's zero-tolerance policy on torture since its announcement in 2003 and the steps taken to prevent any kind of ill-treatment.[192]

An examination of the reports by various UN Special Rapporteurs, such as Christof Heyns and Martin Scheinin, reveal that most of the allegations against the Turkish security forces, such as ill-treatment and extrajudicial killings, were, in fact, committed by JİTEM, an illegal/clandestine counter-terrorism and intelligence organization nested within the Turkish gendarmerie in 1980s and 1990s.[193] Due to the evolution of the Turkish counter-terrorism measures and Türkiye's commitment to reforms, however, such allegations had virtually come to an end after 2001.

ICC's debatable jurisdiction over the crimes that began prior to the entry into force of the Rome Statute but have continued afterwards (so-called "continuing crimes") should not be a concern for Türkiye because of the laws enacted by Türkiye to redress those incidents and compensate the victims of the counter-terrorism measures.[194] For example, "Law on the Compensation of Losses Resulting from Terrorist Acts and the Measures Taken Against Terrorism," which entered into force on July 27, 2004, provides remedies to the displaced people and supports their return on a voluntary basis.[195] Special Rapporteur Martin Scheinin praised the law as being "an example of 'best practice' to be studied by other States."[196] The Special Rapporteur also praised adoption of "Measures on the issue of internally displaced persons and the return to village and rehabilitation project in Turkey" on August 17, 2005.[197]

There are also ECtHR decisions that confirm the efficiency and operability of the Turkish domestic remedies available to the victims of counter-terrorism practices. In *Aydin Icyer v. Turkey*, for example, the ECtHR has unanimously found that the remedies available to Aydin Icyer, whose house was evacuated by Turkish armed forces in 1994 "on account of intense terrorist activities in the region and threats issued by the PKK," were "not only in theory but also in practice" and that they are capable of providing adequate redress.[198] The ECtHR also noted that "there was no obstacle preventing [Aydin Icyer and

192 Scheinin, *supra* note *supra* note 191, at 3, para. 9.

193 Directorate for EU Affairs, *Jitem Terörü Yargıda*, https://www.ab.gov.tr/p.php?e=31047 (10 December 2004).

194 Alan Nissel, Continuing Crimes in the Rome Statute, 25 *Michigan Journal of International Law* 653, 687 (2004).

195 Republic of Türkiye Ministry of Foreign Affairs, *Internally Displaced Persons (IDPs) and the "Return to Village and Rehabilitation Program" in Turkey*, www.mfa.gov.tr/internally-displaced-persons-_idps_-and-the-_return-to-village-and-rehabilitation-program_-in-turkey.en.mfa (accessed 1 January 2024).

196 Scheinin, *supra* note 191, at 2, para. 12.

197 Scheinin, *supra* note 191, at 2, para. 12.

198 *Aydin Icyer v. Turkey*, Appl. No. 18888/02, Third Section Decision As To the Admissibility, (ECtHR, 12 January 2006), http://hudoc.echr.coe.int/sites/eng/pages/search.aspx?i=001-72123.

other] villagers from returning to their homes."[199] These restitutions would prevent the incidents of the 1980s and 1990s from being classified as continuing acts. As for the future, given the aforementioned importance of combating the PKK in accordance with the established principles of international law for the speedy and final elimination of terrorism in Türkiye, it is highly unlikely (and unwise) for Türkiye to carry out actions that could be considered as violation of a law under the Rome Statute.

It should also be noted that, under international humanitarian law and the Rome Statute, not all kinds of displacements of the civilian population constitute a war crime. According to Article 8(2)(e) (viii) of the Rome Statute, "ordering the displacement of the civilian population" is not a war crime when "the security of the civilians involved or imperative military reasons so demand."[200] The resettlements in Türkiye aimed, in compliance with the Rome Statute, to gain concrete and direct military advantage, deprive the PKK of its environment and, at the same time, maintain the safety of the inhabitants.[201] Türkiye's village evacuations, therefore, could not be considered to constitute one of enumerated war crimes of the Rome Statute and would not be found admissible before the Court, even if the conflict was classified as an armed conflict and the temporal jurisdiction requirement was satisfied.

Although the latest version of the Turkish Criminal Code that was adopted in 2005 regulates crimes against humanity and the crime of genocide, it does not define war crimes. Adopting a legislation that would allow its domestic courts to interpret war crimes is of great importance in order to invoke the principle of complementarity, which grants primary responsibility for prosecution to national courts. Türkiye could, upon ratification, declare that it does not accept the ICC's jurisdiction over war crimes for a seven-year-period in accordance with Article 124, which would provide Türkiye with even more time to strengthen its capacity to administer justice for the most serious crimes of international concern so as to meet the needs of investigating and prosecuting allegations of war crimes in accordance with the Rome Statute. Such transition period is also important for Türkiye to communicate with the Office of the Prosecutor to present the reasons why its counter-terrorism measures against the PKK should not, in its view, be classified as an armed conflict subject to international humanitarian law and, in the meanwhile, demonstrate that its counter-terrorism measures are completely aligned with the provisions of the Rome Statute.

3. The Other High Threshold Criteria of the Rome Statute

Unlike the ECtHR, the ICC is not a human rights court, and thus, the human rights violations that do not meet the high threshold of the Rome Statute

199 *Aydin Icyer v. Turkey*, *supra* note 198.
200 Rome Statute, *supra* note 37, art. 8(2)(e)(viii).
201 Jongerden, *supra* note 107, at 82.

will not be prosecuted by the Court. When the OTP decides that there is a reasonable basis to believe that a Rome Statute crime has been committed, it then moves to consider admissibility of the case before the Court in light of "complementarity" and "gravity" – two overall safeguards of the Statute. Even if Türkiye's integral struggle against the PKK were classified as an armed conflict subject to international humanitarian law and the temporal jurisdiction requirement were satisfied, the acts forming the basis of past allegations against the Turkish security forces would not satisfy the high threshold criteria set out in the Rome Statute and would fail to be grave enough to trigger a formal ICC investigation.

3.1. Complementarity

As discussed in Chapter 2, the ICC is complementary to the national courts, and it will only act when the domestic authorities are unable and/or unwilling to do so.[202] Türkiye has taken many steps not only to prevent the kind of crimes that JİTEM committed in 1990s but also to bring the perpetrators to justice. In this regard, 11 special prosecution offices in different regions in Türkiye were assigned to investigate killings of 1990s, the dark period in country's history.[203] Given Türkiye's long-standing efforts to better its national criminal justice to ensure accountability for the acts that could (if other thresholds were met) rise to the level of crimes against humanity or war crimes, it is highly unlikely that the Turkish national courts would be deemed "unwilling" or "unable" to prosecute perpetrators of these crimes. There exists a range of investigative bodies for human rights violations in Türkiye, such as Gendarmerie Human Rights Violations Investigation and Examination Centre (JIHIDEM), Parliamentary Human Rights Inquiry Commission and the Human Rights Presidency. In addition to these mechanisms that aim to investigate serious or minor human rights violations in Türkiye, a Turkish Human Rights Institution (TİHK) was established in June 2012 to receive complaints against public officials at every level.[204] The UN Special Rapporteur Christof Heyns viewed the creation of this institution as "an important step in strengthening the protection of human rights, including the right to life, in Türkiye, in particular in terms of efforts to ensure accountability and redress in cases of violations."[205]

Improvements in the fight against impunity are also confirmed by the European Commission's annual progress reports for Türkiye. For example, the Commission's latest report (2014) commended the decision of the Turkish

202 Rome Statute, *supra* note 37, art. 17(1)(a).

203 Milliyet, *JİTEM Davasında Ölen Albayın Tanıklığı İstendi*, www.milliyet.com.tr/jitem-davasinda-olen-albayin-tanikligi-istendi-gundem-1055115/ (03 February 2009).

204 Christof Heyns, *Report of the Special Rapporteur on Extrajudicial, Summary or Arbitrary Executions*, p. 16, para. 82, U.N. Doc. A/HRC/23/47/Add.2 (18 March 2013).

205 Christof Heyns, *supra* note 204, at 16, para. 83.

Court of Cassation to uphold "the convictions of 11 public officials, following the death in custody of Engin Çeber in 2008," in which "[a] prison director and two prison guards received life sentences."[206] The 2010 constitutional amendment, which allowed the Turkish nationals who claim that any of their rights under the ECHR have been violated to file an individual complaint with the Constitutional Court, is another positive step that demonstrates Türkiye's ability to address violations by public authorities. Justified concerns and criticisms regarding the issues related to judiciary, such as the increasing number of jailed journalists, mass dismissals and arrests of public officials without judicial review, poor oversight of LGBTQ rights, increasing number of corruption cover-up incidents and some other measures that fall short of basic human rights safeguards are not the subjects of the Rome Statute, which only covers the most serious crimes of international concern (namely, genocide, war crimes, crimes against humanity and crime of aggression), but of international human rights law.

3.2. The Gravity Threshold

The ICC's jurisdiction is limited to "the most serious crimes of concern to international community as a whole."[207] The Rome Statute refers to these crimes as "unimaginable atrocities that deeply shock the conscience of humanity"[208] and "threaten the peace, security and well-being of the world."[209] The court will not exercise its jurisdiction over the crimes that are below this gravity threshold. The Office of the Prosecutor stresses that "while, in a general sense, any crime within the jurisdiction of the Court is 'grave,'" "the Statute clearly foresees and requires an additional consideration of 'gravity' whereby the Office must determine that a case is of sufficient gravity to justify further action by the Court."[210] This gravity threshold that the OTP seeks to find before starting a formal investigation is not satisfied in the incidents, for which Türkiye has been accused of committing one of the ICC crimes.

The Court has jurisdiction over the war crimes enumerated under Article 8 of the Rome Statute, "in particular when committed as part of a plan or policy or as part of a large-scale commission of such crimes."[211] Although the words "in particular" suggest that "plan or policy" or "large scale commission" thresholds are not prerequisite, Article 17 (1) (d) of the Statute brings

206 European Commission, *Turkey Progress Report* (October 2014), ec.europa.eu/enlargement/pdf/key_documents/2014/20141008-turkey-progress-report_en.pdf. at 50.

207 Rome Statute, *supra* note 1 at *preamble,* para. 4.

208 Rome Statute, *supra* note 1 at *preamble,* para. 2.

209 Rome Statute, *supra* note 1 at *preamble,* para. 3.

210 International Criminal Court-The Office of the Prosecutor, *Annexe 10*, p. 8 (16 March 2010), *available at* www.icc-cpi.int/iccdocs/doc/doc844043.pdf.

211 Rome Statute, *supra* note 37, art. 8(1).

an additional threshold of gravity for all the crimes over which the Court has jurisdiction.[212]

In order to assess the gravity in a given situation, the OTP considers various factors, such as the number of the victims of serious crimes, manner of commission of the crimes and their impact.[213] The situations that have been found admissible before the ICC involves "thousands of willful killings as well as intentional and large-scale sexual violence and abductions."[214] An examination of the EU and UN reports on Türkiye reveal that the number of the allegations against the Turkish security forces remained very low in 2000s as compared to cases found admissible by the OTP. Thus, alleged crimes committed by the Turkish Armed Forces as part of counter-terrorism operations against the PKK would not be of sufficient gravity to justify a formal investigation, even if the other criteria were to be met.

In the Uganda case, the Office has indicted Joseph Kony and other leaders of the terrorist LRA but has not started a formal investigation into the crimes committed by the Ugandan government agencies and Ugandan national military (UPDF; Uganda People's Defence Force) because of the relative gravity of the crimes.[215] Despite the accusations by different groups and organizations, like Human Rights Watch, that Ugandan government and military has committed serious atrocities, such as extrajudicial executions, rape, children recruitment and torture, the Office has only brought charges against the rebel leaders of the LRA on the grounds that "crimes committed by the LRA were much more numerous and of much higher gravity than alleged crimes committed by the UPDF."[216] Similarly, the OTP has declined to open an investigation into the crimes committed on the flotilla of vessels carrying humanitarian assistance for Gaza Strip (Humanitarian Aid Flotilla) by Israeli Defence Forces (IDF) and the crimes committed in Iraq by British soldiers on the grounds that the crimes committed were not sufficiently grave.[217]

212 Rome Statute, *supra* note 37, art. 17(1)(d).

213 International Criminal Court, *Regulations of the Office of the Prosecutor*, ICC-BD/05-01-09, reg. 29, para. 2 (23 April 2009).

214 International Criminal Court, *Prosecutor v. Charles Ble Goude, Prosecution's Response to the Defence Application Pursuant to Articles 19(4) and 17(1)(d) of the Rome Statute*, Case No. ICC-02/11–02/11–181, para. 30 (20 October 2014), *available at* http://www.icc-cpi.int/iccdocs/doc/doc1853270.pdf.

215 Alana Tiemessen, *Defying Gravity: Seeking Political Balance in ICC Prosecutions*, justiceinconflict.org/2013/04/22/defying-gravity-seeking-political-balance-in-icc-prosecutions/ (accessed 22 April 2013).

216 Michael A. Newton, The Complementarity Conundrum: Are We Watching Evolution or Evisceration? 8 Santa Clara Journal of International Law 115, 158 (2010).

217 ICC-OTP, *Report on Preliminary Examination Activities 2014, supra* note 77, at p. 62, para. 262.

4. Uludere Incident

While most of the serious allegations against Turkish Armed Forces concern the incidents that occurred before the entry into force of the Rome Statute, some allegations concern the acts that occurred after 2002. Most notable among those is the "Uludere incident," one of the most debated acts by the Turkish Armed Forces. The incident has been the subject of very serious allegations against the Turkish Armed Forces. Although the ICC would not have jurisdiction with respect to the allegations that concern the incidents that occurred before the entry into force of the Rome Statute for Türkiye, a brief analysis of the Uludere incident may be helpful in understanding the possibility that an investigation is initiated by the OTP against the senior Turkish officials for the acts carried out as part of Türkiye's fight against PKK.

In the Uludere incident, 34 civilians, a group of civilian smugglers who were, as a result of false intelligence, believed to be PKK members in the preparation of an attack, were killed in a military airstrike near the Turkish-Iraqi border in December 2011.[218] The incident was caused by deceptive intel that a group of armed terrorists was set to stage an attack on Turkish military posts, which led to the bombardment of the group that turned out to be civilian smugglers crossing the Iraqi border into Türkiye. It is the most tragic incident caused by the operations of the Turkish Armed Forces since the PKK's first terrorist attack in 1984.

The regional commander was removed from his post, and several investigations were conducted into the incident. The government's offer for compensation were rejected by the families of the victims.[219] Though the domestic authorities are obliged, under international and domestic law, to prosecute those who are responsible for providing the false intelligence and those who abused/neglected their duty, no one has been convicted so far. While the applications to take the case to the Constitutional Court and to the ECtHR have been rejected on procedural grounds, another application has been filed to the Constitutional Court, rejection of which will pave the way for the ECtHR. If the Turkish authorities fail to carry out effective investigations into the incident, the ECtHR will inevitably find Türkiye guilty of violating Article 2 of the ECHR, which protects the right to life, and of inadequate investigation into the incident.

Sanctions or measures to address the incident, such as the removal of regional commander from his post, are welcomed; however, the investigations into the incident must lead to the prosecution of the official/s who provided the false intelligence and misused/neglected their duties. The prosecution of

218 Sait Yılmaz, *PKK Terör Örgütü ve KCK'da Son Durum*, 4 Journal of Turan Center for Strategical Researches 15, 12 (2012); CNN, *Turkish PM Erdogan Regrets Kurdish Civilian Airstrike Deaths*, edition.cnn.com/2011/12/30/world/meast/turkey-air-strike/index.html (30 December 2011).

219 İnternet Haber, *İşte Uludere'nin Tazminat Miktarı*, www.internethaber.com/iste-uluderenin-tazminat-miktari-397097h.htm (accessed 24 January 2012).

those responsible is vital not only for the establishment of justice for the victims and their families but also for the protection of the credibility of the Turkish Armed Forces.

From an ICC jurisdiction standpoint, it is clear that the Uludere incident, which (not surprisingly) has been used as a propaganda by the PKK and served to the aims of the organization, was not committed as part of a plan or policy of the Turkish Armed Forces. Even if the national investigations do not lead to convictions and sentences, the ICC would not likely open a formal investigation into an individual crime committed by (most likely) non-senior officials – in this case, the official/s who provided the false intelligence or misused their duties to destroy the peace and security of the country.

Unlike the ECtHR, the ICC has jurisdiction over individuals rather than states, and it only prosecutes senior officials who bear the greatest responsibility intentionally. In the same vein, unlike the ECtHR, the ICC cannot try states for their inadequate investigations into such incidents. Furthermore, under the "interests of justice" criterion of the Rome Statute, the ICC is less likely to initiate an investigation into a situation in which finding the real perpetrators seems extremely challenging. Thus, even if the ICC were to treat Türkiye's fight against the PKK as an armed conflict subject to international humanitarian law norms and within the jurisdiction of the Court, it would not initiate an investigation into the Uludere incident, the most tragic incident (with the highest number of civilian casualties) caused by the operations of the Turkish Armed Forces since the beginning of its fight against the PKK terrorism.

5. Possible Allegations of Excessive Use of Force

Possible allegations over disproportionate use of force also should not be considered as an obstacle to Türkiye's accession to the Rome Statute because, as the 2013 OTP Preliminary Examinations Report stressed, "in the context of a non-international armed conflict, the Rome Statute does not contain a provision for the war crime of intentionally launching a disproportionate attack."[220] The Rome Statute's war crime provision that criminalizes the use of force that is "clearly excessive in relation to the concrete and direct overall military advantage anticipated" applies only to international armed conflicts.[221] Therefore, Türkiye's counter-terrorist operations would not face such accusations even if a non-international armed conflict characterization was made.

Aside from the PKK issue, it should be noted that civilian deaths occurred during the military operations as part of either internal or international armed conflicts would not "in itself constitute a war crime" under international

220 International Criminal Court – Office of the Prosecutor, Report on Preliminary Examination Activities 2013, (November 2013), at 12 para. 47, http://www.icc-cpi.int/en_menus/icc/press%20and%20media/press%20releases/Documents/OTP%20Preliminary%20Examinations/OTP%20-%20Report%20%C20Preliminary%C20Examination%C20Activities% 202013.pdf.

221 Rome Statute, *supra* note 37, art. 8(2)(b)(iv).

humanitarian law.[222] Though (personally) it is morally unacceptable, it is permissible under the international humanitarian law and the Rome Statute (as the ICC prosecutor pointed out) "to carry out proportionate attacks against military objectives, even when it is known that some civilian deaths or injuries will occur."[223] A war crime is established when the attack is "clearly excessive" as compared to the "military advantage anticipated."[224]

6. Fighting Against Terrorism in Compliance with International Law

Article 8 (3) of the Rome Statute states that the provisions applicable to war crimes in non-international armed conflicts shall not "affect the responsibility of a government to maintain or re-establish law and order in the state, or to defend the unity and territorial integrity of the State, by all legitimate means."[225] Thus, contrary to concerns raised by the opponents of the Statute, the ICC will not weaken Türkiye's lawful efforts against terrorism. Türkiye can continue its effective fight against terrorism "by all legitimate means."[226] In fact, Türkiye's serious efforts to fight against terrorism without committing abuses and without victimizing indigenous civilians has been complementary to its efforts to reduce the ability of the PKK to recruit new members and to resolve the decades-long conflict.

Türkiye is already a party to a significant number of international human rights instruments, including the European Convention for the Protection of Human Rights and Fundamental Freedom; the International Covenant on Civil and Political Rights; the International Covenant on Economic, Social and Cultural Rights; and the Convention against Torture and Other Cruel, Inhuman or Degrading Treatment or Punishment, etc., as part of its policy to remain engaged with the international human rights mechanisms. A number of United Nations experts who visited Türkiye in 2000s praised Türkiye's deep engagement with the European regional human rights system and constructive cooperation with United Nations mechanisms since 2001.[227] Although the fight against the PKK has admittedly been the main challenge for Türkiye's compliance with international humanitarian law standards,[228] Türkiye's reform experience shows that eradication of the kind of abuses that occurred in the

222 International Criminal Court-The Office of the Prosecutor, *supra* note 210, at p. 5, www.icc-cpi.int/iccdocs/doc/doc844043.pdf.
223 International Criminal Court-The Office of the Prosecutor, *supra* note 210, at p. 5.
224 Rome Statute, *supra* note 37, art. 8(2)(b)(iv).
225 Rome Statute, *supra* note 37, art. 8(3).
226 Rome Statute, *supra* note 37, art. 8(3).
227 Heyns, *supra* note 204, at 3, para. 5.
228 Heyns, *supra* note 204, at 4, para. 9.

1990s and adherence to human rights treaties "are not obstacles to the effectiveness of counter-terrorism measures."[229]

Türkiye's efforts to comply strictly with the established international humanitarian law principles enhances the effectiveness of the measures designed to root out terrorism in Türkiye. First, counter-terrorism measures that respect the law and do not victimize the local civilians reduce both the ability of the PKK to recruit new members and the number of enraged populations who sympathize with this terrorist organization. Türkiye has learnt from the fact that the kind of abuses committed in the 1990s, such as inhuman treatment and enforced disappearance of persons, had made it easier for the PKK to recruit new members and to earn more local sympathy and support.

Second, Türkiye's strong efforts to strictly comply with the international human rights standards, such as elimination of the abuses that constitute inhuman treatment and strengthening of procedural safeguards available to terror suspects, encourages more PKK militants to give up arms. In this regard, judicial reform packages passed into law by the Turkish Parliament serve, *inter alia*, the purpose of encouraging more PKK militants to lay down their arms.

Third, Türkiye's success in bringing its counter-terrorism laws and practices in line with the international standards has been instrumental in gaining further assistance and closer cooperation from other countries in its fight against the PKK. For example, Türkiye's adoption of zero-tolerance policy on torture has been instrumental in preventing the PKK from using the torture claims to earn international sympathy and to block extradition of its senior members from European countries to Türkiye. Although some European states have used the "ill-treatment argument" as justification for their unwillingness to cooperate with the Turkish authorities,[230] adherence to international treaties and to the zero-tolerance policy on torture would allow Türkiye to allay, at least, the genuine fears. In this regard, adherence to international law is essential if Türkiye wants to rally greater support of the international community in its fight against terrorism.

As detailed in the previous chapter, Türkiye would not be eager to trigger an ICC jurisdiction over the terrorist crimes of the PKK because of the possibility that the Court could treat Türkiye's counter-terrorism operations against the PKK as an armed conflict within the meaning of international humanitarian law. Yet even in the highly unlikely event that a preliminary examination is initiated – against Türkiye's will – by the Prosecutor *proprio motu*[231] and in the worst-case scenario where the Court characterizes Türkiye's struggle against

229 Scheinin, *supra* note 191, at 2, para. 5.

230 *See, e.g.*, Devorah Lauter, *Turkey Demands Answers over Kurdish Activist's life in Paris*, www.telegraph.co.uk/news/worldnews/europe/turkey/9798830/Turkey-demands-answers-over-Kurdish-activists-life-in-Paris.html (accessed 13 January 2013).

231 As will be detailed in the Chapter 4, when there is, in the eyes of the Office of the Prosecutor, "reasonable basis to believe" crimes within the subject matter and temporal jurisdiction of the ICC have been or are being committed on the territory or by a national of a State

the PKK as an armed conflict subject to international humanitarian law norms, Türkiye's fight against terrorism would still not be undermined.

In fact, a preliminary examination into the situation regarding the PKK could even be conducive to Türkiye's effective fight against terrorism because a Preliminary Examination Report would articulate the atrocities committed by the PKK since its establishment, from indiscriminate suicide attacks in metropolitan centers to the mass killings of civilians in rural areas, to the recruitment of children. Articulation of the PKK's most serious crimes in the Preliminary Examinations Reports by the OTP would remind the European countries of their responsibilities regarding the unlawful PKK activities taking place in their territory, and it would send a clear signal that the international community is watching. In this regard, as detailed in the previous chapter, Türkiye's ability to trigger investigations could have a deterrent effect on the states that solicit, abet or fund the crimes of the PKK, as they would fear facing charges before the ICC.

It is usually expected that most of the states that prefer to ratify the Rome Statute are intent to promote peace and the rule of law at the international level or that they have confidence in their national criminal system. Türkiye's accession to the Rome Statute, as a demonstration of its confidence in its own national criminal justice system, could also help Türkiye to speedily utilize international cooperation measures, such as extradition of PKK members. Securing the extradition of terror suspects from the European countries is of great importance for Türkiye's fight against terrorism given the large number of the PKK members who reside there. European countries have so far granted less than 3% of the extradition requests by Türkiye.[232] Any step that would enhance Türkiye's reputation internationally, such as ratification of the Rome Statute, could serve as an extra incentive for European countries to arrest and extradite the indicted PKK members to Türkiye.

Bibliography

Al Jazeera, *Turkish Army Says 13 Civilians Killed as Anti-PKK Operation Ends*, www.aljazeera.com/news/2021/2/14/turkey-completes-northern-iraq-operation-against-pkk-minister (accessed 14 February 2021).

Amnesty International, *Turkey: A Policy of Denial*, https://www.amnesty.org/en/documents/eur44/001/1995/en/ (accessed 8 February 1995).

Anadolu Agency, *Top EU Court Rejects PKK's Request Seeking Removal from Terror List*, www.aa.com.tr/en/europe/top-eu-court-rejects-pkk-s-request-seeking-removal-from-terror-list/2764022 (accessed 14 December 2022).

Australian National Security, *Listed Terrorist Organisations*, https://www.nationalsecurity.gov.au/what-australia-is-doing/terrorist-organisations/listed-terrorist-organisations.

Party, the Prosecutor may *proprio motu* open a preliminary examination, absent a State Party referral.

232 Europe Refuses To Extradite Terror Suspects To Turkey, *T-Vine*, 5 February 2017, www.t-vine.com/europe-refuses-to-extradite-terror-suspects-to-turkey/ (accessed 1 January 2024).

Aydın, Kubilay, PKK Operasyonlarının Bilançosu [Consequences of the PKK Operations], *Sözcü*, www.sozcu.com.tr/2016/gundem/pkk-operasyonlarinin-bilancosu-1131227/ (accessed 11 March 2016).

Balik, Gürcan, *Turkey and the US in the Middle East: Diplomacy and Discord during the Iraq Wars* (London and New York: Bloomsbury Publishing: 2016).

Barkey, Henri J. and Graham E. Fuller, *Turkey's Kurdish Question* (Lanham, MD: Rowman & Littlefield Publishers 1998).

Casey-Maslen, Stuart and Steven Haines, *Hague Law Interpreted the Conduct of Hostilities under the Law of Armed Conflict* (Oxford: Hart Publishing 2018).

CNN, Turkish PM Erdogan Regrets Kurdish Civilian Airstrike Deaths, edition.cnn.com/2011/12/30/world/meast/turkey-air-strike/index.html (accessed 30 December 2011).

CNN Türk, En fazla şehit verilen 4'üncü saldırı [The Fourth Attack with the Highest Number of Martyrs]. www.cnnturk.com/turkiye/en-fazla-sehit-verilen-4uncu-saldiri (accessed 19 October 2011).

Convention for the Amelioration of the Condition of the Wounded and Sick in Armed Forces in the Field, 12 August 1949, art. 3, 75 U.N.T.S. 31, 32.

Convention for the Amelioration of the Condition of the Wounded, Sick and Shipwrecked Members of Armed Forces at Sea, 12 August 1949, art. 3, 75 U.N.T.S. 85, 86–88.

Convention relative to the Protection of Civilian Persons in Time of War, 12 August 1949, art. 3, 75 U.N.T.S. 287, 288–290.

Convention relative to the Treatment of Prisoners of War, 12 August 1949, art. 3, 75 U.N.T.S. 135, 136–138.

Criss, Nur Bilge, The Nature of PKK Terrorism in Turkey, (18) *Studies in Conflict and Terrorism* (1995).

Cullen, Anthony, The Definition of Non-International Armed Conflict in the Rome Statute of the International Criminal Court: An Analysis of the Threshold of Application Contained in Article 8(2)(f), 12(3) *Journal of Conflict and Security Law* (2008).

Çiçek, Cuma and Vahap Coşkun, *The Peace Process from Dolmabahçe to Present-Day: Understanding Failure and Finding New Paths* (Barış Vakfi 2016).

Directorate for EU Affairs, *Jitem Terörü Yargıda*, https://www.ab.gov.tr/p.php?e=31047 (accessed 10 December 2004).

Dörtkardeş, İhsan, Irak'a yapılan en büyük kara harekatı [The Largest Ground Operation into Iraq], *Doğan Haber Ajansı*, https://web.archive.org/web/20160207064531/http://www.dha.com.tr/iraka-yapilan-en-buyuk-kara-harekati_223858.html (accessed 20 October 2011).

Eren, Yunus, *The Impact of Land Border Security on Terrorism Financing: Turkey's Southeast Land Border and the PKK*, Master Thesis, Naval Postgraduate School (2013).

European Commission, *Turkey Progress Report*, ec.europa.eu/enlargement/pdf/key_documents/2014/20141008-turkey-progress-report_en.pdf. at 50 (accessed October 2014).

European Court of Human Rights, *Aydin Icyer v. Turkey*, Appl. No. 18888/02, Third Section Decision as to the Admissibility, http://hudoc.echr.coe.int/sites/eng/pages/search.aspx?i=001-72123 (accessed 12 January 2006).

European Court of Human Rights, *Benzer and Others v. Turkey*, Appl. No. 23502/06, Judgment Final, http://hudoc.echr.coe.int/sites/eng/pages/search.aspx?i=001-128036 (accessed 24 March 2014).

Geiß, Robin and Heike Krieger, eds., *The "Legal Pluriverse" Surrounding Multinational Military Operations* (Oxford: Oxford University Press 2019).

Guan, Jing, The ICC's Jurisdiction over War Crimes in Internal Armed Conflicts: An Insurmountable Obstacle for China's Accession? 28 *Penn State International Law Review* 703, 721 (2010).

Habertürk, *En kanlı üçüncü saldırı* [The Third Bloodiest Attack]. https://www.haberturk.com/gundem/haber/680803-en-kanli-ucuncu-saldiri (accessed 19 October 2011).

Hebel, Herman A.M. von, Johan G. Lammers and Jolien Schukking, eds., *Reflections on the International Criminal Court Essays in Honour of Adriaan Bos* (The Hague: TMC Asser Press 1999).

Heyns, Christof, *Report of the Special Rapporteur on Extrajudicial, Summary or Arbitrary Executions*, p. 16, para. 82, U.N. Doc. A/HRC/23/47/Add.2 (18 March 2013).

Human Rights Watch, *Background*, www.hrw.org/legacy/reports/1997/turkey/Turkey-02.htm.

Human Rights Watch, *The Kurds of Turkey: Killings, Disappearances and Torture* (March 1993).

International Committee of the Red Cross, How Is the Term "Armed Conflict" Defined in International Humanitarian Law? *Opinion Paper* (2008).

International Committee of the Red Cross, *Treaties, States Parties and Commentaries*, https://ihl-databases.icrc.org/applic/ihl/ihl.nsf/INTRO/615?OpenDocument.

International Criminal Court, Pre-Trial Chamber II, Situation in the Central African Republic, *The Prosecutor v. Jean-Pierre Bemba Gombo*, Decision Pursuant to Article 61(7)(a) and (b) of the Rome Statute on the Charges of the Prosecutor against Jean-Pierre Bemba Gombo, ICC-01/05–01/08 (15 June 2009).

International Criminal Court, Pre-Trial Chamber II, *Prosecutor v. Jean-Pierre Bemba Gombo*, Decision on the Charges, Case No. ICC-01/05–01/08 (15 June 2009).

International Criminal Court, Pre-Trial Chamber III, The Situation in the Republic of Côte d'Ivoire, Decision Pursuant to Article 15 of the Rome Statute on the Authorisation of an Investigation into the Situation in the Republic of Côte d'Ivoire, ICC-02–11-Corr (15 November 2011).

International Criminal Court, Trial Chamber I, Situation in the Democratic Republic of the Congo, *Prosecutor v. Thomas Lubanga Dyilo*, Judgment pursuant to Article 74 of the Statute (14 March 2012).

International Criminal Court, *Prosecutor v. Charles Ble Goude*, Case No. ICC-02/11–02/11–181, Prosecution's Response to the Defence Application Pursuant to Articles 19(4) and 17(1)(d) of the Rome Statute, http://www.icc-cpi.int/iccdocs/doc/doc1853270.pdf (accessed 20 October 2014).

International Criminal Court, *The Office of the Prosecutor*, Annex 10, www.icc-cpi.int/iccdocs/doc/doc844043.pdf (accessed 16 March 2010).

International Criminal Court, *The Office of the Prosecutor, Report on Preliminary Examination Activities 2014*, http://www.icc-cpi.int/iccdocs/otp/OTP-Pre-Exam-2014.pdf (accessed December 2014).

International Criminal Court, *The Office of the Prosecutor, Situation in Colombia, Interim Report* (November 2012).

International Criminal Court, *The Office of the Prosecutor, Situation in Mali Article 53(1) Report* (16 January 2013).

International Criminal Court, Trial Chamber VI, Situation in the Democratic Republic of the Congo, *Prosecutor v. Bosco Ntaganda*, Judgment, ICC-01/04–02/06 (8 July 2019).

International Criminal Tribunal for the Former Yugoslavia, Haradinaj Case, IT-04–84-T, Judgment (3 April 2008).

International Criminal Tribunal for the Former Yugoslavia, *The Prosecutor v. Ljube Boškoski and Johan Tarčulovski*, Judgement, Case No. IT-04–82-T (10 July 2008).

International Criminal Tribunal for the Former Yugoslavia, Trial Chamber II, *The Prosecutor v. Dusko Tadić*, Opinion and Judgment, Case No. IT-94–1-T (7 May 1997).

International Crisis Group, *Managing Turkey's PKK Conflict: The Case of Nusaybin*, www.crisisgroup.org/europe-central-asia/western-europemediterranean/turkey/243-managing-turkeys-pkk-conflict-case-nusaybin (accessed 2 May 2017).

İnternet Haber, *İşte Uludere'nin Tazminat Miktarı*, www.internethaber.com/iste-uluderenin-tazminat-miktari-397097h.htm (accessed 24 January 2012).

Jongerden, Joost, *The Settlement Issue in Turkey and the Kurds: An Analysis of Spatial Policies, Modernity and War* (Brill, Han 1, 2007).

Korkmaz, Sertaç Canalp, *Meskûn Mahal Muharebesini Anlamak* [Understanding Urban Warfare] (ORSAM 2018).

Küçükali, Adnan and Mehmet Balıkçılar, Hendek Terörü Olaylarının Nusaybin'deki Küçük ve Orta Ölçekli İşletmelere Etkisi [Effects of the Trench Terrorism on the Small and Medium-Sized Enterprises in Nusaybin], (2) *Emek ve Toplum* (2019).

Lauter, Devorah, *Turkey Demands Answers over Kurdish Activist's Life in Paris* www.telegraph.co.uk/news/worldnews/europe/turkey/9798830/Turkey-demands-answers-over-Kurdish-activists-life-in-Paris.html (accessed 13 January 2013).

Lootsteen, Yair M., The Concept of Belligerency in International Law, 166 *Military Law Review* (2000).

Lundgren, Asa, *The Unwelcome Neighbour: Turkey's Kurdish Policy* (London and New York: Bloomsbury Publishing 2007).

Marcus, Aliza, *Blood and Belief: The PKK and the Kurdish Fight for Independence* (New York and London: New York University Press 2007).

Meron, Theodor, *The Humanization of International Law* (Martinus Nijhoff Publishers 2006).

Milliyet, *JİTEM Davasında Ölen Albayın Tanıklığı İstendi*, www.milliyet.com.tr/jitem-davasinda-olen-albayin-tanikligi-istendi-gundem-1055115/ (accessed 3 February 2009).

Milliyet, *PKK operasyonlarında 103 günde neler yaşandı?* [What Happened in the 103 Days of PKK Operations], www.milliyet.com.tr/gundem/pkk-operasyonlarinda-103-gunde-neler-yasandi-2207223 (accessed 10 March 2016).

Ministry of Interior of the Republic of Türkiye, *Uluslararası Af Örgütü'nün Raporuna İlişkin Basın Açıklaması* [Press Release on the Report of the Amnesty International]. www.icisleri.gov.tr/uluslararasi-af-orgutunun-raporuna-iliskin-basin-aciklamasi (accessed 23 January 2017).

Newton, Michael A., The Complementarity Conundrum: Are We Watching Evolution or Evisceration? 8 *Santa Clara Journal of International Law*, 115, 158 (2010).

Nissel, Alan, Continuing Crimes in the Rome Statute, 25 *Michigan Journal of International Law* 653, 687 (2004).

NorthAtlantic Treaty Organization, *Press Conference by NATO Secretary General Jens Stoltenberg Following the First Session of NATO Ministers of Foreign Affairs*, Bucharest, Romania, www.nato.int/cps/en/natohq/opinions_209381.htm?selectedLocale=en (accessed 29 November 2022).

Official Records of the U.N. Diplomatic Conference of Plenipotentiaries on the Establishment of an Int'l Criminal Court, 7th plen. mtg., U.N. Doc. A/CONE 183/SR.7.

Özdağ, Ümit, *Türkiye'de Düşük Yoğunluklu Çatışma ve PKK* [Low Intensity Conflict in Türkiye and the PKK] (İstanbul: Üç Ok Yayıncılık 2005).

Özdağ, Ümit and Ersel Aydınlı, Winning a Low Intensity Conflict: Drawing Lessons from the Turkish Case, 2(3) *The Review of International Affairs* (2003).

Poecke, Thomas Van, Frank Verbruggen and Ward Yperman, Terrorist Offences and International Humanitarian Law: The Armed Conflict Exclusion Clause, 103 *International Review of the Red Cross* 916–917 (2021).

Police, *Lists Associated with Resolutions 1267/1989/2253 and 1988*, www.police.govt.nz/advice/personal-community/counterterrorism/designated-entities/lists-associated-with-resolutions-1267-1989-2253-1988.

Pope, Hugh, Most Turkish Troops Said to Be Out of Iraq: Mideast: Ankara's Army Says It Killed 555 Kurdish Militants and Lost 61 Soldiers, *Los Angeles Times*, www.latimes.com/archives/la-xpm-1995-05-05-mn-62674-story.html (accessed 5 May 1995).

Protocol Additional to the Geneva Conventions of 12 August 1949, and relating to the Protection of Victims of Non-International Armed Conflicts (Protocol II), 8 June 1977, 1125 U.N.T.S. 609.

Public Safety Canada, *Currently Listed Entities*, www.publicsafety.gc.ca/cnt/ntnl-scrt/cntr-trrrsm/lstd-ntts/crrnt-lstd-ntts-en.aspx.

公安調査庁 [Public Security and Intelligence Agency], 地域別テロ情勢等中東・北アフリカ [Terrorism Situation by Region, Middle East/North Africa], 地域別テロ情勢 [Terrorism Situation by Region], トルコ [Türkiye], クルド労働者党 [PKK], https://www.moj.go.jp/psia/ITH/area/ME_N-africa/index.html.

Republic of Türkiye Ministry of Foreign Affairs, *Internally Displaced Persons (IDPs) and the "Return to Village and Rehabilitation Program" in Turkey*, www.mfa.gov.tr/internally-displaced-persons-_idps_-and-the-_return-to-village-and-rehabilitation-program_-in-turkey.en.mfa.

Republic of Türkiye Ministry of Foreign Affairs, *PKK*, www.mfa.gov.tr/pkk.en.mfa.

Rubin, Michael A., Rebel Territorial Control and Civilian Collective Action in Civil War: Evidence from the Communist Insurgency in the Philippines, 64(2–3) *Journal of Conflict Resolution* (2020).

Sassoli, Marco, Use and Abuse of the Laws of War in the War on Terrorism, (22) *Law & Inequality: A Journal of Theory and Practice* (2004).

Sassoli, Marco, Antoine A. Bouvier and Anne Quintin, *How Does Law Protect in War? Cases, Documents and Teaching Materials on Contemporary Practice in International Humanitarian Law* (vol. 1, 3rd ed.) (Geneva: International Committee of the Red Cross 2011).

Scheinin, Martin, Preliminary Note by the Special Rapporteur on the Promotion and Protection of Human Rights and Fundamental Freedoms While Countering Terrorism, U.N. Doc. E/CN.4/2006/98/Add.2, https://documents-dds-ny.un.org/doc/UNDOC/GEN/G06/119/83/PDF/G0611983.pdf?OpenElement (accessed 24 March 2006).

Sivakumaran, Sandesh, *The Law of Non-International Armed Conflict* (Oxford: Oxford University Press 2012).

Soylu, Ragıp, Turkey: Hundreds Arrested After PKK's Execution of 13 Hostages, *Middle East Eye*, www.middleeasteye.net/news/turkey-pkk-execution-hostages-erdogan-lashes-out (accessed15 February 2022).

Sözcü, *Terör yüzünden 355 bin kişi göç etti* [355,000 People Migrated because of Terrorism], www.sozcu.com.tr/2016/gundem/muezzinoglu-teror-yuzunden-355-bin-kisi-goc-etti-1111739/ (accessed 27 February 2016).

Statute of the International Court of Justice, U.N. Charter, Annex I, at 21–30 (1945).

The New York Times, 82 Are Reported Dead as Kurds Battle Turks, www.nytimes.com/1992/09/30/world/82-are-reported-dead-as-kurds-battle-turks.html (accessed 30 September 1992).

The Washington Post, Kurdistan Workers' Party (PKK), https://www.washingtonpost.com/wp-srv/inatl/daily/feb99/pkkprofile.htm.

Tiemessen, Alana, *Defying Gravity: Seeking Political Balance in ICC Prosecutions*, justiceinconflict.org/2013/04/22/defying-gravity-seeking-political-balance-in-icc-prosecutions/ (accessed 22 April 2013).

TRT Haber, *PKK 1984'ten Beri 7 Bin Sivili Katletti*, http://www.trthaber.com/haber/turkiye/pkk-1984ten-beri-7-bin-sivili-katletti-200648.html (accessed 27 August 2015).

Turns, David, At the "Vanishing Point" of International Humanitarian Law: Methods and Means of Warfare in Non-international Armed Conflicts, (45) *German Yearbook of International Law* (2002).

Türkiye Gazetesi, *Hainlere çok yakıştı, 58 terörist etekle yakalandı!* [It Looked Well on Traitors: 58 Terrorists Have Been Captured with Skirts on!], www.turkiyegazetesi.com.tr/gundem/337479.aspx (accessed 9 January 2016).
U.S. Department of State, *Country Reports on Terrorism 2020* (December 2021).
Vienna Convention on the Law of Treaties, 23 May 1969, UN Doc. A/Conf.39/27.
Vite, Sylvain, Typology of Armed Conflicts in International Humanitarian Law: Legal Concepts and Actual Situations, 91(873) *International Review of the Red Cross* (2009).
Wilmshurst, Elizabeth, ed., *International Law and the Classification of Conflicts* (Oxford: Oxford University Press 2012).
Yeğen, Mesut (Project Coordinator), Uğraş Ulaş Tol and Mehmet Ali Çalışkan (Researchers), *Kürt Seçmenlerin Oy Verme Dinamikleri: Kuzeydoğu-Ortadoğu ve Güneydoğu Anadolu Alt Bölgelerinde Seçmenin Siyasal Tercihlerinin Sosyolojik Analizi* [Voting Dynamics of Kurdish Voters: Sociological Analysis of the Voters in the Northeastern, Middleastern and Southeastern Sub-regions] (January 2015).
Yılmaz, Sait, PKK Terör Örgütü ve KCK'da Son Durum, 4 *Journal of Turan Center for Strategic Research* 15, 12 (2012).

4 The Prosecutor's Powers and the Possibility of Politicized Prosecutions

In order for a case to be considered as meeting the legal criteria to warrant a formal ICC investigation, it must 1) fall within the Court's jurisdiction (which requires consideration of subject matter, temporal and either territorial or personal jurisdiction),[1] 2) "be admissible in terms of complementarity and gravity" criteria[2] and 3) "serve the interests of justice."[3] It is the task of the Prosecutor to conduct an initial examination of the available information to determine whether a given situation meets these legal criteria and thus whether or not "there is a reasonable basis to proceed with an investigation" in a given situation.[4] This initial process, in which the available evidence and information are analyzed by the Prosecutor with a view to determining whether they constitute reasonable grounds to initiate a formal investigation, is called "preliminary examination."[5]

Pursuant to the Article 13 of the Rome Statute, a preliminary examination process may be initiated by a) State Party referral,[6] b) United Nations Security Council referral[7] or c) the Prosecutor of the ICC acting *proprio motu* based on the information on the alleged crimes that fall within the jurisdiction of the Court.[8] That is to say, the jurisdiction of the ICC may be triggered not only as a result of a referral of a situation to the ICC by a State Party or the Security Council but also by the Prosecutor *proprio motu*. The focus of this chapter is the Prosecutor's authority to open a preliminary examination into a situation and to seek the initiation of an investigation without a referral from a State

1 See "Preconditions to the exercise of jurisdiction" under article 12 of the Rome Statute. United Nations Treaty Collection, Rome Statute of the International Criminal Court, U.N. Doc. A/CONF.183/9, 17 July 1998, art. 11(2).

2 International Criminal Court – Office of the Prosecutor, *Policy Paper on Case Selection and Prioritisation* (15 September 2016) 9, para. 24 [hereinafter the OTP Policy Paper].

3 Rome Statute, *supra* note 1, art. 53 (1) (c).

4 Rome Statute, *supra* note 1, art. 15 (4).

5 Rome Statute, *supra* note 1, art. 15 (6).

6 Rome Statute, *supra* note 1, art. 13 (a).

7 Rome Statute, *supra* note 1, art. 13 (b).

8 Rome Statute, *supra* note 1, art. 13 (c).

DOI: 10.4324/9781003641643-4

Party or the Security Council. In other words, this chapter does not focus on the process of "case selection"[9] for investigation and prosecution but on the authority to trigger this process.

During the Rome negotiations, the ICC Prosecutor's right to investigate complaints without any referral from a State Party or from the Security Council was among the matters of dispute. While more than 85 States made statements in favor of the Prosecutor having the power to activate the trigger mechanism,[10] around 30 States expressly opposed such power.[11] Moreover, three of the P5 members of the Security Council (namely, the United States, China and Russia) were, and still are, among the opposing States. There were also some hesitant States, such as Jamaica[12] or Slovakia,[13] which doubted whether the ICC Prosecutor's power to act *proprio motu* would yield the anticipated benefits, yet they were "prepared to join in any consensus on the issue."[14]

Among those that opposed the Prosecutor's right to activate the trigger mechanism of the Rome Statute, some States, such as Israel, believed that the ICC Prosecutor, if entitled to the right to act *proprio motu*, would be overburdened by frivolous or political complaints, which could "adversely affect the Prosecutor's independence and standing."[15] Similarly, Malaysia feared "the danger of . . . possible accusations of bias." Representatives of some states, such as Japan, drew attention to the need for a "proper balance" between the ICC's jurisdictional powers and the States Parties' legitimate interests regarding the trigger mechanism of the Court's activities.[16]

9 The OTP Policy Paper, *supra* note 2, at 1.

10 Portugal, Italy, Togo, Sierra Leona, the Philippines, Namibia, Guinea, Sierra Leone, Hungary, the Netherlands, Samoa, Niger, Malta, Belarus, Cyprus, Lesotho, Thailand, Jordan, Mexico, Costa Rica, Venezuela, Ireland, Senegal, Czech Republic, Romania, Australia, Uganda, New Zealand, Belgium, Trinidad and Tobago, Netherlands, Norway, South Africa, Brazil, Denmark, Madagascar, Andorra, Germany, Sweden, Slovenia, Greece, Canada, Chile, Switzerland, Burkina Faso, Namibia, Poland, Argentina, Liechtenstein, Gabon, Mali, Guinea-Bissau, Austria, Ukraine, Cote d'Ivoire, Benin, Finland, Djibouti, Spain, Botswana, Togo, Ecuador, Kuwait, Congo, Armenia, Ethiopia, San Marino, Croatia, Hungary, Croatia, Lithuania, the Republic of Korea, Mozambique, Estonia, Swaziland, Peru, Solomon Islands, Angola, Bosnia and Herzegovina, Egypt, Tanzania, Lithuania, Kyrgyzstan, the Former Yugoslav Republic of Macedonia (with its new name, North Macedonia) and Morocco. See generally, Official Records of the United Nations Diplomatic Conference of Plenipotentiaries on the Establishment of an International Criminal Court, Official Records Volume II, A/CONF.183/13, 15 June–17 July 1998 [hereinafter Official Records of the Rome Conference].

11 The United States, Türkiye, Cuba, China, Japan, Vietnam, Russia, Algeria, Israel, Bangladesh, India, Malaysia, Indonesia, Uruguay, Iraq, Yemen, Kenya, Libya, Nigeria, Oman, Pakistan, Qatar, Saudi Arabia, the United Arab Emirates, Tunisia, Sudan, Iran and Sri Lanka. See generally Official Records of the Rome Conference, *supra* note 10.

12 Official Records of the Rome Conference, *supra* note 10, at 306, para. 15.

13 Official Records of the Rome Conference, *supra* note 10, at 308, para. 47.

14 Official Records of the Rome Conference, *supra* note 10, at 306, para. 15.

15 Official Records of the Rome Conference, *supra* note 10, at 201, para. 111.

16 Official Records of the Rome Conference, *supra* note 10, at 67, para. 46.

The Turkish delegation to the Rome Conference, too, raised concerns regarding the ICC Prosecutor's *proprio motu* power to initiate investigation. The delegation voiced the opinion that "[t]he right to lodge a complaint should be reserved for States and the Security Council" because, it believed, granting the Prosecutor *proprio motu* power would risk "submerging him with information concerning charges of a political, rather than a juridical nature."[17] The delegation considered the prosecutorial authority granted to the ICC Prosecutor to be "unacceptable."[18]

This chapter will first explain that the ICC Prosecutor's powers, including the authority to investigate crimes without a referral from a State Party or the Security Council, are not placed in the hands of the Prosecutor without judicial checks. Article 15 of the Rome Statute provides some procedural safeguards, such as the requirement to seek an authorization from the Pre-Trial Chamber. The judicial scrutiny of the chambers of the Court ensures that the decisions of the ICC Prosecutor are subject to the high threshold criteria set out in the Rome Statute. Safeguards set out in the Rome Statute make it nearly impossible for the unfounded or politically motivated accusations to reach the trial stage.

The chapter will then draw attention to the political restraints placed on the Office of the Prosecutor (OTP) by the States whose cooperation is needed in order to access the defendants and the evidence. The effective functioning of the ICC relies heavily on the cooperation with States, and any unwillingness on the part of the States to cooperate limits the ability of the Prosecutor to bring charges against individuals. Consequently, the chapter will submit that the legal and political restraints placed on the Prosecutor should ally Türkiye's fears about frivolous or political complaints. In this regard, the current and potential challenges the next ICC Prosecutor Karim Khan will face will also be touched upon briefly.

This chapter will claim that the ICC Prosecutor's ability to initiate investigations on his/her own motion is, in fact, a requisite to ensure that the Court is truly effective and free from political interference. The prosecution of the most serious crimes committed in six situations, into which a formal ICC investigation has been initiated by the ICC Prosecutor without any referral from a State Party or the Security Council, have been possible thanks to the Prosecutor's authority to act *proprio motu*. Furthermore, the Prosecutor's *proprio motu* power has been instrumental in encouraging domestic prosecutions. Examination of national proceedings by the Prosecutor who has the power to investigate complaints *proprio motu* sometimes serves as an incentive for national authorities to investigate crimes more carefully and competently.

17 Official Records of the Rome Conference, *supra* note 10, at 124, para. 44.
18 Official Records of the Rome Conference, *supra* note 10, at 211, para. 3.

Finally, this chapter will argue that the ICC Prosecutor's authority to make a determination as to whether or not there is a reasonable basis to proceed with an investigation, in fact, serves as an early filtering mechanism against the politically motivated referrals and against the referrals that fail to meet the high threshold of the Rome Statute. The role given to the Prosecutor under the Rome Statute thus prevents the politically motivated State Party or Security Council referrals from turning into formal investigations.

1. States' Concerns on the Prosecutor's Powers *versus* Rome Statute's Sufficient Safeguards

According to Article 13 of the Rome Statute, an ICC investigation could be triggered either by a State Party or Security Council referral or by the Prosecutor *proprio motu*:

> The Court may exercise its jurisdiction with respect to a crime referred to in article 5 in accordance with the provisions of this Statute if:
>
> (a) A situation in which one or more of such crimes appears to have been committed is referred to the Prosecutor by a State Party in accordance with article 14;
> (b) A situation in which one or more of such crimes appears to have been committed is referred to the Prosecutor by the Security Council acting under Chapter VII of the Charter of the United Nations; or
> (c) The Prosecutor has initiated an investigation in respect of such a crime in accordance with article 15.[19]

Accordingly, the ICC Prosecutor can commence an investigation *proprio motu* only "in accordance with article 15" of the Rome Statute,[20] which provides some procedural safeguards, such as the requirement to seek authorization from the Pre-Trial Chamber.[21] Unlike the trigger mechanisms of a State Party or Security Council referral, Article 15 of the Statute requires the Prosecutor to request authorization from the Pre-Trial Chamber in order to initiate a formal investigation *proprio motu*.[22] The Prosecutor needs to provide his/her analysis of the seriousness of the information collected from reliable sources and convince the Pre-Trial Chamber that "a reasonable basis to proceed with an

19 Rome Statute, *supra* note 1, art. 13.
20 Rome Statute, *supra* note 1, art. 13 (c).
21 Rome Statute, *supra* note 1, art. 15 (c).
22 Rome Statute, *supra* note 1, art. 15 (3). During the Rome negotiations, the proposal requiring the Prosecutor to seek the authorization of the Pre-Trial Chamber if s/he concludes that "there is a reasonable basis to proceed with an investigation" was introduced by Argentina and Germany. See Official Records of the Rome Conference *supra* note 10, at p. 183, para. 38.

investigation" does exist.[23] The Pre-Trial Chamber will examine the request and the supporting material and reject the request for authorization if the situation in question does not appear "to fall within the jurisdiction of the Court."[24]

The Pre-Trial Chamber II's rejection of the Prosecutor's request for the authorization of an investigation into the situation in Afghanistan on 12 April 2019 is an example showing that the Prosecutor's *proprio motu* powers are subject to the judicial scrutiny of the chambers of the Court. The rejection decision, which will be discussed further later, proves that in contrast to the claims brought by some States – such as Sudan – during the Rome Conference,[25] the role assigned to the ICC Prosecutor by the Rome Statute is not beyond the control of the chambers of the Court. As clearly stated in Article 15(3) of the Rome Statute, the Pre-Trial Chamber must consent to an investigation when the jurisdiction of the Court is exercised by the Prosecutor *proprio motu*.

The judicial scrutiny of the chambers of the Court ensures that the decisions of the ICC Prosecutor are subject to the high threshold criteria set out in the Rome Statute. The Prosecutor will not seek authorization to proceed with an investigation and the Pre-Trial Chamber will not grant such authorization if the situation in question does not appear to 1) fall within the Court's jurisdiction (which requires consideration of the subject matter,[26] temporal[27] and either territorial or personal jurisdiction),[28] 2) be admissible in terms of complementarity[29] and gravity[30] criteria and 3) "serve the interests of justice."[31] In fact, the safeguards set out in the Rome Statute, such as the complementarity principle and high gravity threshold, constitute the main restraints on the discretion of the Prosecutor. The Pre-Trial Chamber will authorize the commencement of an investigation only if the crimes in question do appear to be "of sufficient gravity to justify further action by the Court"[32] and only if national courts appear to be "unwilling or unable genuinely" to prosecute the crimes in question.[33] Furthermore, the Pre-Trial Chamber's ruling to authorize an investigation can be appealed to the Appeals Chamber, and admissibility of the case can be challenged by relevant states on the grounds that they are investigating or have investigated the same crimes in question.[34]

23 Rome Statute, *supra* note 1, art. 15 (4).
24 Rome Statute, *supra* note 1, art. 15 (4).
25 Official Records of the Rome Conference, *supra* note 10, at p. 126, para. 77.
26 Rome Statute, *supra* note 1, art. 5.
27 Rome Statute, *supra* note 1, art. 11.
28 Rome Statute, *supra* note 1, art. 12 (2).
29 Rome Statute, *supra* note 1, art. 17 (1) (a).
30 Rome Statute, *supra* note 1, art. 17 (1) (d).
31 Rome Statute, *supra* note 1, art. 53 (1) (c).
32 Rome Statute, *supra* note 1, art. 17 (1) (d).
33 Rome Statute, *supra* note 1, art. 17 (1) (a).
34 Rome Statute, *supra* note 1, art. 18 (4).

As of 30 September 2023, the OTP has received around 18,000 communications on crimes allegedly within the jurisdiction of the Court, calling the Prosecutor to seek an investigation on his/her own initiative.[35] However, the number of the situations, into which a formal ICC investigation has been initiated by the Prosecutor *proprio motu*, remained only six: the situations in Kenya (2010), Côte d'Ivoire (2013), Georgia (2016), Burundi (2017), Myanmar/Bangladesh (2019) and Afghanistan (2020).[36] The overwhelming majority of the communications received by the Office of the Prosecutor are determined to fall manifestly outside the jurisdiction of the ICC, which proves the ICC Prosecutor's cautiousness and prudence in selecting cases. The safeguards/high thresholds set out in the Rome Statute ensure that unfounded or politically motivated accusations will not reach the trial stage.

Depriving the Prosecutor of the authority to act *proprio motu* could, in fact, affect his/her independence adversely. An ICC Prosecutor without the power to initiate investigations *proprio motu* would need to convince States Parties or the members of the Security Council to refer cases to the Court, as a result of which some concessions or guarantees could be sought from the Prosecutor. A member of the Security Council, for example, could attempt to influence or direct the Prosecutor on determining the specific crimes to be investigated or specific individuals to be indicted in exchange for its support for the referral of a situation to the Court. Of course, the filtering mechanism of the ICC would not allow such attempts to yield results, but the confinement of the role of the ICC Prosecutor to receiving complaints from the States Parties or from the Security Council would make the Prosecutor "dependent" on the consent of the States and could consequently undermine the effectiveness and credibility of the Court.

Another Rome Statute–based safeguard on the powers of the ICC Prosecutor is the right of the Security Council to defer the commencement of an investigation for a period of 12 months under Article 16 of the Statute.[37] Moreover, the ICC Prosecutor's subjection to the managerial oversight by the Assembly of States Parties under Article 112(2)(b) of the Rome Statute makes

35 As the reports published in recent years have not declared the up-to-date total number of communications, the current total number has been calculated by addition of the communications received in the last five years to the total number declared in the 2018 report. International Criminal Court – Office of the Prosecutor, "Report on Preliminary Examination Activities 2018" (5 December 2018) 9, para. 18; International Criminal Court – Office of the Prosecutor, "Report on Preliminary Examination Activities 2019" (5 December 2019) 8, para. 23; International Criminal Court – Office of the Prosecutor, "Report on Preliminary Examination Activities 2020" (14 December 2020) 10, para. 30; International Criminal Court – Office of the Prosecutor, "Annual Report of the Office of the Prosecutor" (1 December 2022) 76; International Criminal Court – Office of the Prosecutor, "Office of the Prosecutor Annual Report 2023" (2023) 19.

36 See generally International Criminal Court, *Situations under Investigation*, https://www.icc-cpi.int/pages/situation.aspx (accessed 1 January 2024).

37 Rome Statute, *supra* note 1, art. 16.

the overall "institutional" restraints on the Prosecutor of the ICC exceed those on the prosecutors of *ad hoc* tribunals, such as the International Criminal Tribunal for the Former Yugoslavia.[38]

The ICC prosecutors are elected by secret ballots of States Parties with equally weighted votes. States' fear of politicized prosecution is less meaningful when considering the judicial checks in the Rome Statute and the democratic structure of the Assembly of States Parties. As noted by the Prosecutors of the ICC on many occasions, the ICC will use its limited resources to address only "the most serious crimes of international concern" when the national authorities are unable or unwilling to conduct effective prosecutions, and the OTP will not act based on mere "speculation or suspicion."[39]

1.1. The Situation in Afghanistan: The Most Recent Example of the Strict Scrutiny by the Chambers of the Court

The Pre-Trial Chamber's rejection, on 12 April 2019, of the Prosecutor's request for the authorization of an investigation into the situation in Afghanistan[40] (hereinafter the "Request" or the "Request for Authorization") is a clear example showing that the Prosecutor's *proprio motu* powers are not beyond the control of the Chambers of the Court. The request was rejected by the Pre-Trial Chamber II on the ground that such investigation "at this stage would not serve the interests of justice."[41] Though this decision was amended by the Appeals Chamber, which "decided unanimously to authorise the Prosecutor to commence an investigation into" the Afghanistan situation on 5 March 2020,[42] it is a reminder that chambers of the Court have the final say on whether there is a reasonable basis to proceed with an investigation.

The Request for Authorization was submitted on 20 November 2017, nearly 11 years after the opening of the preliminary examination in 2006.[43] The Request addressed the crimes allegedly committed in the situation in Afghanistan since 1 May 2003 (date of the entry into force of the Rome

38 Mark D. Kielsgard, *Reluctant Engagement: U.S. Policy and the International Criminal Court* (Koninklijke Brill NV 2010) 125.

39 International Criminal Court – Office of the Prosecutor, Report on Preliminary Examination Activities 2014, 2 December 2014, at 56, para. 236.

40 International Criminal Court – Pre-Trial Chamber II, Decision Pursuant to Article 15 of the Rome Statute on the Authorisation of an Investigation into the Situation in the Islamic Republic of Afghanistan (12 April 2019) 3, para. 1, https://www.icc-cpi.int/CourtRecords/CR2019_02068.PDF (accessed 1 January 2024) [hereinafter the Pre-Trial Chamber II's Decision on the Authorisation of an Investigation].

41 International Criminal Court – Pre-Trial Chamber II, *supra* note 40, 32, para. 97.

42 International Criminal Court, *Afghanistan: ICC Appeals Chamber Authorises the Opening of an Investigation*, (5 March 2020), www.icc-cpi.int/Pages/item.aspx?name=pr1516 (accessed 1 January 2024).

43 The Pre-Trial Chamber II's Decision on the Authorisation of an Investigation, *supra* note 40, at p. 3, para. 5.

Statute for Afghanistan) in four categories separately: 1) alleged crimes by the Taliban and other anti-government armed groups,[44] 2) alleged crimes by the Afghan National Security Forces,[45] 3) alleged crimes by the U.S. Forces and the CIA[46] and 4) "other acts" by members of the other international forces deployed in Afghanistan.[47] The Request, while submitting that there was a reasonable basis to believe that crimes falling within the jurisdiction of the Court had been committed by the Taliban and other armed groups,[48] by the Afghan Forces[49] and by the U.S. armed forces and the CIA,[50] noted that the information available was not sufficient to make a determination "at this stage" as to whether or not there were reasonable grounds to believe that members of other international armed forces had committed a crime within the jurisdiction of the Court.[51]

In its rejection decision, the Pre-Trial Chamber II concluded that though "there is a reasonable basis to believe that the contextual elements of both crimes against humanity and war crimes are satisfied in respect of the alleged events,"[52] an investigation into the situation in Afghanistan would not, for the moment, be in the interests of justice[53] due to relevant circumstances that "make such investigation not feasible and inevitably doomed to failure."[54] These relevant circumstances were summarized as follows: 1) the significant time elapsed between the commission of alleged crimes and the submission of the Request in 2017, 2) the lack of cooperation by the most relevant national authorities in respect of surrender of suspects and collection of evidence and 3) low possibility that relevant evidence and suspects would still be available

44 The Pre-Trial Chamber II's Decision on the Authorisation of an Investigation, *supra* note 40, at 6.
45 The Pre-Trial Chamber II's Decision on the Authorisation of an Investigation, *supra* note 40, at 7.
46 The Pre-Trial Chamber II's Decision on the Authorisation of an Investigation, *supra* note 40, at 8.
47 The Pre-Trial Chamber II's Decision on the Authorisation of an Investigation, *supra* note 40, at 9.
48 The Pre-Trial Chamber II's Decision on the Authorisation of an Investigation, *supra* note 40, at 7, para. 20.
49 The Pre-Trial Chamber II's Decision on the Authorisation of an Investigation, *supra* note 40, at 8, para. 22.
50 The Pre-Trial Chamber II's Decision on the Authorisation of an Investigation, *supra* note 40, at 9, para. 24.
51 The Pre-Trial Chamber II's Decision on the Authorisation of an Investigation, *supra* note 40, at 9, para. 25.
52 The Pre-Trial Chamber II's Decision on the Authorisation of an Investigation, *supra* note 40, at 22, para. 66.
53 The Pre-Trial Chamber II's Decision on the Authorisation of an Investigation, *supra* note 40, at 32.
54 The Pre-Trial Chamber II's Decision on the Authorisation of an Investigation, *supra* note 40, at 29, para. 90.

after an 11-year-long preliminary examination.[55] The Chamber's rejection decision drew attention to the fact that the limited resources of the Court require it to focus only on situations where prospects for successful prosecutions appear promising.[56]

The Appeals Chamber, however, found that when deciding on the Prosecutor's request for authorization to open an investigation, the Pre-Trial Chamber erred in considering the interests of justice factor: the Pre-Trial Chamber should have determined only whether or not there was a reasonable factual basis to believe that crimes within the jurisdiction of the Court had been committed and whether or not potential case(s) that would arise appeared to fall within the Court's jurisdiction.[57] The Appeals Chamber also warned that the Rome Statute did not require the Prosecutor to "affirmatively determine that an investigation would be in the interests of justice, as suggested by the Pre-Trial Chamber" because "article 53(1) of the Statute is formulated in the negative":[58] the Prosecutor would seek to initiate an investigation unless she determined that there were "substantial reasons to believe that an investigation would not serve the interests of justice."[59] The Appeals Chamber's unanimous judgment to amend the Pre-Trial Chamber's decision not to authorize an investigation into the situation in Afghanistan did not change the fact that the Prosecutor's decisions and acts were subject to the strict judicial scrutiny of the chambers of the Court.

2. Political Restraints on the ICC Prosecutor

There are also political restraints placed on the ICC Prosecutor by the States whose cooperation is crucial in terms of gathering evidence, arresting suspects and accessing the witnesses and defendants. As the effective functioning of the Court relies heavily on cooperation with the members of the international community, any reluctance on the part of the States to cooperate with the Office of the Prosecutor limits the ability of the Prosecutor to bring charges against the perpetrators. For example, in the case against Uhuru Muigai Kenyatta, then ICC Prosecutor Fatou Bensouda found herself obligated to withdraw the charges against Kenyatta due to insufficient evidence, which was mainly caused by the "failure of the Government of Kenya to cooperate fully

55 The Pre-Trial Chamber II's Decision on the Authorisation of an Investigation, *supra* note 40, at 29, para. 91.

56 The Pre-Trial Chamber II's Decision on the Authorisation of an Investigation, *supra* note 40, at 30, para. 95.

57 International Criminal Court – The Appeals Chamber, Judgment on the Appeal against the Decision on the Authorisation of an Investigation into the Situation in the Islamic Republic of Afghanistan (5 March 2020) 15, para. 34, www.icc-cpi.int/CourtRecords/CR2020_00828.PDF (accessed 1 January 2024).

58 International Criminal Court – The Appeals Chamber, *supra* note 57, 22, para. 49.

59 Rome Statute, *supra* note 1, art. 53(1).

and effectively."[60] The Prosecutor, Bensouda, stressed that her actions could only be "guided by the law and the evidence" and that it was her professional responsibility "to withdraw the charges against the accused" if there is no "reasonable prospect of conviction at trial based on the evidence" available.[61]

Karim Khan (United Kingdom), who was elected by the Assembly of State Parties as the new prosecutor of the ICC, replaced his predecessor, Fatou Bensouda (Gambia), on 16 June 2021 for the new prosecutorial term of nine years.[62] Though the new Prosecutor is left with well-established policies and manuals[63] for the investigation of the most serious crimes of international concern and a well-established office that has accrued the experience of two prosecutorial terms in building cases seeking to establish individual criminal responsibility for the atrocity crimes, he is nevertheless facing significant challenges, such as the possibility of a mass withdrawal by African member states or criticisms over the low number of prosecutions and convictions.[64] There are concerns that if the new Prosecutor fails to chart a path that will enable the Court to meet those challenges, "the institution may never recover."[65] The OTP is expected to improve the quality of its investigations and human resources and enhance its relationship with the judges of the Court to contribute to the efforts[66] aimed at improving the efficiency of the Court's judicial work and expediting proceedings.

Some see the election of Karim Khan, a British barrister, to the position of Prosecutor of the ICC "as a diplomatic win for the UK after Brexit."[67] Though this view is problematic, especially given that the ICC Prosecutor can only represent the interests of justice and of his mandate of independently and impartiality selecting situations for investigation, I believe that the OTP may,

60 International Criminal Court, Press Release – Statement of the Prosecutor of the International Criminal Court, Fatou Bensouda, on the withdrawal of charges against Mr. Uhuru Muigai Kenyatta (12 December 2014), www.icc-cpi.int/en_menus/icc/press%20and%20media/press%20releases/Pages/otp-statement-05-12-2014-2.aspx (accessed 1 January 2024).

61 International Criminal Court, *supra* note 60.

62 International Criminal Court, *"Election of Prosecutor (2020)"* (12 February 2020), https://asp.icc-cpi.int/en_menus/asp/elections/prosecutor/Pages/Prosecutor2020.aspx (accessed 1 January 2024).

63 The International Federation for Human Rights (FIDH), *The Office of the Prosecutor of the ICC – 9 Years On Analysis of the Prosecutorial Strategy and Policies of the Office of the Prosecutor (2003–2011) Recommendations to the Next ICC Prosecutor* (December 2011) 29, www.fidh.org/IMG/pdf/cpiproc579ang.pdf (accessed 1 January 2024).

64 Milena Sterio, The International Criminal Court: Current Challenges and Prospect of Future Success, 52(1) *Case Western Reserve Journal of International Law* 468 (2020).

65 Alex Whiting, A Program for the Next ICC Prosecutor, 52(1) *Case Western Reserve Journal of International Law* 480 (2020).

66 International Criminal Court, *Press Release – ICC Judges Agree on Measures to Improve Efficiency of Criminal Process* (22 June 2015), www.icc-cpi.int/Pages/item.aspx?name=pr1121&ln=en (accessed 1 January 2024).

67 *BBC News*, Karim Khan: UK Lawyer Elected Chief Prosecutor at ICC, www.bbc.com/news/uk-56051110 (accessed 1 January 2024).

nevertheless, enjoy some advantages of being headed by a Prosecutor whose country of nationality is a major global player, especially if that is going to promote greater and continuous support of the UK. The United Kingdom's continuous, stronger support for the efforts of the OTP to bring the perpetrators of the most serious crimes to justice could absorb the negative effects of the hostile campaigns against the ICC, such as the United States' imposition of sanctions in 2020 on court officials engaged in efforts to investigate the situation in Afghanistan.[68] Revocation of the ICC Prosecutor's U.S. travel visa by the White House is an example of how hostile states can get in the face of formal investigation efforts. Greater British political support for the activities of the OTP could also decrease the number of such hostile acts.

In order to deal with current and future challenges and conduct his office's investigations effectively, the new Prosecutor needs, as did his predecessor, the cooperation and support not only of states but also – to a lesser extent – of non-/inter-/supra-governmental organizations.[69] Given the financial constraints and the limited resources of the OTP to gather evidence and intelligence, the support of states and non-governmental organizations is crucial for the effective functioning of the Court, and the lack of support of some opposing global powers (including three of the P5) constitutes a serious restraint on the powers of the ICC Prosecutor.

3. The Role of the Prosecutorial Powers in the Effective Functioning of the ICC

The prosecution of the most serious crimes committed in six situations, into which a formal ICC investigation was initiated by the ICC Prosecutor *proprio motu*, was possible thanks to the Prosecutor's authority to act *proprio motu*. The *proprio motu* power of the ICC Prosecutor, therefore, is of great importance for the effectiveness and credibility of the Court. It would be unrealistic to expect that States Parties or the members of the Security Council would always refer cases to the ICC without taking into account their political agendas. As demonstrated by the Security Council's failure to adopt a draft resolution to refer the situation in Syria to the ICC in May 2014,[70] States often put their own interests above international justice and common interests.

68 Human Rights Watch, *US Sanctions on the International Criminal Court* (14 December 2020), www.hrw.org/news/2020/12/14/us-sanctions-international-criminal-court (accessed 1 January 2024).

69 Whiting, *supra* note 65, at 484; see Zoe Pearson, Non-Governmental Organizations and the International Criminal Court: Changing Landscapes of International Law, 39(2) *Cornell International Law Journal* 243–245 (2006).

70 UN Security Council, Referral of Syria to International Criminal Court Fails as Negative Votes Prevent Security Council from Adopting Draft Resolution, UN doc. SC/11407 (22 May 2014), http://www.un.org/News/Press/docs/2014/sc11407.doc.htm (accessed 1 January 2024).

Neither Syria nor any other State involved in the Syrian conflict is a party to the Rome Statute. Thus, under current conditions, the only way the Prosecutor is authorized to investigate war crimes and crimes against humanity allegedly committed within Syrian borders is by a Security Council referral.[71] Yet heinous crimes committed against civilians since the beginning of the Syrian conflict in March 2011 have not been able to be brought before the ICC due to the veto power of the permanent members, which mostly act to secure their own political partisan interests.

The 2014 draft resolution referring the situation in Syria to the ICC was vetoed by China as well as Russia, a permanent member of the Security Council and a strong supporter of the Syrian regime. Though the UN Secretary-General Antonio Guterres urged in 2015 and 2018[72] that the situation in Syria be referred to the ICC, a new attempt for a Security Council referral is highly likely to face a similar fate in the foreseeable future. Russia alone has, as of 2019, vetoed 13 resolutions relating to the conflict in Syria.[73] The Security Council cannot even condemn the Syrian regime for its violations of war due to the veto power of Russia, whose attitudes in the Council are often guided by *raison d'état*. Similarly, in situations where a State Party (on whose territory heinous crimes have been committed) is not likely to trigger the jurisdiction of the ICC, a Prosecutor without the authority to act *proprio motu* would be subordinated to the veto power of each of the P5. Moreover,

71 Relying on the Pre-Trial Chamber's recent conclusion that ICC has jurisdiction over the alleged deportation of the Rohingya refugees from Myanmar (a non-State Party) to Bangladesh (a State Party), a communication was presented to the Court in March 2019 making a similar argument for the Syrian refugees who have fled to neighbouring Jordan – a State Party, as is Bangladesh. See *The Guardian*, Syrian Refugees Launch Legal Bid to Try Assad for Crimes against Humanity, https://www.theguardian.com/law/2019/mar/07/syrian-refugees-launch-legal-bid-to-try-assad-for-crimes-against-humanity (accessed 1 January 2024).

Pursuant to Article 7(2)(d) of the Rome Statute, in order for an act to constitute the crime of deportation, deportees must be deported "by expulsion or other coercive acts." See Rome Statute, *supra* note 1, art. 7(2)(d). This element of deportation, Pre-Trial Chamber III explains, is met when deportees are removed physically or when they are obliged "to leave the area where they were lawfully present" as a result of coercive acts. See International Criminal Court – Pre-Trial Chamber III, "Decision Pursuant to Article 15 of the Rome Statute on the Authorisation of an Investigation into the Situation in the People's Republic of Bangladesh/Republic of the Union of Myanmar" (14 November 2019) 23, para. 52, available at https://www.icc-cpi.int/CourtRecords/CR2019_06955.PDF (accessed 1 January 2024).

Though the accusations in the communication seem to fall within the jurisdiction of the Court, it remains to be answered whether they could be considered as constituting the elements of the specific crime of deportation against the Syrian refugees who fled to Jordan and whether they could be supported with clear evidence.

72 DW, *Syria Ceasefire Starts Near Damascus as UN Calls for ICC Referral over Aid*, https://www.dw.com/en/syria-ceasefire-starts-near-damascus-as-un-calls-for-icc-referral-over-aid/a-42328500 (accessed 1 January 2024).

73 *Reuters*, Russia Casts 13th Veto of U.N. Security Council action during Syrian War, https://www.reuters.com/article/us-syria-security-un/russia-casts-13th-veto-of-un-security-council-action-during-syrian-war-idUSKBN1W42CJ (accessed 1 January 2024).

even the motives of those States that campaign for a Security Council referral are not always clear, as they could be solely intending to use the Court, via the Security Council, as a forum for putting pressure on States that would oppose such referral.

Like the Security Council's permanent members, which hold the veto power, the State Parties (that are not members of the Security Council) also typically prioritize acting in accordance with their national interests or sometimes solely at the impulse of idiosyncratic preferences of the decision-makers. It would be unrealistic to expect that the head of a State Party who has ordered the commission of the most serious crimes covered in the Rome Statute would be keen on triggering an investigation that could result in him or her standing trial in The Hague. For example, the ousted Syrian President Bashar al-Assad, who (after more than 13 years of a civil war that has left hundreds of thousands of people dead and millions of civilians displaced)[74] still considered himself irreplaceable, would not have been willing to trigger an ICC investigation, even if Syria had been a State Party. Thus, an ICC investigation into the serious crimes committed in Syria would not be likely without the Prosecutor's power to act *proprio motu*, even if Syria had already joined the Court. Given that States' policies towards the ICC are usually driven by national interests or by personal preferences of the decision-makers, the ICC Prosecutor's authority to initiate investigations *proprio motu* is crucial for the credibility and effectiveness of the ICC in addressing the crimes that fall within its jurisdiction.

4. The Prosecutor's Powers as an Incentive for Domestic Prosecutions

Together with the ICC's complementarity principle, which requires the Court to defer to "genuine" national proceedings, the Prosecutor's authority to investigate crimes without a referral from a State Party or the Security Council has been instrumental in encouraging national prosecutions. The Preamble and Article 1 of the Rome Statute emphasize that the ICC "shall be complementary to national criminal jurisdictions."[75] Accordingly, as detailed in Article 17 of the Rome Statute, the ICC can only act when national jurisdictions are either "unwilling or unable" to genuinely investigate or prosecute the crimes in question.[76] Before seeking the authorization of the Pre-Trial Chamber

74 According to the UN High Commissioner for Refugees, the number of Syrians displaced internally and across borders by the Syrian civil war has mounted to nearly 12 million. For the up-to-date figures on the number of Syrians who have fled the country, see Operational Portal Refugee Situations, *Total Persons of Concern*, https://data2.unhcr.org/en/situations/syria (accessed 1 January 2024). For the current figures on the number of internally displaced Syrians, see UN Refugee Agency, *Internally Displaced People*, www.unhcr.org/sy/internally-displaced-people (accessed 1 January 2024).

75 Rome Statute, *supra* note 1, art. 1.

76 Rome Statute, *supra* note 1, art. 17(1) (a).

to commence a formal ICC investigation, the OTP conducts a preliminary examination of situations to determine whether the situations in question "meet the legal criteria, [including the 'complementarity' criteria], to proceed with an investigation."[77] The Prosecutor will not seek to commence an investigation if the national authorities are deemed able and willing to investigate and prosecute. Examination of national proceedings by the Prosecutor who has the power to investigate complaints *proprio motu* sometimes serves as an incentive for national authorities to investigate crimes more carefully and competently.

During preliminary examinations, the OTP gathers and assesses "information relating to the status and progress of national proceedings carried out" by the national authorities.[78] For this purpose, the Prosecutor meets with senior officials from the judiciary and the executive, representatives of non-governmental organizations and civil society.[79] The Prosecutor also communicates with national governments, through reports or formal visitations to support national efforts to fight against impunity. Such activities of the Prosecutor contribute to the efforts to spur States to improve their domestic criminal system and to deter them from committing, abetting or funding serious crimes in the future. In the situation regarding Colombia, for example, the Prosecutor's activities prompted the Colombian authorities to revise the "Justice and Peace Law," which had been adopted by the Congress of Colombia in 2005 to facilitate the demobilization of paramilitary groups in Colombia, so as to ensure greater accountability for the perpetrators of the acts amounting to ICC crimes.[80] A letter sent by the Office of the Prosecutor with a reminder that the Office was monitoring the process of adopting a Justice and Peace Law[81] was even discussed in the Congress.[82] Blocking an ICC prosecution was one of greatest motivating factors for the Colombian government to revise the Justice and Peace Law to provide greater accountability for the perpetrator of the ICC crimes. The preliminary examination of the situation in Colombia was closed in October 2021 with a decision not to proceed with an investigation,[83]

77 ICC-OTP, *Report on Preliminary Examination Activities 2018, supra* note 35, at 32, para. 117.

78 ICC-OTP, *Report on Preliminary Examination Activities 2018, supra* note 35, at 42, para. 160.

79 See for example ICC-OTP, *Report on Preliminary Examination Activities 2018, supra* note 35, at 42, para. 161.

80 William W. Burke-White, Proactive Complementarity: The International Criminal Court and National Courts in the Rome System of International Justice, 49(1) *Harvard International Law Journal* 53, 90 (2008).

81 Alejandro Chehtman, The Impact of the ICC in Colombia: Positive Complementarity on Trial, *Domac Project under the Seventh Framework Programme for EU Research (FP7)*, DOMAC/17 21 (2011).

82 Marieke I. Wierda, *The Local Impact of a Global Court: Assessing the Impact of the International Criminal Court in Situation Countries*, Ph.D. Thesis, University of Leiden (2019) 172.

83 International criminal Court – Office of the Prosecutor, Report on the Situation in Colombia, 30 Nov. 2023, page 2, para. 1, www.icc-cpi.int/sites/default/files/2023-11/2023-11-30-otp-report-colombia-eng.pdf.

accompanied by a Cooperation Agreement, which recalled that the Prosecutor may revisit its prior assessment upon a reversal of circumstances in the national accountability efforts.[84] In this sense, the Prosecutor's authority to either proceed with a formal investigation or to defer to domestic accountability processes encourages States to carry out genuine national proceedings addressing ICC crimes and deter them from committing these crimes in the future.

5. The Prosecutor's Role as Filtering Mechanism

It should be noted that the preliminary examination activities of the OTP are conducted in the same manner "irrespective of whether the Office receives a referral from a State Party or the Security Council" or whether the Prosecutor acts *proprio motu*.[85] The Prosecutor, having reviewed all available information relevant to a situation referred to him/her, may conclude that information available does not provide reasonable grounds to proceed with an investigation. This authority of the Prosecutor to decide as to whether or not there is a reasonable basis to proceed with an investigation serves as an early filtering mechanism against politically motivated referrals or against referrals that fail to meet the high threshold of the Rome Statute.

Of course, the Prosecutor's decision not to proceed is subject to judicial review and can be requested to be reviewed by the Pre-Trial Chamber under Article 53(3)(a), as was done by the Union of Comoros in the situation on Registered Vessels of Comoros, Greece and Cambodia in January 2015.[86] In any event, in contrast to some concerns that the powers of the Prosecutor could result in politicized prosecutions, the role given to the Prosecutor under the Rome Statute actually prevents any politically motivated State Party or Security Council referrals from turning into formal investigations. The most recent example, in which the Prosecutor declined to initiate an investigation, was the situation in the Gabonese Republic, which was referred to the OTP by the Gabonese Republic itself. The Prosecutor announced her decision to close the preliminary examination into the situation in the Gabonese Republic in September 2018 for lack of subject-matter jurisdiction.[87]

84 International Criminal Court – Office of the Prosecutor, Cooperation Agreement between the Office of the Prosecutor of the International Criminal Court and the Government of Colombia, 28 October 2021, art. 6, www.icc-cpi.int/sites/default/files/itemsDocuments/20211028-OTP-COL-Cooperation-Agreement-ENG.pdf

85 International Criminal Court – Office of the Prosecutor, Report on Preliminary Examination Activities 2013 (November 2013), at 4, para. 10.

86 International Criminal Court – Pre-Trial Chamber I, "Application for Review pursuant to Article 53 (3) (a) of the Prosecutor's Decision of 6 November 2014 not to initiate an investigation in the Situation" (29 January 2015) 3, para. 1.

87 ICC-OTP, *Report on Preliminary Examination Activities 2018, supra* note 35, at 71, para. 290.

6. Conclusion

The prosecutorial powers, including the authority to investigate crimes without a referral from a State Party or the Security Council, are not placed in the hands of the ICC Prosecutor without judicial checks. Article 15 of the Rome Statute provides some procedural safeguards, such as the requirement to seek authorization from the Pre-Trial Chamber. The strict judicial scrutiny of the chambers of the Court ensures that the decisions of the ICC Prosecutor are subject to the safeguards set out in the Rome Statute. In fact, the high threshold criteria set out in the Rome Statute make it nearly impossible for unfounded or politically motivated accusations to reach the trial stage.

There are also political restraints placed on the ICC Prosecutor by the States, whose cooperation is crucial in terms of gathering evidence, arresting suspects and accessing the witnesses and defendants. As the effective functioning of the Court relies heavily on cooperation with the members of the international community, any reluctance on the part of the States to cooperate with the Office of the Prosecutor limits the ability of the ICC Prosecutor to bring charges against the perpetrators. Therefore, this chapter concludes that the legal and political restraints placed on the Prosecutor should ally Türkiye's fears about frivolous or political complaints because they avert the possibility of the Prosecutor to bring arbitrary charges against individuals.

The chapter also suggests that the ICC Prosecutor's authority to make a determination as to whether there is a reasonable basis to proceed with an investigation, in fact, serves as an early filtering mechanism against politically motivated referrals or against referrals that do not meet the high threshold of the Rome Statute. The role given to the Prosecutor under the Rome Statute prevents the politically motivated State Party or Security Council referrals from turning into formal investigations.

Bibliography

BBC News, Karim Khan: UK Lawyer Elected Chief Prosecutor at ICC, www.bbc.com/news/uk-56051110 (accessed12 February 2021).

Burke-White, William W., Proactive Complementarity: The International Criminal Court and National Courts in the Rome System of International Justice, 49(1) *Harvard International Law Journal* (2008).

Chehtman, Alejandro, The Impact of the ICC in Colombia: Positive Complementarity on Trial, Domac Project under the Seventh Framework Programme for EU Research (FP7), DOMAC/17 21 (2011).

DW, *Syria Ceasefire Starts Near Damascus as UN Calls for ICC Referral Over Aid*, https://www.dw.com/en/syria-ceasefire-starts-near-damascus-as-un-calls-for-icc-referral-over-aid/a-42328500 (accessed 27 January 2018).

Human Rights Watch, *US Sanctions on the International Criminal Court*, www.hrw.org/news/2020/12/14/us-sanctions-international-criminal-court (accessed 14 December 2020).

International Criminal Court, *Afghanistan: ICC Appeals Chamber Authorises the Opening of an Investigation*, www.icc-cpi.int/Pages/item.aspx?name=pr1516 (accessed 5 March 2020).

International Criminal Court, *Election of Prosecutor* (2020), https://asp.icc-cpi.int/en_menus/asp/elections/prosecutor/Pages/Prosecutor2020.aspx (accessed 12 February 2020).
International Criminal Court, *Office of the Prosecutor, Annual Report of the Office of the Prosecutor* (1 December 2022).
International Criminal Court, *Office of the Prosecutor, Cooperation Agreement between the Office of the Prosecutor of the International Criminal Court and the Government of Colombia*, www.icc-cpi.int/sites/default/files/itemsDocuments/20211028-OTP-COL-Cooperation-Agreement-ENG.pdf (accessed 28 October 2021).
International Criminal Court, *Office of the Prosecutor, Policy Paper on Case Selection and Prioritisation* (15 September 2016).
International Criminal Court, *Office of the Prosecutor, Report on Preliminary Examination Activities 2018* (5 December 2018).
International Criminal Court, *Office of the Prosecutor, Report on Preliminary Examination Activities 2019* (5 December 2019).
International Criminal Court, *Office of the Prosecutor, Office of the Prosecutor Annual Report 2023* (2023).
International Criminal Court, *Office of the Prosecutor, Report on the Situation in Colombia*, www.icc-cpi.int/sites/default/files/2023-11/2023-11-30-otp-report-colombia-eng.pdf (accessed 30 November 2023).
International Criminal Court, *Press Release – ICC Judges Agree on Measures to Improve Efficiency of Criminal Process*, www.icc-cpi.int/Pages/item.aspx?name=pr1121&ln=en (accessed 22 June 2015).
International Criminal Court, *Press Release – Statement of the Prosecutor of the International Criminal Court, Fatou Bensouda, on the withdrawal of charges against Mr. Uhuru Muigai Kenyatta*, www.icc-cpi.int/en_menus/icc/press%20and%20media/press%20releases/Pages/otp-statement-05-12-2014-2.aspx (accessed 12 December 2014).
International Criminal Court, Pre-Trial Chamber I, Application for Review pursuant to Article 53 (3) (a) of the Prosecutor's Decision of 6 November 2014 not to initiate an investigation in the Situation (29 January 2015).
International Criminal Court – Pre-Trial Chamber II, *Decision Pursuant to Article 15 of the Rome Statute on the Authorisation of an Investigation into the Situation in the Islamic Republic of Afghanistan*, https://www.icc-cpi.int/CourtRecords/CR2019_02068.PDF (accessed 12 April 2019).
International Criminal Court – Pre-Trial Chamber III, *Decision Pursuant to Article 15 of the Rome Statute on the Authorisation of an Investigation into the Situation in the People's Republic of Bangladesh/Republic of the Union of Myanmar*, https://www.icc-cpi.int/CourtRecords/CR2019_06955.PDF (accessed 14 November 2019).
International Criminal Court, *Situations under investigation*, https://www.icc-cpi.int/pages/situation.aspx.
International Criminal Court, *The Appeals Chamber, Judgment on the Appeal against the Decision on the Authorisation of an Investigation into the Situation in the Islamic Republic of Afghanistan*, www.icc-cpi.int/CourtRecords/CR2020_00828.PDF (accessed 5 March 2020).
Kielsgard, Mark D., *Reluctant Engagement: U.S. Policy and the International Criminal Court* (Koninklijke Brill NV 2010).
Official Records of the U.N. Diplomatic Conference of Plenipotentiaries on the Establishment of an Int'l Criminal Court, 7th plen. mtg., U.N. Doc. A/CONE 183/SR.7.
Operational Portal Refugee Situations, *Total Persons of Concern*, https://data2.unhcr.org/en/situations/syria (accessed 1 January 2024).
Pearson, Zoe, Non-Governmental Organizations and the International Criminal Court: Changing Landscapes of International Law, 39(2) *Cornell International Law Journal* (2006).

Reuters, Russia Casts 13th Veto of U.N. Security Council Action during Syrian War, https://www.reuters.com/article/us-syria-security-un/russia-casts-13th-veto-of-un-security-council-action-during-syrian-war-idUSKBN1W42CJ (accessed 19 September 2019).
Rome Statute of the International Criminal Court, 17 July 1998, U.N. Doc. A/CONF.183/9.
Sterio, Milena, The International Criminal Court: Current Challenges and Prospect of Future Success, 52(1) *Case Western Reserve Journal of International Law* (2020).
The Guardian, Syrian Refugees Launch Legal Bid to Try Assad for Crimes against Humanity, https://www.theguardian.com/law/2019/mar/07/syrian-refugees-launch-legal-bid-to-try-assad-for-crimes-against-humanity (accessed 7 March 2019).
The International Federation for Human Rights (FIDH), *The Office of the Prosecutor of the ICC – 9 Years On Analysis of the Prosecutorial Strategy and Policies of the Office of the Prosecutor (2003–2011) Recommendations to the Next ICC Prosecutor*, www.fidh.org/IMG/pdf/cpiproc579ang.pdf (accessed December 2011).
UNRefugee Agency, *Internally Displaced People,* www.unhcr.org/sy/internally-displaced-people (accessed 1 January 2024).
UN Security Council, Referral of Syria to International Criminal Court Fails as Negative Votes Prevent Security Council from Adopting Draft Resolution, UN doc. SC/11407, http://www.un.org/News/Press/docs/2014/sc11407.doc.htm (accessed 22 May 2014).
Wierda, Marieke I., *The Local Impact of a Global Court: Assessing the Impact of the International Criminal Court in Situation Countries*, Ph.D. Thesis, University of Leiden (2019).
Whiting, Alex, A Program for the Next ICC Prosecutor, 52(1) *Case Western Reserve Journal of International Law* (2020).

5 The Scope of the ICC's Jurisdiction *Ratione Personae*

Too Broad to Accept?

Pursuant to Article 12 of the Rome Statute, the ICC can exercise its jurisdiction when the crimes in question are a) committed on the territory of a state that is either party to the Court[1] or otherwise accepts the jurisdiction of the Court on an *ad hoc* basis (only for the crimes in question)[2] (territorial jurisdiction), b) committed by the nationals of a state that is either party to the Court[3] or otherwise accepts the jurisdiction of the Court on an *ad hoc* basis (personal jurisdiction)[4] or c) referred to the Court by the Security Council.[5] Accordingly, nationals of a state that is not party to the Rome Statute can also be exposed to the jurisdiction of the ICC in some circumstances, for example, when a non-party state national commits an ICC crime on the territory of a State Party or when a situation is referred to the Court by the Security Council.

Apart from the trigger mechanism of the Rome Statute detailed in the previous chapter, representatives of Türkiye in Rome and Kampala were also concerned about the ICC's jurisdiction over nationals of non-party states. Mr. Güney stated that the jurisdiction of the Court "should be subject to the explicit consent of States."[6] Similarly, the head of the Turkish delegation to the 2010 Kampala Review Conference stated that the Court should not "create obligations or rights for a third state without its consent," citing Article 34 of the Vienna Convention on Law of Treaties.[7] This view, however, should not

1 United Nations Treaty Collection, *Rome Statute of the International Criminal Court*, U.N. Doc. A/CONF.183/9 (17 July 1998), art. 12(2)(a).

2 Rome Statute, *supra* note 1, art. 12(3).

3 Rome Statute, *supra* note 1, art. 12(2)(b).

4 Rome Statute, *supra* note 1, art. 12(3).

5 Rome Statute, *supra* note 1, art. 13(b).

6 Official Records of the United Nations Diplomatic Conference of Plenipotentiaries on the Establishment of an International Criminal Court, Official Records Volume II, A/CONF.183/13 (15 June–17 July 1998), at 124, para. 42 [hereinafter Official Records of the Rome Conference].

7 International Criminal Court, *Statement by Mr. Ismail Aramaz Head of Turkish Delegation*, http://www.icc-cpi.int/iccdocs/asp_docs/RC2010/Statements/ICC-RC-gendeba-Turkey-ENG.pdf (accessed 10 June 2010) [hereinafter Statement by Mr. Ismail Aramaz].

DOI: 10.4324/9781003641643-5

be considered as a legal or political obstacle to Türkiye's accession to the Rome Statute because once the Statute comes into force for Türkiye, the Court's jurisdiction over non-party states will no longer be an issue for Türkiye, as it will no longer be a non-party.

This chapter draws attention to the fact that Türkiye preserves very little by remaining an outsider and that Türkiye's non-accession does not guarantee that the ICC will not exercise jurisdiction over Turkish nationals. The chapter also compares Turkish and American positions with respect to their concerns regarding the ICC's jurisdiction over the nationals of non-party states in an attempt to explain why Türkiye should not follow in the footsteps of the U.S. – its only western ally that has not ratified the Rome Statute – on the issue of ICC accession.

1. Debates in Rome

During the Rome negotiations, two permanent members of the Security Council, the United States[8] and Russia,[9] craftily suggested that "[t]he only way the Court could exercise jurisdiction over a non-party was by means of a Security Council decision."[10] On the contrary, some states, such as India, argued that endowing the Security Council with the power to bind non-party states to the Rome Statute would violate the law of treaties.[11] China, another permanent member of the Security Council, opined that the consent of both the territorial State and the State of nationality should be required.[12]

Some states, such as Sweden, justifiably feared that "[a] consent regime, other than for non-party states, would seriously obstruct justice" and supported the idea that the ICC should be able to act when any of the following are parties to the Rome Statute: "the State where the crime occurred, the State with custody over the suspect, or the State of nationality of the suspect or the victim."[13] The United Kingdom – another permanent member – opined that the consent of the territorial state should be enough to enable an ICC prosecution.[14]

With regard to the exercise of the jurisdiction of the ICC, three options – proposed by different states – were formally considered during the Rome negotiations: a) German proposal, which offered automatic jurisdiction over the core crimes of the Rome Statute; b) Korean proposal, which offered jurisdiction if any of the following are party to the Court: the state on whose territory the crime occurred (the territorial state), the state of which the

8 Official Records of the Rome Conference, *supra* note 6, at 123, para. 28.
9 Official Records of the Rome Conference, *supra* note 6, at 196, para. 40.
10 Official Records of the Rome Conference, *supra* note 6.
11 Official Records of the Rome Conference, *supra* note 6, at 322, para. 34.
12 Official Records of the Rome Conference, *supra* note 6, at 323, para. 41.
13 Official Records of the Rome Conference, *supra* note 6, at 68, para. 54.
14 Official Records of the Rome Conference, *supra* note 6, at 184, para. 45.

accused or the victim was a national or the state with custody over the accused; and c) American proposal, which offered jurisdiction only if the consent of the State of the nationality of the accused is obtained (except for the crime of genocide).[15] While the German and Korean proposals garnered strong support, the American proposal "enjoyed very little support."[16] At the end of the Rome Conference, the current version of the Article 12 of the Rome Statute was adopted as the "compromise approach that would attract the broadest possible support for the statute."[17]

The U.S. attempts to amend the Article 12 of the Statute to exempt non-party states' official actions – such as "humanitarian interventions, peacekeeping actions, or defensive actions to eliminate weapons of mass destruction" – from the jurisdiction of the ICC also did not yield results.[18] The likelihood of the initiation of an investigation that could lead to indictments against the nationals of the United States was the main reason that prompted the United States to be one of the only seven states that voted against adopting the final outcome of the Rome Conference. This likelihood, in the eyes of David Scheffer – the head of the U.S. delegation and the U.S. Ambassador-at-Large for War Crimes Issues – constituted "the single most fundamental flaw in the Rome Treaty that makes it impossible for the United States to sign the present text."[19]

Drawing attention to the need for the cooperation of States for the effectiveness of the ICC, the head of the Turkish delegation to the Rome Conference described the inherent and universal jurisdiction proposals as "unrealistic."[20] Instead, he suggested requiring the consent of not only the state of the nationality of the accused but also of the territorial and custodial states:

> The Court's effectiveness depended on the cooperation of States. The State on whose territory the act or omission had taken place, the State with custody of the person who had committed the crime and the State of which the accused was a national must be parties to the Statute or accept the jurisdiction of the Court for the crime in question.[21]

Although it is true that the cooperation and assistance of states are essential for the operational effectiveness of the ICC, it is also very clear that the consent regime mentioned earlier would often subject the search for justice to the political agendas of individual states that are mostly acting to secure their own

15 Michael P. Scharf, The ICC's Jurisdiction over the Nationals of Non-Party States: A Critique of the U.S. Position, 64 *Law and Contemporary Problems* 67, 77 (2001).
16 Scharf, *supra* note 15, at 71.
17 Scharf, *supra* note 15, at 78.
18 Scharf, *supra* note 15.
19 Steven C. Roach, *Politicizing the International Criminal Court: The Convergence of Politics, Ethics, and Law* (Lanham: Rowman & Littlefield Publishers 2006) 133.
20 Roach, *supra* note 19, at 311, para. 99.
21 Roach, *supra* note 19, at 311, para. 100.

political interests. Confinement of the ICC jurisdiction to obtaining of the consent of both the territorial and custodial states and the state of the nationality of the accused would undermine effectiveness and credibility of the Court by subordinating it to the veto power of each state whose consent is required.

2. Türkiye's Position

Although Türkiye was among states that opposed the ICC's authority to exercise jurisdiction over the nationals of non-party states, such opposition was not the main concern that disappointed the Turkish delegation to the extent that it abstained from voting to adopt the Rome Statute. As explained in the previous chapters, Türkiye's main objections were related to the issues that concern its decades-long fight against terrorism, such as possible implications of Türkiye's ICC accession for its struggle against terrorist organizations. Indeed, while it is understandable for those countries that would most likely not join the Court in the foreseeable future, such as the United States, to perceive the ICC's jurisdiction over non-party states as a threat, it should not be a concern for a state, such as Türkiye, which already stated that it "will soon approve the Rome Statute after completing its internal preparations."[22]

What is significant to recall at this stage is that Türkiye's non-accession does not guarantee that the ICC will not exercise jurisdiction over Turkish nationals and that Türkiye preserves very little by remaining an outsider. First, the ICC will have jurisdiction over the acts committed by Turkish nationals on the territory of a state that is either party to the Court or otherwise accepts the jurisdiction of the Court on an *ad hoc* basis, regardless of whether Türkiye is a party or consents to the jurisdiction of the Court. In such case, an investigation could be triggered by the Prosecutor *proprio motu* or by a State Party referral. Second, the Court would have jurisdiction over the acts committed by Turkish nationals in a situation referred to it by the Security Council, regardless of where the crimes were committed. No precondition is required when a situation, in which an ICC crime appears to be committed, is referred to the Court by the Security Council.

Cyprus is an example where Türkiye could be exposed to the jurisdiction of the ICC as a non-party state. A communication was filed in 2014 requesting the ICC prosecutor to initiate an investigation *proprio motu* into the situation in Cyprus. It was quite obvious that this was a politically motivated referral, especially given the limited subject matter and temporal jurisdiction of the ICC, and it was not surprising that an investigation was not commenced. Nevertheless, what is relevant here is that because "Cyprus" has been declared as a party to the Rome Statute since 2002 as a result of the accession by the

22 Coalition for the International Criminal Court, *Target Countries – URC-Turkey*, http://www.iccnow.org/?mod=urc1010.

de facto administration of Southern Cyprus,[23] a preliminary examination into the situation in Cyprus (including into Türkiye's activities that aimed at protecting Turkish Cypriots as a "Guarantor Power") could be triggered by the Prosecutor *proprio motu* or by a referral of any State Party if high thresholds of the Rome Statute (including the temporal and subject matter jurisdiction, complementarity, gravity and interests of justice criteria) appeared to be satisfied. Thus, by remaining a non-party state, Türkiye does not actually rule out the possibility of the Cyprus question being brought before the Court. The Cyprus question is worthy of its own examination and will be covered in the next chapter.

3. The U.S. Approach to the ICC: An Example to Follow?

A comparison of the positions of Türkiye and the U.S. (Türkiye's only western ally that has not joined the ICC) with respect to the Court's jurisdiction over the nationals of non-party states reveals two critical implications. First, by remaining outside the ICC, Türkiye preserves less than the United States, which enjoys advantages of being a permanent member of the Security Council, such as the power to block any Security Council referrals to the ICC. Second, the United States has much more compelling reasons to fear the ICC's jurisdiction over the nationals of non-party states than Türkiye, such as its expansive military operations across the globe.

3.1. U.S. Objections

The head of the U.S. delegation to the Rome Conference suggested that when the alleged crimes in question are committed by the non-party state nationals, an ICC action should not be possible without the consent of that State.[24] This suggestion, if adopted, would deprive the ICC of the jurisdiction over an ICC crime that is committed on the territory of a State Party but by the nationals of a non-party state, unless the latter grants consent. The U.S. delegation argued that the emergence of the ICC jurisdiction over the nationals of a non-signatory State, in the absence of that State's consent and the Security Council referral, "could not be justified on the basis of existing law."[25]

The U.S. delegation further claimed that an ICC prosecution would be consistent with the fundamental principles of international law only if the consent of the territorial State and the State of the nationality of the accused are obtained.[26] Furthermore, the U.S. delegation supported a case-by-case approach requiring the consent of States in each individual case, even if they

23 International Criminal Court, Assembly of States Parties, *Cyprus*, https://asp.icc-cpi.int/states-parties/asian-states/cyprus.

24 Official Records of the Rome Conference, *supra* note 6, at 195, para. 24.

25 Official Records of the Rome Conference, *supra* note 6, at 195, para. 23.

26 Official Records of the Rome Conference, *supra* note 6, at 322, para. 27.

are parties to the Rome Statute.[27] It goes without saying that a case-by-case mechanism would paralyze the ICC and prevent it from operating effectively.

After realizing that there was "little likelihood of preventing the Rome Treaty from coming into force," the U.S. Administration alternatively attempted to argue that "international law prohibits the ICC from exercising jurisdiction over the nationals of non-parties."[28] Ambassador Scheffer argued, contrary to the belief prevailed at the Rome Conference, that the ICC cannot exercise jurisdiction over the nationals of non-party states on the basis of the "universality" and the "territoriality" principles.[29] With regard to the universality principle, he suggested that "some of the crimes within the subject matter jurisdiction of the ICC are not recognized as crimes of universal jurisdiction under customary international law" and that "universal jurisdiction cannot be delegated to a treaty-based collective international court."[30] With regard to the territoriality principle, he suggested that there is no internationally recognized basis for the delegation of the territorial jurisdiction to an international court without the consent of the accused's state.[31]

However, as highlighted by Professor Scharf, who examined the universal and territorial jurisdictional basis of the Rome Statute – including the issue of the conferral of such jurisdictions to an international court – the jurisdiction of the ICC over the nationals of non-party states is "well-grounded in international law."[32] Professor Scharf explained that the core crimes in the Rome Statute are crimes of universal jurisdiction, which "provides every state with jurisdiction over a limited category of offenses generally recognized as of universal concern, regardless of where the offense occurred, the nationality of the perpetrator, or the nationality of the victim."[33] Indeed, as referred to in the Article 1 of the Rome Statute, crimes within the jurisdiction of the ICC are recognized as "the most serious crimes of international concern"[34] by, including but not limited to, the 124[35] states that have ratified the Rome Statute.

Professor Scharf also noted that the Nuremberg International Military Tribunal and the International Criminal Tribunal for the Former Yugoslavia provided the precedent for the collective delegation of universal jurisdiction to an international court without the consent of accused's state.[36] With respect to

27 Official Records of the Rome Conference, *supra* note 6, at 195, para. 22.
28 Scharf, *supra* note 15, at 69.
29 Scharf, *supra* note 15, at 70.
30 Scharf, *supra* note 15.
31 David Scheffer, International Criminal Court: The Challenge of Jurisdiction, 93 *American Society of International Law Proceedings*, 71–72 (1999).
32 Scharf, *supra* note 15, at 116.
33 Scharf, *supra* note 15, at 76.
34 Rome Statute, *supra* note 1, art. 1.
35 International Criminal Court, *The States Parties to the Rome Statute*, https://asp.icc-cpi.int/en_menus/asp/states%20parties/pages/the%20states%20parties%20to%20the%20rome%20statute.aspx.
36 Scharf, *supra* note 15, at 116.

the territoriality principle, Professor Scharf explained that the territorial states' authority to confer their territorial-based jurisdiction to an international court is recognized by international law.[37] Although addressing these legal arguments is crucial, it is also crucial to bear in mind that the main concern behind the U.S.'s (usually hostile) stance towards the ICC is the fear that large number of American troops could be subject to the Court's jurisdiction.

3.2. A Comparison of the Positions of Türkiye and the U.S.

Permanent members of the Security Council enjoy two kinds of privileges in terms of establishment and enforcement of the ICC's jurisdiction. They can individually block any Security Council referrals to the ICC by using their veto power, and they can collectively defer any investigation for 12 months on a renewable basis.[38] That is to say, the United States, as a permanent member of the Security Council, can veto any resolution that provides the ICC with jurisdiction over its nationals, and it can also try to mobilize the Security Council to defer any investigation triggered by the Prosecutor *proprio motu* or by a State Party referral.

The U.S., in fact, averts, by remaining a non-party, the possibility of the American nationals being brought before the ICC for the acts committed on its own territory (absent its consent) or on the territory of another non-party state (absent the consent of that territorial state). Furthermore, the United States concluded Bilateral Immunity Agreements (BIAs) with over a hundred states to ensure that they would not hand over the U.S. nationals to the ICC without its permission.[39] Türkiye, on the other hand, does not enjoy such protections as BIAs and the privileges of being a permanent member of the Security Council and, therefore, should not follow in the footsteps of the U.S. on the issue of ICC accession.

Moreover, the United States has much more compelling reasons for not joining the ICC than Türkiye, such as its expansive military operations across the globe. As of March 2024, there are approximately 200,000 U.S. troops deployed across the world.[40] The U.S. opposition to the ICC is largely predicated on the fear that a large number of American troops could be subject to the Court's jurisdiction and that its officials could be deprived of the type of due process rights guaranteed to Americans under the U.S. Constitution, such as the right to a jury trial and the protection against self-incrimination.[41] The

37 Scharf, *supra* note 15.

38 Rome Statute, *supra* note 1, art. 16.

39 Central Intelligence Agency, *The World Factbook – Military Deployments*, https://www.cia.gov/the-world-factbook/field/military-deployments (accessed 1 January 2024).

40 Defense Manpower Data Center, *Number of Military and DoD Appropriated Fund (APF) Civilian Personnel Permanently Assigned* (Defense Manpower Data Center 6 May 2021).

41 Mark D. Kielsgar, War on the International Criminal Court, 8 *New York City Law Review* 1, 12 (2005).

"protection" of the American troops from being exposed to the jurisdiction of the ICC has been the main concern that underlies the U.S.'s stance towards the ICC.[42]

Indeed, the OTP, while seeking to open a formal investigation into the situation in Afghanistan, has already identified "the alleged torture or ill-treatment of conflict-related detainees by US armed forces in the period 2003–2008" as a potential case.[43] The OTP has found that "there is a reasonable basis to believe that" members of the U.S. armed forces and of the U.S. Central Intelligence Agency have committed war crimes in Afghanistan in 2003 and 2004.[44] Though the Prosecutor's request for authorization of an investigation was rejected by Pre-Trial Chamber II, in 12 April 2019, on the ground that "the commencement of an investigation would not be in the interests of justice,"[45] this decision was amended by the Appeals Chamber's judgment of 5 March 2020, which authorized the Prosecutor to commence a formal investigation into the alleged crimes committed on the territory of Afghanistan since 1 May 2003, the entry into of force of the Rome Statute for Afghanistan.[46] Authorization of an investigation into the "situation in Afghanistan" is a clear example of the possibility of the U.S. nationals being placed under the jurisdiction of the ICC due to its extensive deployment of troops abroad.

Another compelling U.S. concern that is not shared by Türkiye is the issue of infringement of national sovereignty. Unlike the states that rely on the doctrine of "absolute sovereignty" and "non-interference with international affairs,"[47] Türkiye does not fear that ICC jurisdiction would violate its sovereignty. Infringement of its sovereignty has not been one of the reasons for Türkiye's objections to the ICC's jurisdiction over the nationals of non-parties or to the Prosecutor's powers. Türkiye has already accepted the compulsory jurisdiction of the ECtHR, which hears applications against signatory states

42 *See*, e.g., the statements of the George W. Bush in John P. Cerone, U.S. Attitudes Toward International Criminal Courts and Tribunals, in Cesare P. R. Romano (ed.), *The Sword and the Scales: The United States and International Courts and Tribunals* (Cambridge University Press 2009), at 156.

43 The use of "enhanced interrogation techniques" has been documented, inter alia, in U.S. Department of Defense reports. *See* International Criminal Court, *Office of the Prosecutor, Report on Preliminary Examination Activities 2014* (2 December 2014) 22, para. 94.

44 International Criminal Court, *Office of the Prosecutor, Report on Preliminary Examination Activities 2017* (4 December 2017) 55, para. 254.

45 International Criminal Court – Pre-Trial Chamber II, *Decision Pursuant to Article 15 of the Rome Statute on the Authorisation of an Investigation into the Situation in the Islamic Republic of Afghanistan*, 3, para. 1, https://www.icc-cpi.int/CourtRecords/CR2019_02068.PDF (accessed 12 April 2019).

46 International Criminal Court, *Afghanistan: ICC Appeals Chamber Authorises the Opening of an Investigation* (5 March 2020), www.icc-cpi.int/Pages/item.aspx?name=pr1516 (accessed 1 January 2024).

47 Jing Guan, The ICC's Jurisdiction over War Crimes in Internal Armed Conflicts: An Insurmountable Obstacle for China's Accession? 28(4) *Penn State International Law Review* 754 (2010).

for the breach of a broad range of rights and freedoms and issues binding judgments upon them, at the expense of significant privileges of its sovereignty. Thus, joining a court that tries its nationals would not be an unprecedented "infringement" of Türkiye's sovereignty.

Indeed, the amendment made in the Turkish Constitution in 2004, which paved the way for the extradition of Turkish nationals to the ICC, showed that Turkish lawmakers, unlike the U.S. senators many of whom "believe that sovereignty remains a central issue,"[48] did not consider the ICC jurisdiction as a threat to Türkiye's sovereignty.

It is important to note that accession to the Rome Statute could benefit Türkiye more vis-a-vis the U.S., especially given Türkiye's foreign policy priorities, such as its European Union membership bid. As will be detailed in Chapter 8, Türkiye's accession to the Rome Statute could accelerate its membership negotiations with the EU because joining the ICC is a common policy adopted by all member states under the EU's Common Foreign and Security Policy.

The Council of the European Union has noted that the principles and objectives of the Rome Statute are fully in line with that of the EU and adopted formal decisions "to advance universal support for the Rome Statute . . . by promoting the widest possible participation."[49] The Council has also noted that the EU will follow the developments regarding the cooperation with the ICC closely.[50] Türkiye's accession to this Court would not only enhance its international prestige but would also have positive impact on its membership negotiations with the EU – a critical gain, which would definitely be mentioned in the European Commission's Progress Reports on Türkiye. Such gain is a clear example why Türkiye is likely to benefit more from the ICC accession than the U.S. would and why Türkiye should not follow in the footsteps of the U.S. on the issue of the ICC accession.

4. Conclusion

This chapter first drew attention to the fact that Türkiye's non-party status does not guarantee that the ICC will not exercise jurisdiction over Turkish nationals: the ICC will have jurisdiction over the acts committed by Turkish nationals on the territory of a State Party or in a situation referred to the Court by the Security Council. The chapter then pointed out that extension of the ICC's jurisdiction to the nationals of non-parties should not be considered

48 Samantha Power, The United States and Genocide Law: A History of Ambivalence, in Sarah B. Sewall and Carl Kaysen (eds.), *The United States and the International Criminal Court: National Security and International Law* (Rowman & Littlefield 2000), at 170.

49 The Council of the European Union, *Council Decision 2011/168/CFSP of 21 March 2011 on the International Criminal Court and repealing Common Position 2003/444/CFSP*, art. 1(2) (21 March 2011), https://eur-lex.europa.eu/legal-content/en/TXT/?uri=CELEX%3A32011D0168.

50 The Council of the European Union, *supra* note 49, art. 4(1).

as one of the legal or political obstacles to Türkiye's accession to the Rome Statute because once the Statute comes into force for Türkiye, the Court's jurisdiction over non-party states will be an issue that concerns only non-party states, of which Türkiye will no longer be one.

This chapter also argued that a comparison of the positions of Türkiye and the U.S. with respect to the ICC's jurisdiction over the nationals of non-party states reveals two critical implications. First, Türkiye, by remaining a non-party state, preserves less than the United States, which enjoys advantages of being a permanent member of the Security Council, such as the power to block any Security Council referrals to the ICC. Second, the United States has much more compelling reasons for not joining the ICC than Türkiye, such as its expansive military operations across the globe. This chapter then noted that accession to the Rome Statute could benefit Türkiye more vis-a-vis the U.S., especially given Türkiye's foreign policy priorities, such as its European Union membership bid. Thus, the chapter suggested that Türkiye should not follow in the footsteps of the U.S., its only western ally that has not yet ratified the Rome Statute, on the issue of ICC accession.

Bibliography

Central Intelligence Agency, *The World Factbook*, https://www.cia.gov/library/publications/the-world-factbook/geos/sy.html.

The Council of the European Union, *Council Decision 2011/168/CFSP of 21 March 2011 on the International Criminal Court and Repealing Common Position 2003/444/CFSP*, https://eur-lex.europa.eu/legal-content/en/TXT/?uri=CELEX%3A32011D0168 (accessed 21 March 2011).

Defense Manpower Data Center, *Number of Military and DoD Appropriated Fund (APF) Civilian Personnel Permanently Assigned* (Defense Manpower Data Center 6 May 2021).

Guan, Jing, The ICC's Jurisdiction over War Crimes in Internal Armed Conflicts: An Insurmountable Obstacle for China's Accession? 28 *Penn State International Law Review* 703, 721 (2010).

International Criminal Court, *Afghanistan: ICC Appeals Chamber Authorises the Opening of an Investigation*, www.icc-cpi.int/Pages/item.aspx?name=pr1516 (accessed 5 March 2020).

International Criminal Court, *Assembly of States Parties to the Rome Statute, Cyprus*, https://asp.icc-cpi.int/states-parties/asian-states/cyprus.

International Criminal Court, *Assembly of States Parties to the Rome Statute, the States Parties to the Rome Statute*, https://asp.icc-cpi.int/states-parties.

International Criminal Court, *Office of the Prosecutor, Report on Preliminary Examination Activities 2014*, http://www.icc-cpi.int/iccdocs/otp/OTP-Pre-Exam-2014.pdf (accessed 2 December 2014).

International Criminal Court, *Office of the Prosecutor, Report on Preliminary Examination Activities 2017*, http://www.icc-cpi.int/sites/default/files/itemsDocuments/2017-PE-rep/2017-otp-rep-PE_ENG.pdf (accessed 4 December 2017).

International Criminal Court, *Statement by Mr. Ismail Aramaz Head of Turkish Delegation*, http://www.icc-cpi.int/iccdocs/asp_docs/RC2010/Statements/ICC-RC-gendeba-Turkey-ENG.pdf (accessed 10 June 2010).

Kielsgar, Mark D., War on the International Criminal Court, 8 *New York City Law Review* 1, 12 (2005).

Official Records of the U.N. Diplomatic Conference of Plenipotentiaries on the Establishment of an Int'l Criminal Court, 7th plen. mtg., U.N. Doc. A/CONE 183/SR.7.

Roach, Steven C., *Politicizing the International Criminal Court: The Convergence of Politics, Ethics, and Law* (Lanham: Rowman & Littlefield Publishers 2006), 133.

Romano, Cesare P. R., ed., *The Sword and the Scales: The United States and International Courts and Tribunals* (Cambridge University Press 2009).

Rome Statute of the International Criminal Court (17 July 1998), U.N. Doc. A/CONF.183/9.

Scharf, Michael P., The ICC's Jurisdiction over the Nationals of Non-Party States: A Critique of the U.S. Position, 64 *Law and Contemporary Problems* 67, 77 (2001).

Scheffer, David, International Criminal Court: The Challenge of Jurisdiction, 93 *American Society of International Law Proceedings* 68, 71–72 (1999).

Sewall, Sarah B. and Carl Kaysen, eds., *The United States and the International Criminal Court: National Security and International Law* (Rowman & Littlefield 2000), 170.

6 Implications for the Cyprus Question

A member of the European Parliament and a group of Greek Cypriots have filed a communication with the Prosecutor in 2014, requesting her to use her *proprio motu* power to initiate an investigation into the situation in Cyprus.[1] The Prosecutor, however, has not so far opened a preliminary examination, and it is very unlikely that she will ever be eager to do so due to, *inter alia*, the limited subject matter and temporal jurisdiction of the ICC and the highly controversial and politically sensitive nature of the situation. Nor has the Greek Cyprus, which acceded to the Rome Statute in 2002, so far filed a referral requesting initiation of an investigation.

This chapter explains that, in the highly unlikely event that a preliminary examination into the situation in Cyprus is opened, neither the acts of the Turkish Cyprus (and Türkiye) nor those of the Greek Cyprus (and Greece) in the island of Cyprus would be deemed admissible before the ICC. The limited subject matter and temporal jurisdiction of the ICC, the gravity of the allegations and the remedies that have already been provided to the victims of the acts in question would prevent a preliminary examination from turning into a formal investigation, and the alleged acts of both Greek and Turkish nationals would be found inadmissible before the ICC.

This chapter further submits that given the political constraints, the statehood issues and the risk of obstructing the re-unification talks, the situation in Cyprus would not be a case the Prosecutor would be eager to get involved by a preliminary examination, which is clearly not likely to turn into a formal investigation, even if the preconditions to the exercise of the ICC's jurisdiction were clearly satisfied.

This chapter will focus on the allegations directed against Türkiye. In this regard, the alleged settlement activities in Northern Cyprus in 1970s and alleged violations of the property rights of the Greek Cypriots are the main issues regarding the possibility of the Cyprus question being brought before

1 *See* the communication to the Prosecutor regarding the situation in Cyprus (14 July 2014), https://dl.dropboxusercontent.com/u/92018228/Communication%20-%20ICC%20Turkey.pdf (accessed 1 January 2024).

DOI: 10.4324/9781003641643-6

the ICC as crimes with continuous nature. The chapter explains that these allegations clearly fail to satisfy subject matter and temporal jurisdiction and the gravity requirement of the ICC. This chapter then explains that most of the allegations directed against Türkiye have already been addressed by the ECtHR.

Despite the Rome Statute's high threshold criteria that make an ICC investigation into the situation in Cyprus highly unlikely, some still view the Cyprus question as one of the greatest fears of Türkiye about joining the ICC.[2] In this regard, this chapter draws attention to the fact that even if Türkiye remains a non-party, the Court could still determine that it has territorial jurisdiction over the alleged acts of Türkiye on the island due to the Greek Cyprus's accession to the Rome Statute in 2002.

This chapter will submit that what makes an ICC investigation into the situation in Cyprus very unlikely and almost infeasible is not the preconditions to the exercise of the ICC's jurisdiction but rather the facts, such as the caution of the OTP in selecting cases, the limited temporal/subject matter jurisdiction of the Court, the gravity of the allegations, which clearly falls behind the safeguards/high thresholds of the Rome Statute, the statehood issues, political constraints and the risk of obstructing the re-unification talks. The chapter will finally submit that Türkiye's accession to the Rome Statute is not likely to impact the possibility of the Cyprus issue being brought before the ICC because the Republic of Cyprus is already party to the Rome Statute, and thus, it can already attempt to refer the situation in Cyprus to the ICC regardless of whether Türkiye is a State Party. The Cyprus question, therefore, should not prevent Türkiye from considering the accession to the Rome Statute.

1. Historical and Political Background

Greek and Turkish Cypriots lived together in peace and harmony for more than 300 years under the Ottoman sovereignty between 1571 and 1878.[3] During British rule, however, Greek Cypriots waged an anti-colonial guerilla war against Great Britain in order to facilitate "enosis," the desire to merge the island with Greece.[4] The National Organization of Cypriot Fighters, which was formed by the Greek Cypriots to combat British control over the island[5]

2 Tulin Daloglu, Why Turkey May Not Want to Join the ICC, *Al-Monitor*, www.al-monitor.com/pulse/tr/originals/2014/09/turkey-icc-rome-statue-human-rights.html (accessed 5 September 2014).

3 Jenna C. Borders, Another Door Closed: Resort to the European Court of Human Rights for Relief from the Turkish Invasion of 1974 May No Longer Be Possible for Greek Cypriots, 36 *North Carolina Journal of International Law* 689, 692 (2011).

4 David Wippman, International Law and Ethnic Conflict on Cyprus, 31 *Texas International Law Journal* 41, 144 (1996).

5 Borders, *supra* note 3, at 693.

and supported openly by Greece, conducted a campaign of violence, "making administration of the island extremely difficult."[6]

The idea of merging Cyprus with Greece, of which the island had never been part, was unacceptable to the Turkish Cypriots and Türkiye – the Ottoman Empire's successor.[7] Insistence on enosis, therefore, created animosity between the Turkish and Greek communities.[8] Chaos and bloodshed paved the way for the establishment of a bi-communal republic in 1960 through Zurich and London Agreements, including a Treaty of Guarantee, by Guarantor states Türkiye, Greece and Great Britain.[9] Nonetheless, civil and political unrest between the two communities continued to erupt into violent conflicts, even after Cyprus achieved its independence.[10]

In response to a Greek military coup that overthrew the government of the Republic of Cyprus with the purpose of uniting the island with Greece, Türkiye carried out, as a Guarantor State, a military intervention in 1974 "to restore the status quo" and to prevent Turkish Cypriots from being driven out of the island.[11] After the Greek junta collapsed and the Cypriot president returned to his office, however, Türkiye did not withdraw its troops from the island on the grounds that its military presence was needed in order to protect the Turkish Cypriots "pursuant to its obligations under the 1960 Treaty of Guarantee."[12]

As a result of this military action in the northern part of the island, thousands of Greek Cypriots moved to the south, while thousands of Turkish Cypriots who lived in the south moved to the north.[13] In 1983, after the failure of re-unification talks between the two communities, Turkish Cypriots, "invoking the principle of self-determination," declared independence from the Republic of Cyprus and formed the Turkish Republic of Northern Cyprus,[14] which is not recognized by the international community, except by Türkiye.[15]

The statehood questions, involvement of the Guarantor States and the re-unification efforts between the Greeks and Turks under (or without) auspices of the United Nations make the situation in Cyprus too sensitive to

6 Benjamin M. Meier, Reunification of Cyprus: The Possibility of Peace in the Wake of Past Failure, 34 *Cornell Journal of International Law* 455, 459 (2001).

7 Thomas Ehrlich, Cyprus, The "Warlike Isle": Origins and Elements of the Current Crisis, 18 *Stanford Law Review* 1021, 1025 (1966).

8 Borders, *supra* note 3, at 694.

9 Ehrlich, *supra* note 7, at 1021.

10 Ehrlich, *supra* note 7.

11 Borders, *supra* note 3, at 697; Reeta Paakkinen, *Migration Row Has Two Sides, Turkish Cypriots Say*, http://www.hurriyetdailynews.com/default.aspx?pageid=438&n=migration-row-has-two-sides-turkish-cypriots-say-2009-08-03 (accessed 3 August 2009).

12 Borders, *supra* note 3, at 697.

13 Laura Matson, Competing Land Rights, Legal Redress, and Political Settlement in Cyprus, 31 *Law & Inequality* 199 (2012).

14 Meier, *supra* note 6, at 466.

15 UN Security Council Resolution 541, U.N. Doc. S/RES/541 (18 November 1983).

intervene.[16] If the ICC prosecutor were to open an investigation into the situation in Cyprus *proprio motu*, or if the Greek Cyprus were to refer the situation to the Court, they would most likely come under intense criticism by the EU, UN, U.S. and Türkiye for undermining the re-unification talks on the island irrespective of whether Türkiye is a State Party or not.[17] Such unlikely involvement could even be deferred by the Security Council for a renewable period of 12 months, as envisaged by Article 16 of the Rome Statute,[18] on the grounds that the investigation constitutes a threat to international peace and security under Article 39 of the UN Charter.[19]

2. The ICC's Existing Territorial Jurisdiction Over Türkiye's Activities in Cyprus

In the preliminary examination process of a situation, before proceeding to analyze information on the alleged acts, the OTP needs to determine whether the ICC has jurisdiction over a situation in question. Because Türkiye is currently not party to the Rome Statute, the ICC will only have jurisdiction over the acts of Turkish nationals if they are committed in the territory of a State Party (absent a Security Council referral). Referring to the Greek Cyprus's accession to the Rome Statute in 2002, the ICC could assert territorial jurisdiction over Türkiye's activities on the island.

Most of the alleged acts, committed whether in/by the South or the North, would be considered by the ICC as crimes that started in one part of the island but continued in the other part "if" they appeared to satisfy the limited subject matter/temporal jurisdiction and the gravity requirement of the ICC, and if the victimhood/suffering of the victims continued, because the victims from both sides has moved to the other side as a result of these acts. In such a case, the ICC would have territorial jurisdiction over the alleged acts of Türkiye in Northern Cyprus, and the statehood issues would not deprive the ICC of its

16 BBC, Cyprus Reunification Talks to Resume, *BBC*, www.bbc.com/news/world-europe-26093114 (accessed 2 February 2014).

17 European Commission, Press Release, *Cyprus Steering Group: Commission Enhances Support to the Cyprus Settlement Process*, http://europa.eu/rapid/press-release_IP-14-336_en.htm (accessed 27 March 2014); EurActiv, *US and Turkey Upbeat About Cyprus Reunification*, www.euractiv.com/sections/global-europe/us-and-turkey-upbeat-about-cyprus-reunification-313983 (accessed 22 April 2015).

18 United Nations Treaty Collection, *Rome Statute of the International Criminal Court*, U.N. Doc. A/CONF.183/9 (17 July 1998), art. 16.

19 Article 39 of the U.N. Charter states that "[t]he Security Council shall determine the existence of any threat to the peace, breach of the peace, or act of aggression and shall make recommendations, or decide what measures shall be taken . . . to maintain or restore international peace and security."; *see* Alhagi Marong, Unlocking the Mysteriousness of Complementarity: In Search of a Forum Conveniens for Trial of the Leaders of the Lord's Resistance Army, 40 *Georgia Journal of International and Comparative Law* 98 (2011).

territorial jurisdiction.[20] Türkiye's non-accession, therefore, does not guarantee that the situation in Cyprus will be out of the reach of the ICC Prosecutor. What makes an ICC investigation into the situation in Cyprus very unlikely is not the preconditions to the exercise of the ICC's jurisdiction but rather such facts as the OTP's caution in selecting cases, limited subject matter and temporal jurisdiction of the Court, the gravity of the allegations, the statehood issues, political constraints and the risk of obstructing the re-unification talks.

The OTP's 2013 report on the preliminary examination of activities in Palestine shows how the Office handles the jurisdictional issues originating from statehood ambiguities.[21] The report indicates that it is the practice of the United Nations to make legal determinations on the statehood questions for the purpose of "enabling the exercise of jurisdiction by the Court."[22] Given the Security Council Resolution 541, which found "the declaration by the Turkish Cypriot authorities . . . to create an independent State in northern Cyprus" to be "legally invalid,"[23] the OTP could arguably consider the whole island as a State Party territory due to the deposition of the instrument of ratification of the Rome Statute by an authority from the island. In such a case, accession of Türkiye or the Turkish Republic of Northern Cyprus to the Rome Statute would not be seen as a requisite in order for the Court to exercise jurisdiction over the activities in Northern Cyprus. Instead of being an onlooker to such disputable but possible future considerations, Türkiye should consider being an influential insider of the ICC to better explain its legitimate legal arguments on the issues such as the situation in Cyprus and to make sure that its side of the issues is well understood.

3. The Limited Jurisdiction of the ICC

The Greek Cypriots Group who filed a communication with the ICC Prosecutor linked its settlement claims against Türkiye with the Article 8(2)(b)(viii) of the Rome Statute, which classifies "[t]he transfer, directly or indirectly, by the Occupying Power of parts of its own civilian population into the territory it occupies" as a war crime.[24] However, the migration of Turkish nationals to the Turkish Cyprus could not be categorized as "settlement activities" or as "the transfer of population" within the meaning of Article 8(b)(viii) because Türkiye has never been an "occupying power" in Cyprus, but a Guarantor State using its "legal right to intervene" under the Treaty of Guarantee.[25]

20 William A. Schabas, *The International Criminal Court: A Commentary on the Rome Statute* (Oxford University Press 2010) 285.

21 International Criminal Court, *Office of the Prosecutor, Report on Preliminary Examination Activities 2012* (November 2012), para. 1.

22 International Criminal Court, *supra* note 21, at para. 236.

23 Security Council Resolution 541, *supra* note 15.

24 Rome Statute, *supra* note 18, art. 8(2)(b)(viii).

25 "Turkey intervened as a Guarantor Power on 20 July 1974 in conformity with its rights and obligations deriving from the Treaty of Guarantee. Intervention by Turkey blocked the way

Furthermore, even if Türkiye were to be considered as an occupying power; in order to hold Turkish officials responsible for "settlement" activities in Northern Cyprus, the ICC would need to provide proof of an *actus reus* of the Article 8(b)(viii), which is the "transfer, directly or indirectly, . . . part of its own civilian population."[26] An analysis of the available information, however, reveals that the immigration from Türkiye to the Turkish Cyprus has never been in the way of indirectly transferring population. The immigrants who emigrate from Türkiye to Turkish Cyprus do so on their own initiative in the search of a better future there, and they do not receive privileges or special treatment from Türkiye for emigrating. Given that there is no systematic state policy to compel or induce a population movement to the Turkish Cyprus, the immigration from Türkiye to the island could not be considered as "transfer of population," even if Türkiye was an "occupying power."

The limited subject matter jurisdiction of the ICC aside, an ICC investigation into the alleged acts committed in Cyprus would be inadmissible before the ICC due to the limited temporal jurisdiction of the Court, which cannot prosecute acts that took place prior to 1 July 2002.[27] A comprehensive study published by the Peace Research Institute Oslo (PRIO) in 2007 revealed that most of the migration of Turkish nationals to the Turkish Cyprus occurred in 1970s – outside the time period over which the ICC could possibly act.[28] The number of immigrants dropped significantly in the following decades.[29] The Greek Cypriots Group who filed a communication with the ICC Prosecutor cited this report for some of the figures it provided. In the highly unlikely event that the Prosecutor initiates a preliminary examination into the situation in Cyprus based on the information provided in this communication, the statistical information given in the report of the PRIO would be enough to prevent any further action. The unavailability of high-ranking officials from the relevant period, coupled with the near impossibility of accessing credible evidence and witnesses, constitutes an additional basis for the OTP to regard such applications as lacking in merit.

4. Acts with Continuous Nature

The ECtHR held in *Loizidou v. Turkey* that Türkiye has continuingly violated property rights of Loizidou, a Greek Cypriot, by refusing her access to the

---

to annexation of the Island by Greece and brought security and hope, after eleven years, to the Turkish Cypriots." For more information on the legal aspects of the 1974 intervention, *see* Republic of Türkiye Ministry of Foreign Affairs, *Cyprus*, www.mfa.gov.tr/the-cyprus-issue-overview.en.mfa (accessed 1 January 2024).

26 Rome Statute, *supra* note 18, art. 8(b)(viii).

27 Rome Statute, *supra* note 18, art. 11.

28 Mete Hatay, *Is the Turkish Cypriot Population Shrinking?* (Prio Cyprus Centre 2007) 3.

29 Hatay, *supra* note 28.

property that she abandoned in Northern Cyprus.[30] The ECtHR found that because Türkiye exercises effective control over Northern Cyprus, its obligations under the ECHR extend there since 22 January 1990, the date on which Türkiye recognized ECHR jurisdiction.[31] The *Loizidou* decision has arguably increased the Turkish concerns that some of the acts Türkiye carried out in Cyprus before 2002 could be considered as having continuing nature and, therefore, could be subject to an ICC investigation.

In *Demopoulos and Others v. Turkey*, the ECtHR held that the Immovable Property Commission (IPC), which was created by the Turkish Republic of Northern Cyprus and allowed Greek Cypriots to seek relief for the violation of their property rights, was an "adequate and effective domestic remedy."[32] As a result, applicants can apply to the ECtHR for review only after applying to the IPC and satisfying the ECHR's requirement of exhaustion of local remedies.

The Rome Statute is "undecided" on whether to prosecute continuing crimes, and "it will be for the Court to determine how it should be handled."[33] If the OTP considers that a crime within the jurisdiction of the Court is committed prior to 1 July 2002 but maintained after that date, it will take into account other considerations to determine whether to proceed with an investigation. Cyprus is not a case the Prosecutor would be eager to take on because of the politically sensitive nature of the situation, the risk of obstructing the peace talks and the remedies that the Turkish Republic of Northern Cyprus provided to those who cannot access their properties in Northern Cyprus.

Given the already existing remedies and effective role of the ECtHR in protecting human rights and freedoms of Cypriots, it is highly unlikely that the ICC would be interested in initiating a preliminary examination into the acts that could be considered as having continuing nature. Furthermore, alleged continuing acts in question are far less grave than the crimes committed in the situations currently under ICC investigation, which involve "thousands of willful killings as well as intentional and large-scale sexual violence and abductions."[34] This makes the situation in Cyprus even less attractive for the ICC, whose jurisdiction is limited to "the most serious crimes of concern to the international community as a whole."[35]

Migration activities and the alleged violations of the property rights of the Greek Cypriots in the northern portion of the island have been the most

30 Borders, *supra* note 3, at 725.

31 Borders, *supra* note 3, at 726.

32 Borders, *supra* note 3, at 738.

33 William A. Schabas, *An Introduction to the International Criminal Court* (Cambridge University Press 2011) 75.

34 International Criminal Court, *Prosecutor v. Charles Ble Goude, Prosecution's Response to the Defence Application Pursuant to Articles 19(4) and 17(1)(d) of the Rome Statute,* Case No. ICC-02/11-02/11-181, para. 30, http://www.icc-cpi.int/iccdocs/doc/doc1853270.pdf (accessed 20 October 2014).

35 Rome Statute, *supra* note 18, art. 5(1).

debated issues related to the possibility of the Cyprus question being brought before the ICC as crimes with continuous nature. Some may claim that another Turkish concern regarding the Cyprus question could be the possibility of the 1974 military intervention itself being classified as a continuing crime of aggression. This possibility, however, could not be a concern for Türkiye not only because of Türkiye's legal justifications for its intervention (mentioned earlier) but also because, as will be elaborated in the following chapter, even as a State Party to the Rome Statute, Türkiye would not be bound by the jurisdiction of the Court over the crime of aggression as long as it does not ratify the Kampala Amendments.

5. Conclusion

This chapter has argued that Türkiye's accession to the Rome Statute is not very likely to impact the possibility of the Cyprus issue being brought before the ICC. The Republic of Cyprus, which is recognized by the international community as the legitimate government of the entire island, is already party to the Rome Statute, and thus, it can already attempt to refer the situation in Cyprus to the ICC regardless of whether Türkiye is a State Party. In other words, even if Türkiye remains a non-party, the Court could still determine that it has territorial jurisdiction over Türkiye's activities in the northern part of Cyprus due to the Republic of Cyprus's status as a State Party.

Given the limited subject matter and temporal jurisdiction of the ICC, safeguards of the Rome Statute, the caution of the OTP in selecting cases and the political reality that makes an ICC investigation into the situation in Cyprus almost infeasible, the ICC Prosecutor is highly unlikely to be interested in initiating an investigation into the situation there. In the highly unlikely event that, following Türkiye's accession, a preliminary examination into Cyprus is initiated by the Prosecutor *proprio motu* or the situation is referred to the Court by the Greek Cyprus (after 13 years of being a State Party) or any other State Party, the high threshold criteria set out in the Rome Statute would prevent the OTP from pursuing charges against the nationals of Türkiye. It is in Türkiye's interest to accede to the Rome Statute and influence the Court as an insider. The Greek Cyprus has so far done this pretty well, for example, by using the Court as a platform to impact the international community's perception of the Cyprus question on its behalf or by having its former Supreme Court President elected as one of the Court's judges for a six-year term between 2003 and 2009.[36]

36 International Criminal Court, *Judge Georghios M. Pikis (Cyprus), Judge Pikis Was Elected for a Six-Year Term from the Asian Group of States (Asian States)*, www.icc-cpi.int/en_menus/icc/structure%20of%20the%20court/chambers/the%20judges/Pages/judge%20georghios%20pikis.aspx (accessed 1 January 2024).

If Türkiye, despite the discussions made in this chapter, still believes that acceding to the Rome Statute could weaken its hand against the threat of an ICC investigation, it could, upon ratification of the Rome Statute, opt out of the Court's jurisdiction over war crimes for a period of seven years, as stipulated in Article 124 of the Statute. This would provide the parties to the Cyprus question with even more time to reach a peaceful settlement on the island. Instead of focusing on the nightmare-case scenarios that are highly unlikely to come true due to the high threshold criteria set out in the Rome Statute, Türkiye should discover the benefits of joining the ICC and realize the costs of remaining a non-party, both of which will be elaborated ahead.[37]

Bibliography

BBC, Cyprus Reunification Talks to Resume, *BBC*, www.bbc.com/news/world-europe-26093114 (accessed 2 February 2014).

Borders, Jenna C., Another Door Closed: Resort to the European Court of Human Rights for Relief from the Turkish Invasion of 1974 May No Longer Be Possible for Greek Cypriots, 36 *North Carolina Journal of International Law and Commercial Regulation* 689, 692 (2011).

Daloglu, Tulin, *Why Turkey May Not Want to Join the ICC*, www.al-monitor.com/pulse/tr/originals/2014/09/turkey-icc-rome-statue-human-rights.html (accessed 5 September 2014).

Ehrlich, Thomas, Cyprus, the "Warlike Isle": Origins and Elements of the Current Crisis, 18 *Stanford Law Review* 1021, 1025 (1966).

EurActiv, *US and Turkey Upbeat About Cyprus Reunification*, www.euractiv.com/sections/global-europe/us-and-turkey-upbeat-about-cyprus-reunification-313983 (accessed 22 April 2015).

European Commission, *Press Release – Cyprus Steering Group: Commission Enhances Support to the Cyprus Settlement Process*, http://europa.eu/rapid/press-release_IP-14-336_en.htm (accessed 27 March 2014).

Hatay, Mete, *Is the Turkish Cypriot Population Shrinking?* (Prio Cyprus Centre 2007).

International Criminal Court, *Judge Georghios M. Pikis (Cyprus), Judge Pikis Was Elected for a Six-Year Term from the Asian Group of States (Asian States)*, www.icc-cpi.int/en_menus/icc/structure%20of%20the%20court/chambers/the%20judges/Pages/judge%20georghios%20pikis.aspx.

International Criminal Court, *Office of the Prosecutor, Report on Preliminary Examination Activities 2012*, http://www.icc-cpi.int/NR/rdonlyres/C433C462-7C4E-4358-8A72-8D99FD00E8CD/285209/OTP2012ReportonPreliminaryExaminations22Nov2012.pdf (accessed 22 November 2012).

International Criminal Court, *Prosecutor v. Charles Ble Goude, Case No. ICC-02/11-02/11-181, Prosecution's Response to the Defence Application Pursuant to Articles 19(4) and 17(1)(d) of the Rome Statute*, http://www.icc-cpi.int/iccdocs/doc/doc1853270.pdf (accessed 20 October 2014).

Marong, Alhagi, Unlocking the Mysteriousness of Complementarity: In Search of a Forum Conveniens for Trial of the Leaders of the Lord's Resistance Army, 40 *Georgia Journal of International and Comparative Law* 67, 73 (2011).

Matson, Laura, Competing Land Rights, Legal Redress, and Political Settlement in Cyprus, 31 *Law & Inequality* 199 (2012).

37 *See infra* Chapter 8.

Meier, Benjamin M., Reunification of Cyprus: The Possibility of Peace in the Wake of Past Failure, 34 *Cornell International Law Journal* 455, 459 (2001).

Paakkinen, Reeta, *Migration Row Has Two Sides, Turkish Cypriots Say*, http://www.hurriyetdailynews.com/default.aspx?pageid=438&n=migration-row-has-two-sides-turkish-cypriots-say-2009-08-03 (accessed 3 August 2009).

Republic of Türkiye Ministry of Foreign Affairs, *Cyprus*, www.mfa.gov.tr/the-cyprus-issue-overview.en.mfa.

Rome Statute of the International Criminal Court (17 July 1998), U.N. Doc. A/CONF.183/9.

Schabas, William A., *The International Criminal Court: A Commentary on the Rome Statute* (Oxford University Press 2010), 285.

Schabas, William A., *An Introduction to the International Criminal Court* (Cambridge University Press 2011), 75.

United Nations Security Council Resolution 541, *U.N. Doc. S/RES/541*, https://digitallibrary.un.org/record/58970?v=pdf (accessed 18 November 1983).

Wippman, David, International Law and Ethnic Conflict on Cyprus, 31 *Texas International Law Journal* 141, 144 (1996).

7 Concerns Regarding the Crime of Aggression

During the Rome negotiations, inclusion of the crime of aggression in the Rome Statute was a matter of dispute due to issues such as the difficulty of reaching a consensus on a generally acceptable definition of the crime or on the role envisaged for the United Nations Security Council. Nevertheless, there was a widespread desire to extend the ICC's jurisdiction to the crime of aggression. At the end of the Rome Conference, the crime of aggression was included within the list of punishable offenses, but no agreement was reached as to its definition and jurisdictional conditions due to the highly contentious nature of the crime.[1] While the definition and jurisdictional conditions of the crime of aggression were finally adopted at the Kampala Review Conference in June 2010, the jurisdiction of the ICC over this crime was activated by the Assembly of States Parties through a resolution adopted by consensus in New York in December 2017.[2] The New York resolution not only activated the jurisdiction of the ICC over the crime of aggression but also settled some disputes over who could be subject to the Court's jurisdiction when triggered by a State Party referral or the Prosecutor acting *proprio motu*. The resolution confirmed that, in the case of a State Party referral or *proprio motu* investigation, the ICC would not have the authority to prosecute a crime of aggression if the state of the nationality of the accused or the territorial state had not ratified the Kampala Amendments.

This chapter will draw attention to the narrow applicability of the ICC's jurisdiction over the crime of aggression, explore the implications for new and non-State Parties and conclude that the jurisdiction of the Court over this crime should not dissuade Türkiye from considering accession to the Rome Statute. It will explain that, absent a Security Council referral, the ICC may exercise jurisdiction over the crime of aggression only if it is committed on the

1 Johan D. van der Vyver, Prosecuting the Crime of Aggression in the International Criminal Court, 1 *University of Miami National Security & Armed Conflict Law Review* 1 (2011).

2 Assembly of States Parties, *Resolution on the Activation of the Jurisdiction of the Court over the Crime of Aggression*, art. 2, Doc. ICC-ASP/16/Res.5 (14 December 2017), https://asp.icccpi.int/iccdocs/asp_docs/Resolutions/ASP16/ICC-ASP-16-Res5-ENG.pdf (accessed 1 January 2024) [hereinafter New York Resolution].

DOI: 10.4324/9781003641643-7

territory "and" by the nationals of a State Party that has accepted the Kampala Amendments. The chapter will show that the states' concerns regarding the ICC's jurisdiction over the crime of aggression are less meaningful given that even the States Parties are afforded the right to opt out of the jurisdiction of the Court over this crime.

This chapter will also explain that the states that join the ICC after the adoption or the entry into force of the Kampala Amendments will not be regarded as having ratified these amendments and thus will not be bound by them. The chapter will conclude that Türkiye's accession to the Rome Statute would not impact the possibility of it being exposed to the jurisdiction of the ICC in respect of an act of aggression as long as Türkiye does not opt in to the aggression amendments and thus that Türkiye's possible fears that its nationals could face accusations of the crime of aggression should not hinder its consideration of accession to the Rome Statute.

1. Debates in Rome

Most of the delegations present at the Rome Conference expressed their support for the inclusion of the crime of aggression on condition that a clear and generally accepted definition adopted and the role of Security Council is respected.[3] Drawing attention to the responsibility of the Security Council for maintaining international peace and security, some states, such as Japan[4] and Macedonia,[5] even suggested that a prior determination of an act of aggression by the Security Council should be a condition for initiating a formal investigation.

Some states, such as Cuba, rightly warned that the ICC's ability to prosecute the crime of aggression should not be subordinate to the role of the Security Council.[6] Some states, such as Korea, which might have expected that the ICC's jurisdiction over the crime of aggression could protect them from the acts of aggression, went further and suggested that the ICC "must" have automatic jurisdiction over the crime.[7]

In Rome, there were also states that expressly opposed the inclusion of the crime of aggression in the Rome Statute. The USA,[8] Israel[9] or Morocco,[10] for

3 See, e.g., statements made by the representatives of Sweden, at Official Records of the United Nations Diplomatic Conference of Plenipotentiaries on the Establishment of an International Criminal Court, *Official Records Volume II, A/CONF.183/13* (15 June–17 July 1998), at 68, para. 60 [hereinafter Official Records of the Rome Conference].
4 Official Records of the Rome Conference, *supra* note 3, at 67, para. 45.
5 Official Records of the Rome Conference, *supra* note 3, at 86, para. 45.
6 Official Records of the Rome Conference, *supra* note 3, at 93, para. 36.
7 Official Records of the Rome Conference, *supra* note 3, at 69, para. 82.
8 Official Records of the Rome Conference, *supra* note 3, at 95, para. 61.
9 Official Records of the Rome Conference, *supra* note 3, at 99, para. 41.
10 Official Records of the Rome Conference, *supra* note 3, at 103, para. 106.

example, opined that it was "premature" to add the crime to the list of punishable offenses of the Rome Statute. While the United States delegation found it "premature" "to attempt to define a crime of aggression in terms of individual criminal responsibility,"[11] Israeli delegation "was not persuaded that conditions were yet ripe for the inclusion of the crime of aggression in the Statute of the Court."[12] Israeli delegation also asserted that it feared the possibility of the manipulation of the Court for political ends.[13] As is seen, reservations and concerns voiced during the Rome negotiations concerning the ICC's jurisdiction over the crime of aggression varied from state to state. These concerns and reservations can be summarized as follows:

- The lack of a clear and generally acceptable definition of the crime of aggression and the difficulty of reaching a consensus on such a definition;
- The difficulty of reaching a consensus on the role to be afforded to the Court in determining the existence of an act of aggression at the expense of the Security Council's role;
- The difficulty of translating the crime of aggression, which is essentially a state act, into an individual criminal liability; and
- The lack of consensus on the Court's jurisdiction over the aggressors who are nationals of the states that are not State Parties or have not accepted the amendments on aggression.

Türkiye, too, was among states that voiced reservations regarding the ICC's jurisdiction over the crime of aggression. The representatives of Türkiye in Rome (and Kampala) expressed their concerns about the difficulty of translating the crime of aggression into individual criminal liability,[14] the role to be granted to the ICC in determining the existence of an act of aggression[15] and the situation of the aggressors who are the nationals of the states that have not accepted the amendments on aggression.[16]

Among the concerns noted earlier, the issues of achieving a consensus regarding a generally acceptable definition and the jurisdiction conditions, in particular, provoked heated debates. At the end of the conference, the crime of aggression was included within the list of punishable offenses of the Rome Statute, but no agreement was reached as to its definition and jurisdictional

11 Official Records of the Rome Conference, *supra* note 3, at 95, para. 61.

12 Official Records of the Rome Conference, *supra* note 3, at 99, para. 41.

13 Official Records of the Rome Conference, *supra* note 3.

14 Mr. Güney stated during the Rome negotiations that "it was difficult to see how an act imputable to a State could become imputable to an individual." *See* Official Records of the Rome Conference, *supra* note 3, at 179, para. 143.

15 International Criminal Court, *Statement by Mr. Ismail Aramaz Head of Turkish Delegation*, http://www.icc-cpi.int/iccdocs/asp_docs/RC2010/Statements/ICC-RC-gendeba-Turkey-ENG.pdf (accessed 10 June 2010) [hereinafter Statement by Mr. Ismail Aramaz].

16 Statement by Mr. Ismail Aramaz, *supra* note 15.

conditions. Instead, a Preparatory Commission was set up in the closing plenary session of the Conference to draft proposals regarding the crime to be considered at a future Review Conference.[17]

2. Kampala Amendments: Definition and Jurisdictional Conditions of the Crime of Aggression

The definition of the crime of aggression and the conditions under which the ICC could exercise jurisdiction over that crime were adopted at the Kampala Review Conference that took place on 11 June 2010.[18] Accordingly, the crime of aggression has been described as follows:

> the planning, preparation, initiation or execution, by a person in a position effectively to exercise control over or to direct the political or military action of a State, of an act of aggression, which, by its character, gravity and scale, constitutes a manifest violation of the Charter of the United Nations.[19]

An act of aggression, on the other hand, has been defined as "the use of armed force by a State against the sovereignty, territorial integrity or political independence of another State, or in any other manner inconsistent with the Charter of the United Nations."[20] Given that the definition adopted at the Kampala Review Conference requires the act of aggression in question to, "by its character, gravity and scale, constitute a manifest violation of the Charter of the United Nations,"[21] an investigation is not likely to lead to charges unless the act in question is a manifestly "serious and dangerous" unlawful use of force.[22]

It was agreed at the Kampala Review Conference that the ICC would have jurisdiction over the crime of aggression referred to it by the Security Council irrespective of whether the aggressor or the victim state is a State Party (just like the jurisdictional regime for the other core crimes of the Rome Statute).[23] However, in the case of an investigation triggered by a State Party referral or by the Prosecutor acting *proprio motu*, unlike the jurisdictional regime for the other core crimes of the Rome Statute, commission of the crime of aggression on the territory or by the national of a state party is not enough for the ICC

17 Vyver, *supra* note 1, at 5.
18 Vyver, *supra* note 1, at 1.
19 United Nations Treaty Collection, *Rome Statute of the International Criminal Court*, U.N. Doc. A/CONF.183/9 (17 July 1998), art. 8 bis (1).
20 United Nations Treaty Collection, *supra* note 19, art. 8 bis (2).
21 Jennifer Trahan, A Meaningful Definition of the Crime of Aggression: A Response to Michael Glennon, 33 *University of Pennsylvania Journal of International Law* 907, 936 (2012).
22 Vyver, *supra* note 1, at 25.
23 Rome Statute, *supra* note 19, art. 15 ter.

to exercise its jurisdiction: both the territorial and the suspect's states must be States Parties,[24] and they both must have ratified the Kampala Amendments.[25]

In other words, in contrast to the other three core crimes in the Rome Statute, the ICC will not have jurisdiction, absent a Security Council referral, over the crime of aggression committed by the nationals of a State Party a) if that state has not ratified the Kampala Amendments or b) if the state on whose territory the crime has been committed has not ratified the Kampala Amendments. These preconditions are consistent with Türkiye's own emphasis that "the Court should not exercise its jurisdiction concerning the crime of aggression if the alleged aggressor has not accepted the amendment or is not a State Party to the Rome Statute."[26] The requirement that both the territorial state and the state of the nationality of the accused must have ratified the Kampala Amendments serves to satisfy the Article 121(5) of the Rome Statute, which provides that "the Court shall not exercise its jurisdiction regarding a crime covered by" "[a]ny amendment to articles 5, 6, 7 and 8 of this Statute" when committed by the nationals or on the territory of "a State Party which has not accepted the amendment."[27]

Kampala Amendments have also provided the States Parties with the right to formally decline to accept the ICC's jurisdiction over the crime of aggression by lodging an opt-out declaration with the Registrar of the ICC.[28] A State Party, which still fears that an ICC investigation accusing its nationals of a crime of aggression is likely, despite the absence of a Security Council referral, could avoid this fear simply by lodging an opt-out declaration with the Registrar of the ICC. Similarly, a State Party that categorically objects the ICC's jurisdiction over the crime of aggression could simply lodge an opt-out declaration, instead of remaining a non-party or assuming hostile attitude towards the Court.

With regard to the determination of the existence of aggression, on the other hand, the provisions adopted by the Kampala amendments require the Prosecutor, before proceeding with an investigation, to "ascertain whether the Security Council has made a determination of an act of aggression."[29] If the Security Council determines that the act in question constitutes an act of aggression, the Prosecutor can proceed with an investigation.[30] If the Security Council does not make such a determination within the following six months, the Prosecutor can still launch an investigation provided that the Pre-Trial Chamber grants an authorization to do so.[31] This is, in fact, contrary

24 Rome Statute, *supra* note 19, art. 15 bis (5).
25 Rome Statute, *supra* note 19, art. 121(5).
26 Statement by Mr. Ismail Aramaz, *supra* note 15.
27 Rome Statute, *supra* note 19, art. 121(5).
28 Rome Statute, *supra* note 19, art. 15 bis (4).
29 Vyver, *supra* note 1, at 34.
30 Vyver, *supra* note 1.
31 Vyver, *supra* note 1.

to the expectations of the representatives of Türkiye, who had felt that "an investigation into an alleged case of aggression should only be initiated where the UN Security Council has determined that an act of aggression has taken place."[32]

3. The New York Resolution: Activation of the Crime of Aggression

It was agreed that the ICC's jurisdiction over the crime of aggression would be activated following ratification of the Kampala Amendments by no less than 30 States Parties[33] and subject to a decision to be taken after January 2017 by a two-thirds majority of the ASP.[34] The 30th state deposited its instrument of ratification of the Kampala Amendments in June 2016,[35] and the decision to activate the ICC's jurisdiction over the crime of aggression was made through an ASP resolution, which was adopted in New York on 14 December 2017.[36] The New York Resolution, which was adopted by consensus, activated the "Court's jurisdiction over the crime of aggression as of 17 July 2018."[37]

Before the adoption of the New York Resolution by the ASP, there was a dispute regarding the exercise of the jurisdiction of the Court over the crime of aggression when it was committed on the territory of a State Party that had ratified the Kampala Amendments but by nationals of a State Party that had not ratified the amendments.[38] According to one of the two conflicting views, the ICC would not have jurisdiction over an act of aggression when the state of the nationality of the accused "or" the state where the act was committed were States Parties that have not ratified the Kampala amendments. This view

32 Statement by Mr. Ismail Aramaz, *supra* note 15.

33 Rome Statute, *supra* note. 19, art. 15 bis (2), 15 ter (2).

34 Rome Statute, *supra* note. 19, art. 15 bis (3), 15 ter (3).

35 Denmark became the 47th State to ratify the Kampala Amendments on the crime of aggression. See Global Institute for the Prevention of Aggression, The Global Campaign for Ratification and Implementation of the Kampala Amendments on the Crime of Aggression, *News*, https://crimeofaggression.info. As of today, 47 states have ratified the amendments. These are, respectively, Liechtenstein, Samoa, Trinidad and Tobago, Luxembourg, Estonia, Germany, Botswana, Slovenia, Cyprus, Uruguay, Andorra, Belgium, Slovakia, Croatia, Austria, Poland, Spain, Latvia, San Marino, Georgia, Malta, Costa Rica, Czech Republic, Switzerland, Lithuania, Finland, Macedonia, El Salvador, Iceland, the State of Palestine, The Netherlands, Chile, Portugal, Argentina, Panama, Ireland, Guyana, Paraguay, Ecuador, Bolivia, Mongolia, Italy, Sweden, Peru, Niger, Ukraine and Denmark. See United Nations Treaty Collection, *Amendments on the crime of aggression to the Rome Statute of the International Criminal Court*, https://treaties.un.org/Pages/ViewDetails.aspx?src=TREATY&mtdsg_no=XVIII-10-b&chapter=18&clang=_en#1 (accessed 11 June 2010).

36 New York Resolution, *supra* note 2.

37 New York Resolution, *supra* note 2, art. 1.

38 Dapo Akande and Antonios Tzanakopoulos, Treaty Law and ICC Jurisdiction over the Crime of Aggression, 29 *European Journal of International Law* 941 (2018).

was referred to as "narrow view"[39] and was based on Article 121(5) of the Rome Statute, which provides that "the Court shall not exercise its jurisdiction regarding a crime covered by" "[a]ny amendment to articles 5, 6, 7 and 8 of this Statute" when committed by the nationals or on the territory of "a State Party which has not accepted the amendment."[40]

The other view, however, claimed that when the territorial state is a state party that has ratified the Kampala amendments, the ICC could exercise its jurisdiction irrespective of whether the state of the nationality of the accused has ratified the Kampala amendments, provided that the latter has not previously opted out of the Court's jurisdiction over the crime of aggression. According to this view, states that wish to rule out the possibility of their nationals being brought before the ICC for the crime of aggression, absent a Security Council referral, need to opt out of the Court's jurisdiction over that crime. This view was referred to as "broad view"[41] and was based on Article 12(2) of the Rome Statute, which provides the Court with the jurisdiction over the crimes committed on the territory of a state party, even if the state of the nationality of the accused is a non-party.[42]

New York Resolution, however, rightly confirmed the narrow view and made it clear:

> in the case of a State referral or *proprio motu* investigation the Court shall not exercise its jurisdiction regarding a crime of aggression when committed by a national or on the territory of a State Party that has not ratified or accepted these amendments.[43]

Though the Prosecutor and the judges of the ICC are not bound to adhere to the decisions of the ASP, they are very likely to take the same stand on this issue because the view confirmed by the ASP is line with the Article 121(5) of the Rome Statute, which states that "[i]n respect of a State Party which has not accepted the amendment, the Court shall not exercise its jurisdiction regarding a crime covered by the amendment when committed by that State Party's nationals or on its territory."[44] In any event, a State Party, which fears that an ICC investigation accusing its nationals of a crime of aggression is probable despite the absence of a Security Council referral, could avoid this fear simply by lodging an opt-out declaration with the Registrar of the ICC.[45]

39 Akande and Tzanakopoulos, *supra* note 38.
40 Rome Statute, *supra* note. 19, art. 121(5).
41 Akande and Tzanakopoulos, *supra* note 38, at 941.
42 Rome Statute, *supra* note. 19, art. 12(2).
43 New York Resolution, *supra* note 2, art. 2.
44 Rome Statute, *supra* note. 19, art. 121(5).
45 The Republic of Kenya became the first State Party to do so in November 2015. See International Criminal Court, *Declaration of Non Acceptance of Jurisdiction of the International Criminal Court Pertaining to the Crime of Aggression Pursuant to Paragraph*

4. The Status of the States that Join the ICC after the Adoption of the Kampala Amendments

The question remains, nevertheless, whether the states that ratify the Rome Statute after the adoption and the entry into force of the Kampala Amendments could thereby be regarded as having ratified the amendments. One might, at first, expect that new states must be regarded as having ratified the amended/latest version of the Rome Statute unless they express a different intention,[46] in accordance with Article 40 (5) of the Vienna Convention on the Law of Treaties (Vienna Convention), which states that "[a]ny State which becomes a party to the treaty after the entry into force of the amending agreement shall, failing an expression of a different intention by that State, . . . be considered as a party to the treaty as amended."[47]

Alas, this is not the case here. As evidenced by the records of U.N. Treaty Collection, states that joined the ICC after the adoption of the Kampala Amendments have not been recognized as having ratified the Kampala Amendments despite their failure to express not to be bound by the amendments. Among 15 states that ratified the Rome Statute since the adoption of the Kampala Amendments,[48] only two states (Palestine and El Salvador) have been declared to be bound by the amendments on the crime aggression (as they deposited their instrument of ratification of the amendments).[49] The State of Palestine, for example, joined the ICC in January 2015[50] but ratified the Kampala Amendments in June 2016.[51] El Salvador, on the other hand, became the first country to ratify the Rome Statute and the Kampala

4 of Article 15bis of the Rome Statute (30 November 2015), www.icc-cpi.int/iccdocs/other/2015_NV_Kenya_Declaration_article15bis-4.pdf (accessed 1 January 2024).

46 *See*, e.g., Andreas Zimmermann, Does 19 + 11 Equal 30? The Nitty Gritty of the Law of Treaties and the Kampala Amendment to the Rome Statute on the Crime of Aggression, *EJIL: Talk!*, www.ejiltalk.org/does-19-11-equal-30-the-nitty-gritty-of-the-law-of-treaties-and-the-kampala-amendment-to-the-rome-statute-on-the-crime-of-aggression/ (accessed 27 November 2014).

47 Vienna Convention on the Law of Treaties, U.N. Doc. A/CONF.39/27, 1155 U.N.T.S. 331, 8 I.L.M. 679, opened for signature 23 May 1969, entered into force on 27 January 1980, art. 40(5).

48 These are respectively Seychelles (2010), St. Lucia (2010), Moldova (2010), Grenada (2011), Tunisia (2011), Philippines (2011), Maldives (2011), Cabo Verde (2011), Vanuatu (2011), Côte d'Ivoire (2013), Guatemala (2012), State of Palestine (2015), El Salvador (2016), Kiribati (2019) and Armenia (2023). See United Nations Treaty Collection, *Rome Statute of the International Criminal Court*, https://treaties.un.org/Pages/ViewDetails.aspx?src=TREATY&mtdsg_no=XVIII-10&chapter=18&clang=_en (accessed 17 July 1998).

49 *Amendments on the Crime of Aggression to the Rome Statute of the International Criminal Court*, *supra* note 35.

50 *Rome Statute of the International Criminal Court*, *supra* note 48.

51 *Amendments on the Crime of Aggression to the Rome Statute of the International Criminal Court*, *supra* note 35.

Amendments simultaneously.[52] Kiribati and Armenia, the states that joined the ICC after the Kampala Amendments came into effect, likewise have not been recognized as having ratified the amendments despite their failure to express their intention not to be bound by the amendments.[53]

The reason behind this deviation from the principle established by Article 40(5) of the Vienna Convention may be the categorical language of Article 121(5) of the Rome Statute which dictates that "[i]n respect of a State Party which has not accepted the amendment, the Court shall not exercise its jurisdiction regarding a crime covered by the amendment when committed by that State Party's nationals or on its territory."[54] In other words, the deviation from Article 40(5) of the Vienna Convention may well be explained by the fact that, unlike the amendments which fall under Article 121(4) of the Rome Statute and bind all States Parties, the Kampala Amendments on the crime of aggression fall under Article 121(5) of the Rome Statute and bind only "those States Parties which have accepted" them.[55]

5. Conclusion

Reservations and concerns regarding the ICC's jurisdiction over the crime of aggression varied from state to state. While some states such as China and the U.S. were more concerned about "the challenge the court poses to the Security Council's primacy over peace and security issues,"[56] Türkiye feared that "some of the drafting alternatives on this issue may, if adopted, lead to the politicization of the Court."[57]

Despite all these concerns and objections, the ICC's jurisdiction over the crime of aggression is now a reality. While the main issues surrounding the ICC's jurisdiction over the crime of aggression, such as the definition and jurisdictional conditions of the crime, were resolved by the Kampala Amendments, the activation of that jurisdiction was achieved by the New York Resolution. The New York resolution has also settled some disputes over who could be subject to the jurisdiction of the ICC when triggered by a State Party referral or the Prosecutor acting *proprio motu*. The resolution made it clear that, absent a Security Council referral, the ICC may exercise jurisdiction over

52 Global Institute for the Prevention of Aggression, The Global Campaign for Ratification and Implementation of the Kampala Amendments on the Crime of Aggression, *El Salvador Ratifies Amended Version of the Rome Statute*, https://crimeofaggression.info/page/3/ (accessed 3 March 2016).

53 Kiribati and Armenia joined the ICC in November 2019 and November 2023, respectively. *Rome Statute of the International Criminal Court, supra* note 48, https://treaties.un.org/pages/ViewDetails.aspx?src=TREATY&mtdsg_no=XVIII-10&chapter=18&lang=en#13.

54 Rome Statute, *supra* note 19, art. 121(5).

55 Rome Statute, *supra* note 19.

56 Allison Marston Danner, Navigating Law and Politics: The Prosecutor of the International Criminal Court and the Independent Counsel, 55 *Stanford Law Review* 1633, 1635 (2003).

57 Statement by Mr. İsmail Aramaz, *supra* note 15.

the crime of aggression only if it is committed on the territory "and" by the nationals of a State Party that has accepted the Kampala Amendments.

This chapter has shown that the states' concerns regarding the ICC's jurisdiction over the crime of aggression are less meaningful given that even the States Parties are afforded the right to opt out of the jurisdiction of the Court over this aggression. This chapter has also shown that, as evidenced by the practice of the U.N. Office of Legal Affairs, the states that join the ICC after the adoption or the entry into force of the Kampala Amendments are not regarded as having ratified these amendments and thus are not automatically bound by them.

Türkiye's reservations over the crime of aggression presumably spring from the concerns that its occasional military operations against the PKK camps in northern Iraq in pursuit of PKK members or that its continuing military presence in Cyprus would come under the judicial scrutiny of the ICC. Given the narrow applicability of the crime of aggression, which allows States Parties to decline to accept the jurisdiction of the Court over that crime, however, such concerns should not be considered as an obstacle to Türkiye's consideration of accession to the Rome Statute. Türkiye could, as a State Party, avert the possibility of its nationals being subject to the jurisdiction of the Court with respect to an alleged act of aggression simply by not ratifying the Kampala Amendments or by lodging an opt-out declaration, absent a Security Council referral.

Even in the case of a Security Council referral, which is the only way a state could be subject to the ICC's aggression jurisdiction absent its consent, an investigation is not likely to lead to charges unless the act in question is a manifest violation of the Charter of the United Nations"[58] and a manifestly "serious and dangerous" unlawful use of force.[59] In any event, because a Security Council referral of a situation would provide the ICC with the competence to prosecute even the nationals of non-State Parties, Türkiye's accession to the Rome Statute would not impact the possibility of it being exposed to the jurisdiction of the Court in respect of an act of aggression as long as it does not opt in to the aggression amendments. Of course, the acceptance of the Kampala Amendments by all states is what international community wishes to see, but given that some accession is better than non-accession, the safeguards provided for under the Rome Statute should at least allay genuine concerns of the states that are pondering to join the ICC.

Bibliography

Akande, Dapo and Antonios Tzanakopoulos, Treaty Law and ICC Jurisdiction over the Crime of Aggression, 29 *European Journal of International Law* (2018).

58 Trahan, *supra* note 21, at 936.
59 Vyver, *supra* note 1, at 25.

Danner, Allison Marston, Navigating Law and Politics: The Prosecutor of the International Criminal Court and the Independent Counsel, 55 *Stanford Law Review* 1633, 1635 (2003).

Global Institute for the Prevention of Aggression, The Global Campaign for Ratification and Implementation of the Kampala Amendments on the Crime of Aggression, *El Salvador Ratifies Amended Version of the Rome Statute*, https://crimeofaggression.info/page/3/ (accessed 3 March 2016).

Global Institute for the Prevention of Aggression, The Global Campaign for Ratification and Implementation of the Kampala Amendments on the Crime of Aggression, *News*, https://crimeofaggression.info.

International Criminal Court, *Assembly of States Parties, Resolution on the Activation of the Jurisdiction of the Court over the Crime of Aggression*, art. 2, Doc. ICC-ASP/16/Res.5 https://asp.icccpi.int/iccdocs/asp_docs/Resolutions/ASP16/ICC-ASP-16-Res5-ENG.pdf (accessed 14 December 2017).

International Criminal Court, *Declaration of Non Acceptance of Jurisdiction of the International Criminal Court Pertaining to the Crime of Aggression Pursuant to Paragraph 4 of Article 15bis of the Rome Statute*, www.icc-cpi.int/iccdocs/other/2015_NV_Kenya_Declaration_article15bis-4.pdf (accessed 30 November 2015).

International Criminal Court, *Statement by Mr. Ismail Aramaz Head of Turkish Delegation*, http://www.icc-cpi.int/iccdocs/asp_docs/RC2010/Statements/ICC-RC-gendeba-Turkey-ENG.pdf (accessed 10 June 2010).

Trahan, Jennifer, A Meaningful Definition of the Crime of Aggression: A Response to Michael Glennon, 33 *University of Pennsylvania Journal of International Law* 907, 936 (2012).

United Nations, *Official Records of the U.N. Diplomatic Conference of Plenipotentiaries on the Establishment of an Int'l Criminal Court*, 7th plen. mtg., U.N. Doc. A/CONE 183/SR.7.

United Nations Security Council Resolution 541, U.N. Doc. S/RES/541 (18 November 1983).

United Nations Treaty Collection, *Amendments on the Crime of Aggression to the Rome Statute of the International Criminal Court*, https://treaties.un.org/Pages/ViewDetails.aspx?src=TREATY&mtdsg_no=XVIII-10-b&chapter=18&clang=_en#1 (accessed 11 June 2010).

United Nations Treaty Collection, *Rome Statute of the International Criminal Court*, https://treaties.un.org/Pages/ViewDetails.aspx?src=TREATY&mtdsg_no=XVIII-10&chapter=18&clang=_en (accessed 17 July 1998).

Vienna Convention on the Law of Treaties (23 May 1969), UN Doc. A/Conf.39/27.

Vyver, Johan D. van der, Prosecuting the Crime of Aggression in the International Criminal Court, 1 *University of Miami National Security & Armed Conflict Law Review* 1 (2011).

Zimmermann, Andreas, Does 19 + 11 Equal 30? The Nitty Gritty of the Law of Treaties and the Kampala Amendment to the Rome Statute on the Crime of Aggression, *EJIL: Talk!* www.ejiltalk.org/does-19-11-equal-30-the-nitty-gritty-of-the-law-of-treaties-and-the-kampala-amendment-to-the-rome-statute-on-the-crime-of-aggression/ (accessed 27 November 2014).

8 Benefits

Why Should Türkiye Join the ICC?

All the previous chapters have shown that the exercise of the ICC's jurisdiction over Turkish nationals is highly unlikely and that the concerns presented against Türkiye's accession are not so serious as to justify Türkiye's avoidance of the Court's jurisdiction. This chapter explores some of the compelling benefits for Türkiye to join the Court. These are, first, acquiring the rights that would allow Türkiye to participate in the further shaping of the Court; second, enjoying positive political impacts of being a State Party, such as enhancing its reputation internationally; and third, having a stronger hand in its European Union full-membership negotiations.

1. Being an Influential Insider

The ICC is an independent, treaty-based institution, whose legislative and governing body is the Assembly of States Parties (ASP). Members of the ASP, the states that have ratified the founding treaty of the Court, have the right to participate in the further shaping of the law and procedures and the staffing of this institution. Instead of postponing accession to the Court and passively remaining a non-Party State, Türkiye could become an active participant of the determination process of critical issues simply by joining the Court.

First, every member of the ASP has the right to propose amendments[1] and equally vote on the amendments proposed by the other members.[2] Türkiye, by being a State Party to the Court, could more effectively suggest amendments to the Rome Statute and cast its vote on the proposals in a way to accomplish changes it considers important for the protection of its interests. As a member of the assembly, Türkiye would not only be able to actively participate in the further shaping of the definitions and the elements of the crimes and procedures through casting its vote but it would also have the opportunity to sway other countries as an insider.

1 United Nations Treaty Collection, Rome Statute of the International Criminal Court, U.N. Doc. A/CONF.183/9 (17 July 1998), art. 9(2)(a), 51(2)(a).

2 Rome Statute, *supra* note 1, art. 112(7).

DOI: 10.4324/9781003641643-8

With regard to inclusion of terrorism within the Statute, for example, staying out of the Court does not provide any contribution to the efforts to add terrorism to the list of punishable offenses. As a member of the ASP, Türkiye could propose and vote on behalf of any amendment to include terrorism *per se* as a crime within the jurisdiction of the Court and sway other countries in this direction. Likewise, Türkiye would be able to cast its vote on the final adoption of the Kampala Amendments on the crime of aggression after January 2017. As a State Party, Türkiye could engage the Assembly over critical amendments to the Statute, making it more palatable to itself.

Second, as a State Party, Türkiye would acquire the right to participate in electing and removing the judges and the prosecutor of the Court and put forward its nationals as candidates for these positions. The election of Greek Cypriot judge Georghios Pikis, nominated by the Republic of Cyprus, as a member of the Appeals Chamber is a clear example of how a State Party could benefit from accession to the Court. Likewise, the election of a Turkish national as a judge would grant Türkiye the privilege of providing the Court with the Turkish perspective on the issues, such as Cyprus.

Third, by being a State Party to the Rome Statute, Türkiye would also have the opportunity to create more meaningful communication with the Court and the OTP in particular. Türkiye's closer dialogue with the OTP is of great importance given the primary responsibility of the Office for conducting the preliminary examinations and initiating formal investigations. For example, with regard to the communication that was filed with the Prosecutor requesting her to initiate an investigation *proprio motu* into the settlement activities of Türkiye in Northern Cyprus, Türkiye could more effectively provide the Office with the aforementioned statistical information that would refute most of the claims brought up in the communication.

Furthermore, as a member of the ASP, Türkiye could more effectively bring issues that bother it to the Court's agenda. It could, for example, provide more information to the ASP and the OTP regarding the atrocities occurring on its Iraqi and Syrian borders and use the Court as a platform to show the world how Türkiye bears the greatest burden not only in accommodating hundreds of thousands of refugees fleeing these atrocities each year[3] but also in global counter-terrorism efforts, such as deporting "more than a thousand foreign fighters from almost 75 countries" who were travelling to join the ISIS terrorist organization.[4]

In this regard, Türkiye could strengthen its counter-terrorism dialogue with the members of the ASP against the terrorist groups, such as ISIS. This would

3 UNICEF, *Humanitarian Action for Children – Syrian Refugees*, www.unicef.org/appeals/syrianrefugees.html.

4 Republic of Türkiye Ministry of Foreign Affairs, *Turkey and the USA Co-Chaired the Global Counter-Terrorism Forum in New York*, www.mfa.gov.tr/turkey-and-the-usa-co_chaired-the-global-counter_terrorism-forum-in-new-york-2014.en.mfa (accessed 1 January 2024).

also help Türkiye disprove the speculative allegations that Türkiye neglected its responsibility to fight against the ISIS when it was first formed. *It goes without saying that speculative allegations* are unlikely to be considered by the ICC, as the OTP has made it clear on many occasions that it will not act on the information based on mere "speculation or suspicion."[5]

Lastly, should Türkiye finally ratify the Rome Statute and become an integral member of the ICC, it would acquire the ability to trigger the Prosecutor's preliminary examination actions with respect to the crimes committed by the nationals of other states on its territory or on a vessel and aircraft under its registration. For example, the aforementioned Humanitarian Aid Flotilla incident, which had resulted in the death of ten Turkish activists and serious injuries to more than 50 civilians, was referred to the Court by the Union of the Comoros, a State Party in which one of the vessels was registered.[6] If all the vessels on which the crimes were committed had been registered in Türkiye, the Court's territorial jurisdiction could not have been invoked.

A preliminary examination into the incident was opened in May 2013, but it was only expanded to include conduct occurred on the vessels bearing State Party flags, namely, the Union of the Comoros, Cambodia and Greece. The jurisdiction of the Court did not extend to conduct occurred on the vessels registered in Türkiye because of Türkiye's non-party status. Although the OTP's preliminary examination into the incident, which was concluded in November 2014, did not result in an investigation on the grounds that it was not "of sufficient gravity to justify further action by the Court," it was important in that it enumerated the war crimes believed to be committed against Turkish nationals.[7]

Türkiye's ability to trigger investigations could also have a deterrent effect on the PKK's senior members, their abettors and the states that solicit or fund the crimes of the PKK, as they would fear facing charges before the Court. As detailed in Chapter 2, some acts of the PKK constitute crimes against humanity. As a State Party to the Court, Türkiye could also use its strengthened corporate dialogue with the European members of the ASP to develop closer cooperation in combatting the funding networks of the PKK in European countries.

2. Political Implications

Establishment of the world's first permanent international criminal tribunal has been described as a "great victory" for humanity in the fight against impunity for the gravest crimes.[8] Though Türkiye was an active participant of the

5 International Criminal Court, *Office of the Prosecutor, Report on Preliminary Examination Activities 2014* (2 December 2014), 56, para. 236.
6 International Criminal Court, *supra* note 5, at 59, para. 246.
7 International Criminal Court, *supra* note 5, at 62, para. 262.
8 Hakan Karakehya, International Criminal Court and Turkey, 12(10) *US-China Law Review* (2015) 781.

efforts to create an independent international court that would try the perpetrators of the most serious crimes, its decision in 2004 to shelve the issue of the Rome Statute ratification left its commitment to the pursuit of international criminal justice incomplete. Ratification of the Rome Statute is an opportunity for Türkiye to demonstrate its political will to fight against atrocities and bring the perpetrators of the heinous crimes to justice.

Many believe that Türkiye's influence in its region and popularity in the world has seriously dwindled in the past few years. Indeed, Türkiye's failure on 16 October 2014 to gain a nonpermanent seat at the Security Council supports this view.[9] Despite its intensive lobbying efforts, Türkiye received less than half of the 151 votes it received in its previous successful bid in 2008.[10]

Accession to the Rome Statute, as a demonstration of Türkiye's commitment to further contribute to international peace and the rule of law, could help Türkiye garner greater support from the members of the ASP and the UN General Assembly when contesting prestigious seats. If Türkiye wants to engage more actively in cooperation with international organizations and play a greater role in international relations, it should first show the world that it has confidence in its own national criminal justice system and that it shares the commitment to put an end to impunity for the perpetrators of grave crimes that threaten the peace and security of the world.

Türkiye's accession to the Rome Statute could also motivate its southern and eastern neighbors to consider ratification and thus could significantly contribute to the advancement of the international rule of law in the Middle East. Given the high costs of living in a neighborhood where serious crimes are committed frequently, advancing justice, accountability and the fight against impunity in this region aligns with Türkiye's best interests. The bloody civil war in Syria, which lasted over a decade, or emergence of terrorist groups such as ISIS are examples of how Türkiye pays the price of having unstable neighbors, where the rule of law is not established. Türkiye is not only *concerned about* the large number of refugees flowing into Türkiye but also about small-scale violations of its territorial integrity by these unstable states or groups emerging there.

Syria, for example, hit Türkiye with a mortar bomb on 4 October 2012, killing five Turkish citizens in the southern border town of Akçakale.[11] Syria also shot down a Turkish warplane while it was flying in international airspace

9 Semih Idiz, *UN Vote Confirms Turkey's Waning Influence*, www.al-monitor.com/pulse/originals/2014/10/turkey-united-nations-security-council-vote.html# (accessed 17 October 2014).

10 Harut Sassounian, *Why the UN Rejected Turkey's Bid for a Security Council Seat?* www.huffingtonpost.com/harut-sassounian/why-the-un-rejected-turke_b_6036878.html (Updated 23 December 2014).

11 Matthew Weaver and Brian Whitaker, *Turkey-Syria Border Tension*, http://www.guardian.co.uk/world/2012/oct/04/turkey-syria-threat-security-live (accessed 4 October 2012).

on June 2012.[12] On 11 June 2014, ISIS raided Türkiye's Consulate General in the Iraqi city of Mosul and held 49 Turkish citizens, including Turkish diplomats, as hostage for over three months.[13] These are only some of the most recent prices that Türkiye has paid for living in an environment where the rule of law is not established. Ratifying the Rome Statute would eventually benefit Türkiye by contributing to the restoration of peace and the rule of law in the region, which would also eventually make it easier for Türkiye to develop stronger relations with its neighbors.

3. Stronger European Union Candidacy

Türkiye, an associated member of the European *Union since 1963*, has been knocking on the *Union's* door *for full membership since* 1987.[14] Among all EU members and membership candidates, Türkiye is the only country that has not yet joined the ICC.[15] Türkiye's accession to the founding treaty of the ICC, of which the European Commission and the European Parliament have been strong supporters, would have a very positive impact on the Türkiye-EU full membership negotiations because accession to the Rome Statute is considered "as an essential component of the Union's democratic model and values."[16]

In June 2003, the Council of the European Union adopted its second formal "Common Position" on the ICC, which imposed obligations on the EU members "to support the effective functioning of the Court and to advance universal support for it."[17] The Council also called on the associated members of the Union, including Türkiye, to align with the objective of this Common Position "by promoting the widest possible participation in the Rome Statute."[18]

ICC accession is not one of the criteria for joining the EU (so-called Copenhagen criteria), but it is a common policy adopted by all members of the Union under the "Common Foreign and Security Policy," which is

12 David Blair and Barney Henderson, *Syria Shoots Down Turkish Fighter Jet*, http://www.telegraph.co.uk/news/worldnews/middleeast/syria/9349777/Syria-shoots-down-Turkish-fighter-jet.html (accessed 22 June 2012).

13 Republic of Türkiye Ministry of Foreign Affairs, *No: 196, 11 June 2014, Press Release Regarding the Raid on Our Consulate General in Mosul*, www.mfa.gov.tr/no_-196_-11-june-2014_press-release-regarding-the-raid-on-our-consulate-general-in-mosul.en.mfa (accessed 1 January 2024).

14 Ali Çarkoğlu and Barry M. Rubin, *Turkey and the European Union: Domestic Politics, Economic Integration and International Dynamics* (Frank Cass 2003) 141.

15 Council of Europe: Parlimentary Assembly, *Documents: Working Papers* (Council of Europe 2002) 196.

16 Coalition for the International Criminal Court, *Target Countries – URC-Turkey*, http://www.iccnow.org/?mod=urc1010.

17 Council of the European Union, *Council Common Position 2003/444/CFSP of 16 June 2003 on the International Criminal Court*, art. 1(2), www.consilium.europa.eu/uedocs/cmsUpload/l_15020030618en00670069.pdf (accessed 18 June 2003).

18 Council of the European Union, *supra* note 17.

a mechanism developed by the Union for adopting common guidelines on external policy and security issues. According to this policy, all members of the EU agree that objectives adopted in the Rome Statute are fully in line with those of the Union and that crimes within the jurisdiction of the Court are also of concern for the members of the Union. In this regard, Türkiye's Rome Statute ratification would go a long way in proving that Türkiye shares the commitment of the Union to justice and the prevention of serious crimes.

The EU addresses the accession to the Rome Statute as an improvement in the area of human rights.[19] Although the European Commission commended, in its 2014 Progress Report, on Türkiye's implementation of reforms in the area of human rights, such as "the Action Plan for the Prevention of Violations of the European Convention on Human Rights," Türkiye is required to make more progress on human rights issues in order to continue with full-membership negotiations.[20] Because the Union sees the ICC ratification as a human rights issue, Türkiye's accession to the Court would represent another important step ahead in strengthening the protection of human rights, providing a significant boost to the negotiation process.

Bibliography

Blair, David & Barney Henderson, *Syria Shoots Down Turkish Fighter Jet*, http://www.telegraph.co.uk/news/worldnews/middleeast/syria/9349777/Syria-shoots-down-Turkish-fighter-jet.html (accessed 22 June 2012).

Çarkoğlu, Ali and Barry M. Rubin, *Turkey and The European Union: Domestic Politics, Economic Integration and International Dynamics* (Frank Cass 2003).

Coalition for the International Criminal Court, *Target Countries – URC-Turkey*, http://www.iccnow.org/?mod=urc1010.

Council of Europe: Parliamentary Assembly, *Documents: Working Papers* (Council of Europe 2002), 196.

Council of the European Union, *Action Plan to Follow-Up the Decision on the International Criminal Court* 9, http://register.consilium.europa.eu/pdf/en/11/st12/st12080.en11.pdf (accessed 12 July 2011).

Council of the European Union, *Council Common Position 2003/444/CFSP of 16 June 2003 on the International Criminal Court*, art. 1(2), www.consilium.europa.eu/uedocs/cmsUpload/l_15020030618en00670069.pdf (accessed 18 June 2003).

European Commission, *Turkey Progress Report*, 50, http://ec.europa.eu/enlargement/pdf/key_documents/2014/20141008-turkey-progress-report_en.pdf (accessed October 2014).

Idiz, Semih, *UN Vote Confirms Turkey's Waning Influence*, www.al-monitor.com/pulse/originals/2014/10/turkey-united-nations-security-council-vote.html# (accessed 17 October 2014).

19 Council of the European Union, *Action Plan to Follow-Up the Decision on the International Criminal Court*, 9, http://register.consilium.europa.eu/pdf/en/11/st12/st12080.en11.pdf (accessed 12 July 2011).

20 European Commission, *Turkey Progress Report*, ec.europa.eu/enlargement/pdf/key_documents/2014/20141008-turkey-progress-report (accessed October 2014).

International Criminal Court, *Office of the Prosecutor, Report on Preliminary Examination Activities 2014*, at 62, para. 262, http://www.icc-cpi.int/iccdocs/otp/OTP-Pre-Exam-2014.pdf) (accessed 2 December 2014).

Karakehya, Hakan, International Criminal Court and Turkey, 12(10) *US-China Law Review* (2015).

Republic of Turkey Ministry of Foreign Affairs, No: 196, *Press Release Regarding the Raid on Our Consulate General in Mosul*, www.mfa.gov.tr/no_-196_-11-june-2014_press-release-regarding-the-raid-on-our-consulate-general-in-mosul.en.mfa (accessed 11 June 2014).

Republic of Turkey Ministry of Foreign Affairs, *Turkey and the USA Co-Chaired the Global Counter-Terrorism Forum in New York*, www.mfa.gov.tr/turkey-and-the-usa-co_chaired-the-global-counter_terrorism-forum-in-new-york-2014.en.mfa.

Sassounian, Harut, *Why the UN Rejected Turkey's Bid for a Security Council Seat?* www.huffingtonpost.com/harut-sassounian/why-the-un-rejected-turke_b_6036878.html (Updated 23 December 2014).

UNICEF, *Humanitartian Action for Children – Syrian Refugees*, www.unicef.org/appeals/syrianrefugees.html.

United Nations Treaty Collections, *Rome Statute of the International Criminal Court* (17 July 1998), U.N. Doc. A/CONF.183/9.

Weaver, Matthew and Brian Whitaker, *Turkey-Syria Border Tension*, http://www.guardian.co.uk/world/2012/oct/04/turkey-syria-threat-security-live (accessed 4 October 2012).

9 Conclusion

States that refrain from joining the ICC usually have multiple reasons for that. While some of these reasons may be common for certain states, some will definitely differ from state to state. For example, even though Türkiye shares most of China's reasons for voting against the Rome Statute (such as the Court's jurisdiction over war crimes committed in internal armed conflicts, the *proprio motu* power of the Prosecutor to investigate or the Court's jurisdiction over the nationals of non-party states), Türkiye's objections to the exclusion of terrorism from the Rome Statute are not shared by China. Similarly, China's reservations on the ICC's jurisdiction over the crimes against humanity committed during peacetime are not shared by Türkiye.

Türkiye, unlike most of the States Parties of the ICC, is already a party to several key international human rights instruments, including the ECHR, which imposes much more extensive obligations than the Rome Statute and lacks its procedural safeguards, to maintain its international image and European relations. Its counter-terrorism operations are, therefore, already subjected to close judicial scrutiny of the ECtHR as well as national accountability mechanisms. In addition, due to its European Union membership bid, Türkiye's counter-terrorism practices are also subjected to political scrutiny of the European institutions. The European Commission's annual progress reports for Türkiye, for example, address all allegations of individual abuse. That is to say, a non-national and non-domestic scrutiny over Türkiye's counter-terrorism operations would not be new.

Possibility of facing politically motivated allegations should not hinder Türkiye's consideration of accession to a court, to which all its European counterparts have already joined. Procedural safeguards and the thresholds of the Rome Statute make it nearly impossible for the unfounded or politically motivated allegations to reach the formal investigation stage before the ICC. In order to avoid being portrayed as unwilling to commit itself to further promote the fight against impunity, Türkiye should promptly join the Court and stay in solidarity with the members of the ASP.

This book has shown that Türkiye's objections to the Rome Statute are not so serious as to justify Türkiye's avoidance of the ICC's jurisdiction because, given the procedural protections of the Statute, the exercise of ICC jurisdiction

DOI: 10.4324/9781003641643-9

over Turkish nationals is highly unlikely. It examined the concerns that lie at the bottom of Türkiye's fears about joining the ICC and suggested that limited subject matter and temporal jurisdiction of the Court and the high threshold criteria set out in the Rome Statute should allay Türkiye's concerns about the final outcome of the Rome Conference. This book has also shown that remaining a non-party is not an effective way of achieving the changes that Türkiye wants to see in the Rome Statute. Furthermore, this book established that remaining outside the Court does not guarantee that the Court will not exercise jurisdiction over Turkish nationals.

In this regard, **Chapter 2** suggested that exclusion of the crime of terrorism from the subject matter jurisdiction of the ICC, which was one of the biggest disappointments of the Turkish delegation to the Rome Conference, should not hinder Türkiye's consideration of accession to the Rome Statute. First, irrespective of whether the PKK's terrorist acts, which prompted Türkiye's efforts to include terrorism in the Rome Statute, would fall within the subject matter jurisdiction of the Rome Statute, such jurisdiction would not be triggered by Türkiye because it could lead the ICC to characterize the conflict between Türkiye and the PKK as an armed conflict subject to international humanitarian law norms – a characterization that Türkiye has strongly opposed. Chapter 2 explained that it is highly likely that the OTP would treat Türkiye's counter-terrorism operations against the PKK as an armed conflict if a preliminary examination were to be started. Because of the possibility of such classification, which Türkiye strongly opposes, Türkiye would not wish to trigger an ICC investigation into the crimes committed by the PKK, even if terrorism was expressly included in the Rome Statute.

Second, Chapter 2 has submitted that most of the terrorist acts of the PKK appear to fall within one of the already existing core crimes of the Rome Statute. The lack of the reference to terrorism in the Rome Statute does not prevent the ICC from investigating and prosecuting the terrorist acts. If an investigation were to be triggered today, the ICC would most likely consider most of the terrorist attacks of the PKK as falling within the subject-matter jurisdiction of the ICC.

Third, Chapter 2 has shown that regardless of whether the terrorist acts that targeted Türkiye would fall within the subject matter jurisdiction of the Rome Statute, an ICC investigation into those acts would be found inadmissible before the Court because Türkiye has already been conducting genuine criminal investigations against the perpetrators. An examination of the existing national proceedings and investigations against PKK members show that Türkiye is able and willing to conduct effective prosecutions against terrorist crimes taking place in its territory. Thus, even if the crime of terrorism *per se* had been included in the Rome Statute in a way to cover the PKK's crimes that do not amount to any of the currently existing crimes, those acts would most likely be inadmissible under the complementarity principle of the Court because of Türkiye's ability and willingness to prosecute them.

Chapter 2 finally attempted to explain that Türkiye could, in fact, benefit from joining the ICC by acquiring the right to trigger a preliminary examination. Although it is true that Türkiye would not be eager to trigger a preliminary examination into the activities of the PKK for the reasons detailed in Chapter 2, Türkiye's ability to trigger such examination could still have a deterrent effect on the PKK's senior members, their abettors and the states that solicit, abet or fund the crimes of the PKK, as they would fear facing charges before the Court. Moreover, in the highly unlikely event that a preliminary examination is triggered by Türkiye or by the Prosecutor *proprio motu*, articulation of the PKK's most serious crimes in the Preliminary Examination Reports by the Office of the Prosecutor would remind the European countries of their responsibilities regarding the unlawful PKK activities taking place in their territory, and it would send a clear signal that the international community is watching. Thus, Chapter 2 concluded that the lack of the reference to terrorism in the Rome Statute should not hinder Türkiye's consideration of accession.

Chapter 3 has established that the ICC's jurisdiction over war crimes committed as part of an internal armed conflict, which was another objection that Türkiye voiced during the Rome negotiations, would not undermine Türkiye's fight against the terrorist groups, contrary to concerns raised by the opponents of the Statute. The chapter focused on Türkiye's worst-case scenario, in which the Court considers the situation in southeastern Türkiye as an internal armed conflict subject to Article 8(2)(c) and (e) – the articles that deal with the crimes committed as part of an armed conflict not of an international character – and explained that the ICC's jurisdiction over internal armed conflicts should not hinder Türkiye's consideration of accession to the Rome Statute because possible allegations against the Turkish security forces would not meet the legal criteria to justify the initiation of a formal investigation. Thus, joining the Court would not hamper Türkiye in its measures of legitimate repression.

First, Chapter 3 has explained that most of the allegations against Turkish security forces concern the incidents that occurred prior to the entry into force of the Rome Statute in 2002, and thus, they are outside the temporal jurisdiction of the Court. Furthermore, when Türkiye accedes to the Rome Statute, the ICC will have jurisdiction only with respect to the allegations concerning the incidents occurred after the entry into force of the Statute for Türkiye, unless Türkiye accepts the jurisdiction of the Court also for the acts that took place prior to its ratification but after 2002. Second, Chapter 3 submitted that even if even Türkiye's integral struggle against the PKK was classified as an armed conflict and the temporal jurisdiction requirement was satisfied, allegations against Turkish nationals would be found inadmissible before the ICC due to the "complementarity" principle and the "gravity" threshold of the Rome Statue. The chapter drew attention to the fact that the ICC does not intervene when the national authorities are able and willing to prosecute the acts in question and when the acts in question fail to appear to be grave enough to trigger a formal ICC investigation.

Third, Chapter 3 has shown that even if an internal armed conflict characterization was made, Türkiye's counter-terrorist operations would not face accusations of excessive use of force because "in the context of a non-international armed conflict, the Rome Statute does not contain a provision for the war crime of intentionally launching a disproportionate attack."[1] Fourth, Chapter 3 explains that even if other requirements were satisfied, most of the allegations against the Turkish Armed Forces would not satisfy *actus reus* of the crimes enumerated in the Rome Statute. It emphasizes that Türkiye's efforts to fight against terrorism without committing abuses and without victimizing indigenous civilians has been complementary to its efforts to reduce the ability of the PKK to recruit new members. It argues Türkiye's success in bringing its counter-terrorism laws and practices in line with the international standards has been instrumental in gaining closer cooperation from other countries in its fight against the PKK. After arguing that joining the ICC could even be conducive to Türkiye's effective fight against terrorism, Chapter 3 concludes that the ICC's jurisdiction over internal armed conflicts should not hinder Türkiye's consideration of accession to the Rome Statute.

Chapter 4 dealt with Türkiye's hesitations about the ICC Prosecutor's *proprio motu* powers to initiate an investigation. Chapter 4 first argued that the Prosecutor's power to initiate investigations *proprio motu* is not only crucial for the effective operation of the Court but also instrumental in encouraging domestic prosecutions. Chapter 4 then explained that prosecutorial powers are not placed in the hands of the Prosecutor without judicial checks. First, the Rome Statute requires the prosecutor to request authorization from the Pre-Trial Chamber before initiating a formal investigation on her own motion. The Prosecutor cannot proceed with an investigation without an authorization from the Pre-Trial Chamber of the Court.

Second, the safeguards and the high threshold criteria set out in the Rome Statute, which are the main restraints placed on the Prosecutor's discretion, avert the possibility of the Prosecutor to bring arbitrary charges. Third, there is also political restraint placed on the office of the Prosecutor by the states whose cooperation is needed in order to access the defendants and the evidence. The effective functioning of the ICC relies heavily on the cooperation with states. After drawing attention to the fact that the Prosecutor of the ICC is elected by secret ballots of State Parties with equally weighted votes, Chapter 4 concluded that the judicial checks and the filtering mechanism of the Rome Statute should allay Türkiye's fears over politicized prosecution.

Chapter 5 handled the objections and hesitations of states, including Türkiye, to the ICC's ability to exercise jurisdiction over the nationals of the states

1 International Criminal Court, *Office of the Prosecutor, Report on Preliminary Examination Activities 2013* (November 2013) 12, para. 47, http://www.icc-cpi.int/en_menus/icc/press%20and%20media/press%20releases/Documents/OTP%20Preliminary% 20Examinations/OTP%20-%20Report%20%C20Preliminary%C20Examination%C20Activities% 202013.pdf.

that are not party to the Rome Statute in some circumstances, for example, when a non-party state national commits an ICC crime on the territory of a State Party or when a situation is referred to the Court by the Security Council. The chapter explained why the ICC's jurisdiction over the non-party state nationals is not a legal or political obstacle to Türkiye's accession to the Rome Statute. First, once the Rome Statute comes into force for Türkiye, the Court's jurisdiction over non-party states will no longer be an issue for Türkiye, as it will no longer be a non-party. While it is understandable for those countries that would most likely not join the Court in the foreseeable future, such as the United States, to perceive the ICC's jurisdiction over non-party states as a threat, it should not be a concern for a state, such as Türkiye, which already stated that it "will soon approve the Rome Statute after completing its internal preparations."[2]

Second, Chapter 5 argued that Türkiye preserves very little by remaining an outsider and that Türkiye's non-accession does not guarantee that the ICC will not exercise jurisdiction over Turkish nationals. The ICC would have jurisdiction over the acts committed by Turkish nationals on the territory of a state that is either party to the Court or otherwise accepts the jurisdiction of the Court on an *ad hoc* basis, regardless of whether Türkiye is a party or consents to the jurisdiction of the Court. In such case, an investigation could be triggered by the Prosecutor *proprio motu* or by a State Party referral. The ICC would also have jurisdiction over the acts committed by Turkish nationals in a situation referred to it by the Security Council, regardless of where the crimes were committed, as no precondition is required when a situation, in which an ICC crime appears to be committed, is referred to the Court by the Security Council.

Chapter 5 also compared the Turkish and American positions with respect to their concerns regarding the ICC's jurisdiction over the nationals of non-party states in an attempt to explain why Türkiye should not follow in the footsteps of the U.S. – its only western ally that has not yet ratified the Rome Statute – on the issue of ICC accession. It stated that, as opposed to Türkiye, the United States enjoy the privileges of being a permanent member of the Security Council, such as the right to veto any resolution that provides the ICC with the jurisdiction over U.S. nationals. Furthermore, the United States concluded Bilateral Immunity Agreements with over a hundred states to ensure that they would not hand over the U.S. nationals to the ICC without its permission. Türkiye, on the other hand, does not enjoy such protections as BIAs and the privileges of being a permanent member of the Security Council and, therefore, should not, as some argue, follow in the footsteps of the U.S. on the issue of ICC accession.

2 Coalition for the International Criminal Court, *Target Countries – URC-Turkey*, http://www.iccnow.org/?mod=urc1010 (accessed 1 January 2015).

In the context of the comparison between the Turkish and American positions, Chapter 5 also draws attention to the fact that the United States has much more compelling reasons for not joining the ICC than Türkiye, such as its expansive military operations across the globe. The U.S. fears that a large number of American troops could be subject to the Court's jurisdiction and that its officials could be deprived of the type of due process rights guaranteed to Americans under the U.S. Constitution, such as the right to a jury trial and the protection against self-incrimination.

Another compelling U.S. concern that is not shared by Türkiye is the concerns over the infringement of national sovereignty. Infringement of its sovereignty has not been one of the reasons for Türkiye's objections to the ICC's jurisdiction over the nationals of non-parties or to the Prosecutor's powers. Türkiye has already accepted the compulsory jurisdiction of the ECtHR, which hears applications against signatory states for the breach of a broad range of rights and freedoms and issues binding judgments upon them, at the expense of significant privileges of its sovereignty. Thus, joining a court that tries its nationals would not be an unprecedented (so-called) "infringement" of Türkiye's sovereignty.

Chapter 5 finally noted that accession to the Rome Statute could benefit Türkiye more vis-a-vis the U.S., especially given Türkiye's foreign policy priorities, such as its EU membership bid. For all these reasons detailed in Chapter 5, the chapter concluded that Türkiye's attitude towards the ICC (and towards the issues, such as the ICC's jurisdiction over the nationals of non-parties) should differ from that of the U.S.

Chapter 6 discussed possible implications of Türkiye's ICC accession for the Cyprus question. It argued that Türkiye's accession to the Rome Statute will not likely impact the possibility of the Cyprus question being brought before the Court for several reasons. First, the Republic of Cyprus, which is recognized by the U.N. as the de jure government of the whole island, is already party to the Rome Statute, and thus, it can already attempt to refer the situation in Cyprus to the ICC regardless of whether Türkiye is a State Party or not. In other words, even if Türkiye remains a non-party, the Court could still determine that it has territorial jurisdiction over Türkiye's activities in the northern part of Cyprus because the Republic of Cyprus is internationally recognized as the legitimate government of the entire island.

Second, neither the acts of the Turkish Cyprus (and Türkiye) nor those of the Greek Cyprus (and Greece) on the island of Cyprus would be found admissible before the ICC because they clearly fail to satisfy the subject matter and temporal jurisdiction and the gravity requirement of the ICC. Most notably, Türkiye's military intervention, which ensued following a Greek-led coup that sought to unify the island with Greece, took place in 1974, half a century ago. Therefore, the acts of the parties during and in the aftermath of the intervention fall outside the temporal jurisdiction of the ICC, which cannot prosecute the incidents that occurred prior to the entry into force of the Rome Statute in 2002. Moreover, the unavailability of high-ranking officials from the relevant period, coupled with the near impossibility of accessing credible evidence and witnesses, constitutes an additional basis for the OTP to regard such applications as lacking in merit. The fact that nearly all decision-makers and senior officials from the 1974 events are no longer alive poses an additional jurisdictional challenge, making a formal ICC investigation highly unlikely and nearly unfeasible, particularly due to the near impossibility of gathering evidence, arresting suspects and accessing witnesses and defendants.

Third, Chapter 6 submitted that given the political constraints and the risk of obstructing the re-unification talks, the situation in Cyprus would not be a case the Prosecutor would be eager to get involved by a preliminary examination that is clearly not likely to turn into a formal investigation, even if the preconditions to the exercise of the ICC's jurisdiction were clearly satisfied. The statehood questions, involvement of the Guarantor States and the re-unification efforts between the Greeks and Turks make the situation in Cyprus too sensitive to intervene.

Despite the Rome Statute's high threshold criteria that make an ICC investigation into the situation in Cyprus highly unlikely, some still view the Cyprus question as one of the greatest fears of Türkiye about joining the ICC. Chapter 6, therefore, primarily focused on the allegations against Türkiye, which, as a Guarantor State exercising its legal right under the Treaty of Guarantee, conducted a military intervention in Cyprus in 1974 "to prevent a Greek takeover of the island"[3] and to safeguard the Turkish Cypriots from being driven off the island. Chapter 6 submitted that what makes an ICC investigation into the situation in Cyprus highly unlikely and almost infeasible is not the difficulty of establishing territorial or personal jurisdiction but rather factors such as the OTP's caution in selecting cases, the limited temporal and subject matter jurisdiction of the Court, the gravity of the allegations falling below the high thresholds of the Rome Statute, remedies provided to the victims of some of the acts in question, as well as statehood issues and political constraints. In any event, even if Türkiye remains a non-party, the Court could still assert territorial jurisdiction over the alleged acts of Turkish nationals on the island due to the Greek Cyprus's accession to the Rome Statute in 2002.

Chapter 6, therefore, concluded that the Cyprus question should not be viewed as an obstacle to Türkiye's consideration of accession to the Rome Statute. It recommended that instead of being an onlooker to such disputable but possible future considerations, Türkiye should consider being an influential insider of the ICC to better explain its legitimate legal arguments on the issues such as the situation in Cyprus, to impact the international community's perception of the Cyprus question on its behalf and to make sure that its side of the issues is well understood.

3 Patrick W. Nee, *Key Facts on Turkey: Essential Information on Turkey* (The International Publishing Company 2013) 1.

Chapter 7 has suggested that Türkiye should not be concerned about the Court's jurisdiction over the crime of aggression, as each State Party to the Court has the option not to opt in to such jurisdiction. It has shown that, absent a Security Council referral, the ICC may exercise jurisdiction over the crime of aggression only if it is committed on the territory "and" by the nationals of a State Party that has accepted the Kampala Amendments. The chapter has explained that the states' concerns regarding the ICC's jurisdiction over the crime of aggression are less meaningful given that even the States Parties are afforded the right to opt out of the jurisdiction of the Court over this crime.

Chapter 7 has also shown that the states that join the ICC after the adoption or the entry into force of the Kampala Amendments will not be regarded as having ratified these amendments and thus will not be bound by them. The chapter concluded that Türkiye's possible fears that its nationals could face accusations of the crime of aggression should not hinder its consideration of accession to the Rome Statute because such accession would not impact the possibility of Türkiye being exposed to the jurisdiction of the ICC in respect of an act of aggression as long as Türkiye does not opt in to the aggression amendments.

Chapter 8 explored the benefits that Türkiye could gain by joining the ICC. All the chapters preceding Chapter 8 have shown that the exercise of the ICC's jurisdiction over Turkish nationals is highly unlikely and that the concerns presented against Türkiye's accession are not so serious as to justify Türkiye's avoidance of the Court's jurisdiction. Chapter 8, on the other hand, explored some of the compelling benefits for Türkiye to join the ICC.

First, by acceding to the Rome Statute, Türkiye would acquire the rights that would allow it to participate in the further shaping of the law and procedures and the staffing of the ICC. It could more effectively suggest amendments to the Rome Statute and cast its vote on the proposals in a way to accomplish changes it considers important for the protection of its interests. By being a State Party to the Court, Türkiye would also acquire the right to participate in electing and removing the judges and the prosecutor of the Court and put forward its nationals as candidates for these positions. Furthermore, as a State Party, Türkiye could more effectively bring issues that bother it to the Court's agenda, create more meaningful communication with the Office of the Prosecutor and sway other members of the Court as an insider. It could become an active participant of the determination process of critical issues simply by joining the Court.

Second, by joining the ICC, Türkiye would enjoy positive political impacts of being a State Party, such as enhancing its reputation internationally. Accession to the Rome Statute, as a demonstration of Türkiye's commitment to further contribute to international peace and the rule of law, could help Türkiye garner greater support from the members of the Assembly of State Parties and the UN General Assembly when contesting prestigious seats, such as a nonpermanent seat at the Security Council. Türkiye's accession to the

Rome Statute could also motivate its southern and eastern neighbors to consider ratification and thus could significantly contribute to the advancement of the international rule of law in the Middle East. Given the significant challenges posed by the frequent commission of serious international crimes in its southern neighborhood, advancing justice, accountability and the fight against impunity in this region aligns with Türkiye's best interests.

Third, as a State Party to the Rome Statute, Türkiye would have a stronger hand in its European Union full-membership negotiations. ICC accession is not one of the criteria for joining the EU, but it is a common policy adopted by all members of the Union under the Common Foreign and Security Policy, and it is considered as an essential component of the EU's values. Türkiye's accession to the founding treaty of the ICC, of which the European Commission and the European Parliament have been strong supporters, would have a very positive impact on the Türkiye-EU full membership negotiations. The EU addresses the accession to the Rome Statute as an improvement in the area of human rights. Türkiye's accession to the Court would represent another important step ahead in strengthening the protection of human rights, providing a significant boost to the negotiation process.

This book has finally argued that Türkiye's non-party status to the ICC creates difficulties in its foreign policy and harms its reputation internationally. In concluding that Türkiye's hesitations do not constitute an insurmountable obstacle for its accession to the Rome Statute, the book has encouraged the Turkish government to join the ever-growing ICC family without delay and enjoy the benefits of being an influential insider.

Bibliography

Coalition for the International Criminal Court, *Target Countries – Turkey*, http://www.iccnow.org/?mod=urc1006.

International Criminal Court, *Office of the Prosecutor, Report on Preliminary Examination Activities 2013*, http://www.icc-cpi.int/en_menus/icc/press%20and%20media/press%20releases/Documents/OTP%20Preliminary%20Examinations/OTP%20-%20Report%20%C20Preliminary%C20Examination%C20Activities%202013.pdf (accessed November 2013).

Nee, Patrick W., *Key Facts on Turkey: Essential Information on Turkey* (The International Publishing Company 2013), 1.

Index

FSC
www.fsc.org
MIX
Papier | Fördert gute Waldnutzung
FSC® C083411

Kolibri 360 GmbH
Ferdinand-Jühlke-Straße 7
99095 Erfurt, Deutschland
produktsicherheit@kolibri360.de